FAITH DISCIPLESHIP

Sharing a Living
FAITH

FACILITATOR GUIDE

D.L. Lowrie • Steve Stege • Randy Holman
G. Dwayne McCrary • Jimmy Storrie • John Strappazon

LifeWay Press
Nashville, Tennessee

ISBN 0-7673-9334-1

Dewey Decimal Classification: 248.5
Subject Heading: WITNESSING \ EVANGELISTIC WORK

Unless otherwise indicated, Scripture quotations are from the Holy Bible,
New International Version © copyright 1973, 1978, 1984 by International Bible Society.

The *New King James Version* is the text for Scripture memory in the FAITH gospel presentation.
Scripture quotations marked NKJV are from *New King James Version*,
© 1979, 1980, 1982, Thomas Nelson, Inc. Publishers. Used by permission.

The FAITH Sunday School Evangelism Strategy® is an evangelistic venture of LifeWay Christian Resources
of the Southern Baptist Convention and is endorsed by the North American Mission Board.

Obtain additional copies of this book by writing to Customer Service Center, MSN 113;
127 Ninth Avenue, North; Nashville, TN 37234-0113; by calling toll free (800) 458-2772;
by faxing (615) 251-5933; by ordering online at *www.lifeway.com*; by emailing
customerservice@lifeway.com; or by visiting a LifeWay Christian Store.

For information about adult discipleship and family resources, training, and events,
visit our Web site at *www.lifeway.com/discipleplus*.

For information about FAITH, visit our Web site at *www.lifeway.com/sundayschool/faith*.

Printed in the United States of America

LifeWay Press
127 Ninth Avenue, North
Nashville, Tennessee 37234-0151

*As God works through us, we will help people and churches know Jesus Christ and seek His kingdom
by providing biblical solutions that spiritually transform individuals and cultures.*

Contents

The Writers

The writers of this course are a team of ministers and FAITH practitioners at First Baptist Church in Lubbock, Texas. Early the church captured a vision of what FAITH could do and became one of 27 originator churches that participated in the first FAITH Clinic, hosted by First Baptist Church, Daytona Beach, Florida, in January 1998.

Since implementing FAITH in February 1998, First Baptist Lubbock has experienced the fruit of FAITH: excitement; a sense of expectancy; and increased baptisms, attendance, enrollment, and awareness of lost people. Its Sunday School has been reawakened to its purpose: an evangelism strategy that mobilizes the laity to do the work of ministry.

D. L. Lowrie, Pastor

D. L. knows, practices, and is committed to the principles of Sunday School growth. He teaches the FAITH Basic course each semester and leads the church to be a Great Commission church.

Steve Stege, Associate Pastor for Education and Administration

Steve is committed to Sunday School as the primary evangelistic arm of the church and continually guides the staff and volunteer leaders to keep FAITH focused as the Sunday School evangelism strategy. He teaches the Basic and Advanced courses each semester at First Baptist and is a lead teacher at FAITH Clinics.

Randy Holman, Minister to Senior Adults and Evangelism

Randy is FAITH Director, effectively coordinating the work of FAITH each semester. He teaches the Basic and Advanced courses each semester. He has also served as an administrator of FAITH Clinics.

G. Dwayne McCrary, Minister to Young Adults/Discipleship

Dwayne understands and implements the purpose of Sunday School growth. He understands that two of the greatest benefits of FAITH are discipleship for new believers and the growth of all believers.

Jimmy Storrie, Minister to Youth

Jimmy is committed to Sunday School as the hub of youth ministry. He has implemented and taught Student FAITH. He loves and ministers to students but primarily considers himself an equipper of youth leaders to do the work of ministry.

John Strappazon, Minister to University Students

John has a heart for reaching and discipling today's university student. He is developing a strategy for reaching college students by using FAITH Sunday School Evangelism Strategy.

Expression of Commitment

FAITH Discipleship: Sharing a Living Faith

I commit myself to continue **FAITH** Sunday School
evangelism training in my church.

I recognize **FAITH** training as a way to help my church and Sunday School,

to continue to grow as a Great Commission Christian,

to be obedient to God's command to be an active witness,

and to equip others to share their faith.

Signed: _____

Address: _____

Phone number: _____ Email address: _____

My role in *Sharing a Living Faith*:

❑ Team Leader ❑ Assistant Team Leader

❑ Other: _____

My Sunday School class/department: _____

Dates of my *Sharing a Living Faith* training: _____

Foreword

All over the world I have said, "I would do FAITH even if no one were ever saved or if our Sunday School or worship attendance never increased." Why? Because of the personal spiritual growth that has occurred in the lives of those attending FAITH training. FAITH truly builds believers.

FAITH Discipleship is one of the major reasons I have so emphatically made that statement. FAITH Discipleship is where a new depth of maturity begins to take hold in the lives of FAITH participants. *Sharing a Living Faith* is the subject of this upcoming semester's study. You will discover dynamic spiritual truths that will help you grow in Christ and become a better, more confident witness. *Sharing a Living Faith* is guaranteed to be a thrilling and rewarding journey of faith in your personal walk with Christ as you continue to win and disciple your world.

There is always more in your journey of faith, and you are about to discover more. I wholeheartedly and overwhelmingly endorse FAITH Discipleship, and I applaud your participation in it.

Bobby Welch
Senior Pastor, First Baptist Church
Daytona Beach, Florida

Introduction

Congratulations for completing semesters of FAITH evangelism training and for making a commitment to further growth as a Great Commission Christian through FAITH Discipleship. FAITH Discipleship grows from the same biblical principles your previous FAITH training was based on, including Jesus' Great Commission: " 'Go and make disciples of all nations, baptizing them in the name of the Father and of the Son and of the Holy Spirit, and teaching them to obey everything I have commanded you. And surely I am with you always, to the very end of the age' " (Matt. 28:19-20). Notice Jesus' dual emphasis on going and making disciples. You have concentrated a great deal on going to the lost, and you have already learned many skills and biblical teachings that are important for disciples to know and practice. In FAITH Discipleship courses you will learn more about what it means to be a disciple of Jesus Christ and to make disciples of others.

Here are some specific ways your FAITH Discipleship training will equip you further as a Great Commission witness.

- By teaching you important biblical truths you need to understand and exemplify as a growing disciple
- By equipping you to respond to difficult questions you may encounter in witnessing
- By helping you develop as a life witness for Christ, taking advantage of daily opportunities to share God's love
- By giving you opportunities to practice what you have learned in witnessing situations
- By helping you develop as a Team Leader
- By suggesting ways you can help new Sunday School and church members grow as disciples

The first stop on your FAITH Discipleship journey is this course, *Sharing a Living Faith*. This course will help you clarify your beliefs as a disciple of Jesus Christ. You will receive guidance that will benefit your discipleship journey in the following significant ways.

1. *You will develop a biblical belief system.* Your walk as a disciple will be enriched and strengthened as you incorporate biblical teachings into your life and submit to the transforming power of God's Word.
2. *You will become a more effective witness.* You will be able to explain what you believe when you have opportunities to share in-depth with someone or when you are asked difficult questions.
3. *You will be equipped to disciple others.* You will explore ways to disciple persons who are won to Christ and who become involved in Sunday School and church.

A thorough knowledge of Christian beliefs will serve as a firm foundation not only for your future witnessing experiences but also for your lifelong growth as a disciple of Jesus Christ.

FAITH Visit Outline

Preparation

INTRODUCTION
INTERESTS
INVOLVEMENT

Church Experience/Background

- Ask about the person's church background.
- Listen for clues about the person's spiritual involvement.

Sunday School Testimony

- Tell general benefits of Sunday School.
- Tell a current personal experience.

Evangelistic Testimony

- Tell a little of your preconversion experience.
- Say: "I had a life-changing experience."
- Tell recent benefits of your conversion.

INQUIRY

Key Question: In your personal opinion, what do you understand it takes for a person to go to heaven?

Possible Answers: Faith, works, unclear, no opinion

Transition Statement: I'd like to share with you how the Bible answers this question, if it is all right. There is a word that can be used to answer this question: FAITH (spell out on fingers).

Presentation

F IS FOR FORGIVENESS

We cannot have eternal life and heaven without God's forgiveness.

"In Him [meaning Jesus] we have redemption through His blood, the forgiveness of sins"—Ephesians 1:7a, NKJV.

A is for AVAILABLE

Forgiveness is available. It is—

AVAILABLE FOR ALL

"For God so loved the world that He gave His only begotten Son, that whoever believes in Him should not perish but have everlasting life"—John 3:16, NKJV.

BUT NOT AUTOMATIC

"Not everyone who says to Me, 'Lord, Lord,' shall enter the kingdom of heaven"—Matthew 7:21a, NKJV.

I is for IMPOSSIBLE

It is impossible for God to allow sin into heaven.

GOD IS—

- LOVE

  John 3:16, NKJV

- JUST

  "For judgment is without mercy"—James 2:13a, NKJV.

  MAN IS SINFUL

  "For all have sinned and fall short of the glory of God"—Romans 3:23, NKJV.

  Question: But how can a sinful person enter heaven, where God allows no sin?

T is for TURN

Question: If you were driving down the road and someone asked you to turn, what would he or she be asking you to do? (change direction)

Turn means repent.

TURN from something—sin and self

"But unless you repent you will all likewise perish"—Luke 13:3b, NKJV.

TURN to Someone; trust Christ only

(The Bible tells us that) *"Christ died for our sins according to the Scriptures, and that He was buried, and that He rose again the third day according to the Scriptures"*—1 Corinthians 15:3b-4, NKJV.

"If you confess with your mouth the Lord Jesus and believe in your heart that God has raised Him from the dead, you will be saved"—Romans 10:9, NKJV.

H is for HEAVEN

Heaven is eternal life.

HERE

"I have come that they may have life, and that they may have it more abundantly"—John 10:10b, NKJV.

HEREAFTER

"And if I go and prepare a place for you, I will come again and receive you to Myself; that where I am, there you may be also"—John 14:3, NKJV.

HOW

How can a person have God's forgiveness, heaven and eternal life, and Jesus as personal Savior and Lord?

Explain based on leaflet picture, FAITH (Forsaking All, I Trust Him), Romans 10:9.

Invitation

INQUIRE

Understanding what we have shared, would you like to receive this forgiveness by trusting in Christ as your personal Savior and Lord?

INVITE

- Pray to accept Christ.
- Pray for commitment/recommitment.
- Invite to join Sunday School.

INSURE

- Use *A Step of Faith* to insure decision.
- Personal Acceptance
- Sunday School Enrollment
- Public Confession

FAITH Participation Card

Name: _____ Semester dates: _____

Address: _____ Phone: _____

Sunday School department: _____ Teacher: _____

Other Team members: _____

Check one: ❑ FAITH Team Leader   ❑ FAITH Learner   ❑ Assistant Team Leader

	1	2	3	4	5	6	7	8	9	10	11	12	13	14	15	16	Totals
Class Participation *Place a check to indicate completion for the appropriate session.*																	
Present																	
Home study done																	
Outline recited																	
Visitation *Indicate a number for the following areas.*																	
Number of tries																	
Number visits																	
Number of people talked with																	
Type of Visit *(Assignments)*																	
Evangelistic																	
Ministry																	
Follow-up																	
Opinion Poll																	
Gospel Presented																	
Profession																	
Assurance																	
No decision																	
For practice																	
Gospel Not Presented																	
Already Christian																	
No admission																	
Sunday School Enrollment																	
Attempted																	
Enrolled																	
Life Witness																	
Profession																	
Assurance																	
No decision																	

Sharing a Living Faith: An Orientation

In this session you will—

HEAR IT by learning the purpose of this course, the topics to be covered, and the process to be used in examining each session's topic;

SEE IT by viewing a video segment on the impact this course can have on your growth as a disciple and on your development as a Great Commission witness;

SAY IT by practicing the *Preparation* portion of the FAITH Visit Outline;

STUDY IT by overviewing Home Study Assignments.

In Advance
- Read the introduction. Preview the content of all sessions.
- Read the teaching suggestions and content for session 1. Pay special attention to the distinctives of FAITH Discipleship and to the description of this course (see pp. 12–15). Decide whether to use the session 1 computer slides or the overhead cels.
- Prepare the room for teaching.
- Cue the videotape to the session 1 segment, Lighting the Way.
- Review your Sunday School Testimony and Evangelistic Testimony. Update them to reflect your recent experiences.
- Pray for participants.
- Distribute Journals as participants arrive. When you are ready to begin the orientation, direct participants to open their Journals to page 12.

HEAR IT

Step 1 (5 mins.)

Welcome participants to *Sharing a Living Faith*. Ask participants to recall things God has done in their lives and the skills they have learned through their previous semesters of FAITH. Pray, thanking God for the lives that have been changed forever and that you have another opportunity to grow as Great Commission Christians.

SEE IT

Step 2 (15 mins.)

Introduce the concept of FAITH Discipleship and show the session 1 videotape segment, Lighting the Way.

Where Your Journey in FAITH Has Led

Congratulations for completing semesters of FAITH evangelism training and for making a commitment to further growth as a Great Commission Christian through FAITH Discipleship. Perhaps your journey thus far has taken you to places you had never been before—into the lives of lost persons who need to know our Lord Jesus Christ. Although your way may have been difficult at times, we hope that your journey has also taken you to new heights in your relationship with God as you learned to rely on Him for power and boldness in sharing His love for people.

In *A Journey in FAITH* you learned to use the FAITH Visit Outline to present the gospel to lost persons. You also learned to use your Sunday School testimony in witnessing visits. You learned the value of making Sunday School ministry visits. You gained valuable experience in making witnessing visits, as well as in sharing FAITH in everyday situations.

In *Building Bridges Through FAITH* you learned the importance of following up with new Christians to lead them to their next steps of growth and commitment. You learned and practiced additional skills for connecting people with Christ, the church, and Sunday School. You saw how these vital connections occur in daily life, in intentional visits, in ministry actions, and in other ways.

Now you are ready for the next phase of your journey, FAITH Discipleship.

The Next Step: FAITH Discipleship

FAITH Discipleship grows from the same biblical principles your previous FAITH training was based on, including Jesus' Great Commission: " 'Go and make disciples of all nations, baptizing them in the name of the Father and of the Son and of the Holy Spirit, and teaching them to obey everything I have commanded you. And surely I am with you always, to the very end of the age' " (Matt. 28:19-20). Notice Jesus' dual emphasis on going and making disciples. You have concentrated a great deal on going to the lost, and you have already learned many skills and biblical teachings that are important for disciples to know and practice. In FAITH Discipleship courses you will learn more about what it means to be a disciple of Jesus Christ and to make disciples of others.

Discipleship has been defined as "a personal, lifelong, obedient relationship with Jesus Christ in which He transforms your character into Christlikeness; changes your values into Kingdom values; and involves you in His mission in the home, the church, and the world."[1]

Do you see the way FAITH Discipleship complements FAITH evangelism training? From your growing relationship with Jesus come motivation, skills, and knowledge for witnessing and ministering to others. Here are some specific ways your FAITH Discipleship will equip you further as a Great Commission witness.

- By teaching you important __**biblical**__ __**truths**__ you need to __**understand**__ and __**exemplify**__ as a growing disciple
- By equipping you to __**respond**__ to difficult __**questions**__ you may encounter in witnessing
- By helping you develop as a __**life**__ __**witness**__ for Christ, taking advantage of daily opportunities to share God's love
- By giving you opportunities to __**practice**__ what you have learned in __**witnessing**__ __**situations**__
- By helping you develop as a __**Team**__ __**Leader**__
- By suggesting ways you can __**disciple**__ others

The first stop on your FAITH Discipleship journey is this course, *Sharing a Living Faith*.

What Does It Mean to Share a Living Faith?

Like your previous FAITH training, FAITH Discipleship emphasizes the importance of your personal relationship with God as the basis of a viable Christian testimony. The good news you share is more than a gospel presentation. It is a Person—the Savior who lives in you. Your faith does not consist of an academic recitation of facts but of what the living God is doing in you and through you every day. It's not just words but the living Word whom you share with joy and gratitude! By growing in discipleship, you learn to adopt His mind, His character, His values, and His behavior, so that your life reflects the God who dwells in you. As a result of your relationship with Him, you want to live by His Word, minister to others, worship God, and fellowship with other believers. And you want everyone to know the Savior the way you do. That's what it means to share a living faith!

This course has been designed to help you share a living faith in the following significant ways.

1. You will develop a biblical __belief__ __system__.
To share a living faith, you need to know what you believe. This course will help you clarify your beliefs as a disciple of Jesus Christ. You will discover biblical answers to the following key questions about the Christian faith.

HEAR IT

Ask participants to turn to page 13 in their Journals and to fill in the blanks as you present the benefits of FAITH Discipleship. Use the computer diskette or the overhead cel.

Goals of FAITH Discipleship

Step 3 (10 mins.)

State that *Sharing a Living Faith* has three purposes. Participants will be equipped to share a living faith by—
- developing a biblical belief system;
- becoming a more effective witness;
- learning ways to disciple Team members.

Use the computer diskette or the overhead cel to explain each purpose.

Purposes of *Sharing a Living Faith*

Highlight the questions that will be examined in this course. Use the computer diskette or the overhead cel.

Important Questions

Give participants a moment to respond to the question in writing. Then ask volunteers to share their responses.

- How do I know the __Bible__ is __true__?
- Does __God__ __exist__?
- Is __Jesus__ really __God's__ __Son__?
- Who is the __Holy__ __Spirit__?
- Why does __evil__ exist?
- Why does God permit __suffering__?
- What does it mean to be __lost__?
- What does it mean to be __saved__?
- Why do I need the __church__?
- Are __Bible__ __study__ and __prayer__ important?
- What is the __purpose__ of __life__?
- How can I find __strength__ for __daily__ __living__?
- How can I overcome __spiritual__ __obstacles__?

Your walk as a disciple will be enriched and strengthened as you incorporate biblical teachings into your life and submit to the transforming power of God's Word.

2. You will become a more effective __witness__.

By now you have no doubt encountered individuals who have asked difficult questions, like the ones listed above. Some questions may have seemed to come from nowhere and to have nothing to do with the gospel presentation. Others were so weighty and broad that you didn't know how to begin to respond.

Can you think of any questions you have been asked while witnessing that stumped you or left you feeling inadequate? Write them here.

_____

_____

These questions can make any Christian witness uncomfortable. If you are a Team Leader, you probably feel that Learners expect you to have all of the answers for handling difficult situations like these.

The second purpose of this study is to give you insight for dealing with some of the difficult questions you may face while witnessing.

- Difficult questions can arise in __FAITH__ __visits__. You can never anticipate all of the questions you may be asked while making a visit. However, certain common questions continue to surface for which you can prepare, like the ones listed above. Although this course requires no additional memory work associated with the FAITH Visit Outline, you will gain new insights into ways you can respond when questions arise during specific parts of the outline, as well as in other types of visits you make.

- Difficult questions can arise in _____ **daily** _____ **life** _____.
  Questions of eternal significance can arise in daily life as people
  face stress and crisis.
    —A coworker is reading the newspaper at break, and a discus-
       sion develops about who can be trusted to tell the truth.
    —A long-time acquaintance calls to tell you that his spouse is
       facing cancer and wants to know if your pastor can visit.
    —A neighbor's oldest child is ready to leave for college, and
       your neighbor wonders whether all the extra days and nights
       he clocked at work were worth it.
    —The clerk at the grocery store asks you why you are happy
       when so many bad things are happening in our world.

There are opportunities around us every day to be a life witness—
one who seeks to share Jesus with anyone who needs God's forgiveness
and hope. When people ask difficult questions with eternal significance, like the ones you will study during this semester, they are
opening doors into their lives. These opportunities may well be divine
appointments God has set for us.

3. You will learn ways to _____ **disciple** _____ **others** _____.

The third purpose of this course is for you to explore ways to disciple
others. In FAITH Advanced you learned to use follow-up visits to
begin nurturing new Christians. You also studied ways to assimilate
new members into your Sunday School class or department and
church. It is intended that as you develop a biblical belief system, you
will find ways to incorporate what you have learned into your role as
an active Sunday School member or worker. As a Team Leader, you are
also discipling Team members by leading Team Time, serving as a role
model, and being an encourager and a motivator.

The Roles of a Team Leader

While you are meeting for this *Sharing a Living Faith* orientation, Team
Learners are overviewing many important ingredients of FAITH. They
will learn to depend on you to interpret and reinforce many of the
things they are discovering for the first time. *Sharing a Living Faith* is intentionally designed for someone who has already learned the FAITH
Visit Outline. Everything is planned to help you encourage and train
individuals who are learning the outline for the first time. Although
every participant in this course may not be a Team Leader, the importance of this role will be evident in this course.

If you are participating in this training as a Team Leader, you will
learn specific ways to lead your Team through training. If you are
participating in another way, you still will focus on actions you can

State that these situations are
examples of opportunities for sharing
in daily life.

If leading students, relate daily-life
situations they might face:
- A classmate starts a discussion
  about the biology lesson on
  evolution.
- A friend asks why bad things keep
  happening to his family members.
- A parent worries about paying all of
  the family's bills for the month.
- Having made a big mistake, a friend
  says that she will never be able
  to forgive herself and doesn't see
  why she should keep walking the
  straight path.

Step 4 (10 mins.)

Review the Team Leader's roles from
FAITH Advanced as participants fill in
the blanks on pages 16–17 in their
Journals. Use the computer diskette
or the overhead cel.

Roles of a
Team Leader

Point out that participants can refer to What Learners Need, which also appears in the margin on page 16 of their Journals, during the semester.

WHAT LEARNERS NEED

Learners need a Team Leader who will—

- hear them recite the FAITH Visit Outline every week during Team Time;
- contact and pray for them during the week;
- gently persuade them to share what they have learned in actual visits;
- motivate and encourage them;
- check off memory work every week;
- model the outline in visits;
- use the Opinion Poll correctly in visits;
- know how to adjust the pace of training to meet Learner needs/abilities;
- be with them and encourage them to attend Celebration Time.

State: You will grow in faith as you put into practice 2 Timothy 2:1-2. You have accepted the privilege of mentoring two new Learners. They will be uncertain, concerned, excited— just as you once were. Keep in touch during the week. Explain why you handled a visit a particular way. Pray for Learners and seek to help them.

take to enhance your skills in leading persons to faith in Christ. God may be preparing you for the time when you will lead a Team of Learners through FAITH.

If you are a Team Leader, you will fill several important roles.

1. You are a ____role____ ____model____.
You will serve as a role model in FAITH training by—
- demonstrating how to make a FAITH visit;
- being on time for Team Time;
- learning and demonstrating what you have learned and are learning in FAITH training;
- keeping up with all Home Study Assignments;
- making sure the Team has positive Visitation Time experiences;
- participating in Celebration Time.

You will also serve as a role model in Sunday School by—
- taking leadership roles;
- participating in weekly Sunday School leadership team meetings;
- assimilating people, especially new members, into the class or department;
- looking for ways to disciple new believers through Sunday School.

2. You are an ____encourager____ and a ____motivator____.
As a Team Leader, you are responsible for—
- recognizing Learner needs;
- helping class and department members know about and want to be a part of the FAITH strategy;
- letting Learners know that you are praying for them;
- getting to know Learners and helping them feel comfortable with you during training sessions and throughout the week;
- assisting Learners as they memorize various parts of the FAITH Visit Outline during the week;
- encouraging Team members in things they are doing well before, during, and after visits;
- helping Learners during Team Time recite memory work and share experiences from home study;
- being sensitive to pressure points for Learners during the training;
- recognizing dropout signals;
- celebrating what Learners have memorized and completed by signing off on their assignments during Team Time;
- gently persuading Learners, when they are ready, to take the lead in specific parts of the visit.

3. You are a _____growing_____ _____disciple_____.

Everything you do as a Team Leader assumes that you are growing in your faith. It will be obvious if you are not doing this. Everything done in FAITH Discipleship—witnessing, ministry, mentoring, Bible study, prayer—requires you to grow. Making yourself available to be used by God in these ways is essential.

The Process

Sharing a Living Faith follows the format of FAITH Basic and Advanced courses.

1. Team Time (15 mins.)
   - CHECK IT—Leading Team Time
2. Teaching Time (45 mins.)
   - KNOW IT—review of the previous week's material
   - HEAR IT—presentation of the week's material
   - SEE IT—video segment supporting the week's material (selected sessions only)
   - SAY IT—application of the week's material or practice of the FAITH outline
   - STUDY IT—preview of Home Study Assignments
3. Visitation Time (110 or more minutes, depending on your church's schedule)
   - DO IT
4. Celebration Time (30 mins.)
   - SHARE IT

What Happens During Team Time

Team Time is a very important part of the schedule for FAITH Learners. During these 15 minutes Learners debrief, practice, and recite the portion of the FAITH Visit Outline they have been assigned to learn up to that point. Since learning the entire FAITH Visit Outline is such a significant part of FAITH training, Team Time becomes a time of accountability.

If You Are a Team Leader

Your job is to help Learners rehearse the outline so that they feel more comfortable and natural in making a visit. Although Team Time is only 15 minutes during most sessions, Learners will increasingly see it as a much appreciated checkup and practice time.

Each session of this resource provides help for preparing for and leading Team Time. Although Team Leaders are responsible for conducting Team Time each week, everyone who has completed FAITH Basic will have an important role.

Step 5 (30 mins.)

Recall the FAITH training schedule. Quickly review the parts of the process participants are familiar with. Spend more time on the new features of this course.

Pages 8–9 contain the FAITH Visit Outline in its entirety for participants to refer to throughout *Sharing a Living Faith* as needed. No new memory work is required for *Sharing a Living Faith*. The same FAITH Visit Outline is used in visits. Team Leaders will grow in their understanding of Christian beliefs and will learn ways to present the gospel more effectively in visits and in daily-life settings. Team Leaders will help new Learners become familiar with the presentation for the first time as Learners attend separate training sessions for FAITH Basic (*A Journey in FAITH*). As each Learner recites appropriate points of the FAITH Visit Outline each week, the Team Leader should check off these points in the Learner's *A Journey in FAITH Journal*.

Review the dynamics of Team Time, using the computer diskette or the overhead cel.
• FAITH Visit Outline
• Other Home Study Assignments
• Debriefing of Previous Session
• Help for Strengthening a Visit

Team Time Agenda

Team Time begins in session 2. Because good use of time is extremely important throughout this training, it is vital that you begin and conclude on time each week. (Session 12 is an extended Team Time, in which Learners spend the entire session practicing material they have learned.)

Each week ask Learners to recite the assigned portion of the FAITH Visit Outline as designated in the Team Time portion of *A Journey in FAITH Journal.* Hold the Learner's FAITH Journal and follow the outline as each person recites it.

Notice that these same assignments are capsuled in your resource in the section Leading Team Time, which begins each session. This feature will make you aware of what Learners are expected to know. Your copy of the FAITH Visit Outline is on pages 8–9 in this resource.

During the first few sessions you will likely have adequate time for both Team members to recite. Be aware that the longer the recitation, the greater the likelihood that only one person will be able to complete the outline during the 15 minutes before Teaching Time. Some of this work can continue in the car as the Team travels to and from visits.

In early sessions ask the person who feels most comfortable reciting to share first. Try not to put a Team member on the spot.

As a general rule and especially in later sessions, try to call on the person who most needs practice to share first. Do so with sensitivity and gentleness.

As a Team member correctly recites each line or phrase of the outline, place a check mark in the box beside the phrase. If the Learner has difficulty, does not recite it appropriately, or overlooks any portions, write notes in his copy of the FAITH Journal for his review. Be prepared to answer any questions the Learner might have about the outline and suggest ways to strengthen sharing the outline. When a Team member has successfully recited the assigned portion of the outline, sign off by writing your name or initials in the space provided in the member's Journal.

Overview the Learner's Home Study Assignments from the previous week. Feel free to raise questions and to discuss any aspect of the assignments. Doing so can help reinforce many important concepts taught through these assignments—concepts that may have been only introduced during the session. Again, sign off in the Learner's Journal any assignments that have been completed and that call for your approval.

As you debrief assignments or answer questions about the previous session, highlight ones that will appear on the final written review (ses. 16). Weekly, help reduce Learners' concerns about the final review.

Although you will not read the Learner's Your Journey in Faith pages, it will be significant to check to see that the Learner is keeping a written journal of his experiences throughout FAITH. It is easy to overlook this important aspect of home study.

However, journaling brings an enriching dimension to FAITH training. Suggest that Team members record their experiences and reflections on the Bible study. Encourage Learners to review previous journaling pages, particularly during times of discouragement. At the end of this semester both you and your Learners will be asked to write testimonies of what FAITH has meant personally, so your Journal is a wonderful record.

If You Are Not a Team Leader

Even if you are not a Team Leader, you will still need to participate in Team Time by being prepared to recite the FAITH Visit Outline, review the Home Study Assignments, and discuss ways to strengthen a visit. You may be asked to assist the Team Leader by working with a Team member who needs help and encouragement in learning and reciting the FAITH Visit Outline.

As Team members ride together to and from the visits, Learners can continue to practice sharing the outline and to discuss ways to strengthen a visit.

What Happens During Teaching Time

During Teaching Time you and Team Learners go in separate directions for a focused time to learn new information. While Teaching Time for Team Learners presents the concepts in FAITH Basic, you will study the content in this course, *Sharing a Living Faith*. You will spend 45 minutes each week focusing on a different Christian belief, each framed as a question that might be posed by a lost person. You will receive biblical instruction, followed by suggestions for applying what you have learned in FAITH visits and other witnessing and ministry situations.

The following format will be used for Teaching Time.

A Quick __Review__

The first segment of Teaching Time, A Quick Review, is a five-minute period of accountability. Principles from the previous session will be reviewed. Some of the material in A Quick Review will appear on the final review (ses. 16).

Defining the __Question__

Behind many questions you encounter on a visit or in daily life may lie a variety of other questions that reveal a hunger for Jesus Christ. For example, the situations noted earlier in this session point to questions we will study this semester.

Look at the questions listed in Contents (p. 3) and identify which questions might be suggested by the following situations.

Introduce the segments of Teaching Time, using the computer diskette or the overhead cel. Ask participants to fill in the blanks on pages 19–20 in their Journals. State that the same process is followed in each session's Teaching Time.

Teaching Time Agenda

Give participants time to complete this exercise. Then call for responses. Possible responses:

1. The Bible, God, Jesus, evil, what it means to be lost, what it means to be saved, why Bible study and prayer are important
2. Jesus, suffering, what it means to be lost, what it means to be saved, why Bible study and prayer are important, strength for daily living, purpose of life
3. Jesus, what it means to be lost, what it means to be saved, purpose of life
4. God, Jesus, evil, suffering, what it means to be saved, church, strength for daily living, purpose of life

For students use the alternative questions on page 15 for this exercise.

1. A coworker is reading the newspaper at break, and a discussion develops about who can be trusted to tell the truth.

   _____

2. A long-time acquaintance calls to tell you that his spouse is facing cancer and wants to know if your pastor can visit.

   _____

3. A neighbor's oldest child is ready to leave for college, and your neighbor wonders whether all the extra days and nights he clocked at work were worth it.

   _____

4. The clerk at the grocery store asks you why you are happy when so many bad things are happening in our world.

   _____

Each question being addressed in this study can be asked from a variety of perspectives. Defining the Question, a five-minute segment of Teaching Time, will help you identify these perspectives and understand the issue behind the question.

The Bible ___Speaks___
This 10- to 20-minute segment of Teaching Time examines Scriptures that address the session's topic. Biblical teaching is always the source of truth and authority for our belief system.

___Entry___ ___Points___ in FAITH Visits
This five-minute period identifies points in FAITH visits when questions about that session's topic could arise. Perhaps the person you are witnessing or ministering to will ask a question or mention a problem that indicates the need to address this issue.

How You Can ___Respond___
This five-minute period suggests ways you can respond when the question or issue arises during a FAITH visit.

What Happens During Visitation Time
This period of 110 or more minutes, depending on your church's schedule, is the vital time when you and your Team come back together to practice what you have learned through prayer and training.

FAITH Teams

Three persons are on every FAITH Team. In addition to the Team Leader, who has been trained in the FAITH strategy, two Team Learners have been enlisted to be trained and to visit together. Each Team represents a designated Sunday School division, department, or class.

Write the names of your Team members on the lines provided. If a Team member has already received training but is not participating as a Team Leader, write that member's name and role on the Team (for example, Assistant Team Leader).

_____

_____

_____
                                                    Team Leader

Lead participants to write the names of other members of their FAITH Team on the lines provided.

FAITH Participation Card

One of the first things Team members are doing is preparing their FAITH Participation Cards (p. 10). You will remember that this card is used each week as a name placard and to record numbers and types of visits attempted and made by the Team. If you have not already completed the top portion of your Participation Card, do so now. Make sure your name is printed in large letters on the reverse side of your name placard.

Review the categories of the Participation Card. You will be responsible for helping your Team members understand the categories identified on the card. You will also be responsible for helping them to complete their cards following visits that begin with session 2.

The Participation Card is the basis for information on the FAITH Report Board. Remember that reports from the visits are summarized here. Your job is to orient your Team members to this process so they can eventually report during Celebration Time.

Lead participants to complete the personal information on their cards for the semester. Emphasize the importance of every team's completing a weekly report.

Types of Visits

In all visits you should be ready to share the message of the gospel, as well as to invite unsaved persons to saving faith in Christ. You will look for opportunities to represent Christ by ministering to individuals in need, by enrolling some people in Bible study, and by helping others grow in their journey of faith. Each Team will make four types of visits.
1. Teams will make visits to Sunday School prospects, some of whom have had contact with your church as visitors to Sunday School, worship, or a special event. Some have been referred by a member, and others were discovered through a People Search opportunity. Generally, prospects are those who are open to a contact from or a relationship with your church.

Review the types of visits that can be made.

2. Teams will make ministry visits to Sunday School members.
3. Teams will make visits using the Opinion Poll.
4. Teams will make follow-up visits to persons who have made significant decisions: to trust Christ, join the church, or enroll in Sunday School.

Although you will discover many new experiences when you make visits, Learners will be interested in knowing about each of these types of visits when they receive their assignments. Your experience, as well as what is taught during Teaching Time, will be particularly helpful as Learners determine ways to participate in each type of visit.

Visitation Folder

Each Team will have a visitation folder that has been prepared for that week's visits. Be prepared to explain the significance and use of each item before, during, and after visits.

Contents of the visitation folder may include these and other items designated by the church.

Visitation assignment forms. Each week you should have several of these forms. Some assignments will be to a specific person or family indicated as a prospect. Other forms might be for visits to members. Some forms will indicate the assignment as a follow-up visit. Each form should indicate the general nature of the assigned visit.

If the card does not indicate that the person is a Sunday School member, assume that you are visiting to cultivate a relationship on behalf of the church and the Sunday School. Approach the visit assuming that you may have an opportunity to share the gospel.

Lead your Team to make as many visits as are feasible during the designated time. If you are unable to make assigned visits and/or have extra time, use the Opinion Poll to identify opportunities for evangelism and ministry.

Information about the church and Sunday School. A diagram, list, or information sheet should include a basic overview of Sunday School so that you can help family members identify with and know where Sunday School classes meet.

A *Step of Faith.* Use this leaflet when sharing the gospel with a person and issuing an **Invitation**. Also use it to enroll a person in Sunday School and to record decisions made during a visit.

My Next Step of Faith. In session 3 of FAITH Advanced you received detailed help in using this leaflet to help a new believer take a next step of obedience through believer's baptism.

Opinion Poll cards. Use these forms to ask and record responses when making Opinion Poll visits.

Bible-study material used by your class. During a visit give a copy of current material to new enrollees and to nonattending members.

Believe magazine. This devotional magazine helps new believers understand who they are in Christ and become grounded in their faith.[2]

Highlight resources in the visitation folder that are unique to your church. Encourage participants to record ways these items can help them.

For students who are new believers, *essential connection* devotional magazine is suggested.

Church promotional information about upcoming special events and opportunities.

Identify the items in your packet that are unique to your church. How can these items help you make better visits?

_____

You will be responsible for demonstrating how to use each item in the visitation folder. Until Learners overview how to use these items and complete the forms, you will be responsible for training them in how to use them. Remember that you are the Learners' model, and they will follow the example you set. Whatever you do correctly or incorrectly will be multiplied by them in the future.

Let's briefly review what is expected in completing the visitation forms. No matter what type of record form is used by the church, you need to take the following actions.

1. Fill in every applicable ___**blank**___ in which information is requested.
2. If an assigned person is not at home or is not willing to respond to selected questions for information, ___**initial**___ the card (or blanks left incomplete) and indicate the ___**date**___ of the attempted visit and the ___**reason**___ information was not recorded.
3. ___**Print**___ information ___**legibly**___.
4. Write information discovered from the visit that will help in making any ___**follow-up**___ ___**contact**___.
5. Record information about all other ___**prospects**___ discovered in the home.
6. Turn in the detachable ___**Response**___ ___**Card**___ portion of *A Step of Faith*.

Prayer and Practice

If you have a sufficient number of teams participating in FAITH visits, the work of several teams will be coordinated by a FAITH Group Leader. For the purposes of Prayer and Practice, one group of Teams will remain in the Teaching Time room each week to pray while other Teams make visits. This process will begin no earlier than session 3. Assignments for Prayer and Practice are made on a rotating basis and are noted in your weekly newsletter or in the visitation folder.

As soon as visiting Teams depart to make visits, the assigned Group Leader assembles Teams for prayer. Teams pray throughout Visitation Time specifically for the Team members visiting and for the individuals to be visited. They pray for divine appointments. The Group Leader might call the names of persons visiting and being visited.

During Prayer and Practice the Group Leader can also lead Teams to practice reciting the FAITH Visit Outline with one another. Team

Direct participants to fill in the blanks on page 23 in their Journals as you emphasize the six points of completing all records.

Explain how prayer and practice will be done in your church, as well as how this information will be communicated.

members can also spend time writing notes to prospects and members. When Prayer and Practice is over, the Group Leader leads participants to complete their session Participation and Evaluation Cards.

What Happens During Celebration Time

This is a 30-minute time to report Team and FAITH-strategy victories. Each week you will be responsible for leading your Team to report about visits attempted and visits made. This can become a very meaningful and motivational time. In addition to helping Team members update and submit their Participation Cards, Evaluation Cards, and visitation-assignment cards, help them know how to complete the Report Board.

Particularly during the first few weeks of training, Team members will look to you to share verbal reports during the report time. Even if a Team seemingly has not had a productive visit, Team members share in the ministry's victories during this period.

Keep these guidelines in mind as you lead and help your Team members verbally report.

1. *Be brief.* The amount of time needed will be determined by the number of Teams reporting.
2. *Be precise.* Do not give unnecessary details.
3. *Be positive.* Discuss problems or negatives in another setting, such as with your Group Leader.
4. *Be enthusiastic.* You and your Team have been attempting the greatest opportunity in the world!
5. *Be accurate.* Do not embellish what really happened.
6. *Be careful.* Do not report anything confidential that was shared with your Team. Use only the first names of the persons you visited.
7. *Be thankful.* Even if no decision was made or no one allowed you to share, be grateful for the opportunity to talk.
8. *Be affirming.* If Joe shared a Sunday School testimony for the first time in a visit and did a great job, tell the entire group. You not only encourage Joe but also motivate other Teams.

Your Resources

Sharing a Living Faith will enhance and reinforce your earlier FAITH training. Here are important resources you will use.

FAITH Visit Outline

There is no new memory work; you will continue to practice the FAITH Visit Outline.

Highlight guidelines for giving reports during Celebration Time.

Using the computer diskette or the overhead cel, review the dates this course will begin and end, as well as the times Team Time, Teaching Time, Visitation Time, and Celebration Time will begin each week.

Our Schedule

Break (5 mins.)

Step 6 (10 mins.)

Overview the resources available to participants through their Journals or through the group sessions.

Sharing a Living Faith Journal

As was true in FAITH Basic and Advanced, the Journal will be your main resource. After you have filled in the blanks during each session's Teaching Time, it can be helpful during home study to reread that session to get the big picture. Besides the content studied during Teaching Time, the following sections are included in your Journal.

- *Leading Team Time.* The Leading Team Time suggestions each week will help you as a Team Leader debrief, practice, and review with your Team. Suggestions are based on Learners' *A Journey in FAITH Journal* Team Time agenda for each week.
- *Home Study Assignments.* Each week your Home Study Assignments reinforce the session by helping you apply what you have learned.
—*Your Discipleship Journey.* Assignments in this section focus on your development as a disciple.
—*Growing as a Life Witness.* This section reminds you of your responsibility to witness and minister to others during the week.
—*Your Weekly Sunday School Leadership Team Meeting.* This section allows you to make notes about the way your FAITH Team influences the work of your Sunday School class or department. As you and other leaders meet to plan for next Sunday's Bible-study time, identify actions that need to be taken through Sunday School as a result of prayer concerns, needs identified, visits made by the Team, and decisions made by the persons visited. You may also identify ways you can disciple others in your Sunday School class or department and in your church.
—*Discipling Your Team Members.* This section suggests ways you can disciple your Team members as you prepare to lead your FAITH Team's group time at the beginning of the next session and as you mentor and support members through the week. You will find reminders about the things the Learners have studied, as well as some tips to help you be a better Team Leader.
—*For Further Growth.* This section challenges you with optional long-term reading or discipleship activities.

In-Session Training Resources

Your Facilitator will use these resources to help you learn.

- Videotape segments, in which you will see examples of visits and other witnessing encounters that focus attention on the questions addressed in this course
- Computer diskette or overhead cels to help you fill in the blanks and understand that session's teaching

Sunday School

Your Sunday School class or department is a primary resource. Sunday School is the unique dynamic of FAITH. Your class/department can be

---

These items are provided in your *Sharing a Living Faith Training Pack.*

- *Facilitator Guide.* This guide contains the same sessions trainees have, plus answers and teaching suggestions.
- *Sharing a Living Faith Journal.* Each participant needs a copy of the Journal.
- *Audiotape.* You have permission to duplicate the tape for every participant. These messages by Bobby Welch may be used anytime during the course to motivate Learners and to reinforce teaching content.
- *Videotape.* Video segments give examples of ways participants can express their Christian beliefs in FAITH visits and how they can handle challenges to their beliefs. These segments support selected training sessions. The videotape also provides a brief promotional segment. You have permission to duplicate the video for additional training groups.
- *Overhead cels.* This set of 73 overhead cels is used during Teaching Times to support the sessions' content.
- *Computer diskette.* You may prefer a computer presentation to overhead cels. Choose the medium of teaching support best suited for your church and for the training room. The PC disk provided is compatible with PowerPoint® 1997 software.
- *Order form.* Additional copies of the *Journal,* the *Facilitator Guide,* and the *Training Pack* may be ordered, as well as items introduced in previous FAITH courses.

a place where names become people, needs become visible, and assimilation becomes more than a term. Attending the weekly Sunday School leadership team meeting creates this link.

Your Walk with God

Three components of your walk with God will provide essential spiritual direction as you participate in this course.

- *Your willingness to join God's work.* The work of evangelism is God's activity, and you must be willing to be on His agenda and timetable in this endeavor. Ask that His Holy Spirit will guide you in what you say and do; empower you for divine confidence, strength, and wisdom; and prepare each lost person's heart for the seeds you will sow. During the next 16 weeks, expect God to work in your life, in your Sunday School/church, in the lives of people you meet, and in your Team.
- *Bible study.* You will be exposed to a lot of biblical content during this course. Your Facilitator will not have time to cover in-depth each passage in your Journal. Spend time between sessions reading and reviewing the passages so that you will be better prepared "to give the reason for the hope that you have" (1 Pet. 3:15). Never underestimate the power of God's living and active Word to speak with an authority of its own (see 2 Tim. 3:15-17; Heb. 4:12).
- *Prayer.* Prayer is your most important and most powerful resource. The Lord has promised to hear us when we call on Him (see Matt. 18:19-20; 21:22; Luke 11:9-13). Call on Him throughout *Sharing a Living Faith* and enlist faithful prayer partners to uphold you in prayer for the next 16 weeks.

Your Testimony

By now you have been involved in FAITH training for at least 1½ years, maybe longer. Many things can take place in that length of time.

Think about your Sunday School class when you started FAITH training and the ways FAITH has changed your Sunday School. Who has joined as a result of FAITH?

_____

_____

Step 7 (10 mins.)

Emphasize the importance of current Sunday School and evangelistic testimonies. Give participants an opportunity to identify ways their testimonies need to be updated. Encourage them to update or rewrite their testimonies, if necessary, before session 2.

What members have participated in FAITH training?

_____

_____

Because Sunday School is an essential part of the FAITH process, it is important to keep your Sunday School testimony current. What changes do you need to make in your Sunday School testimony you developed for your first semester of FAITH to better describe what is happening in your class today?

_____

_____

You may also need to update your evangelistic testimony. What has God been teaching you in the past 18 months? How has your spiritual life changed? What adjustments do you need to make in your evangelistic testimony to make it current?

_____

_____

Remind participants that they will assist Team Learners in developing their testimonies as well. Encourage participants to share their updated testimonies with other Team members.

Growing as a Life Witness

While overviewing the Participation Card, you may have noticed the Life Witness line. One goal of FAITH training is to develop Great Commission Christians—believers committed to sharing the gospel in today's world. This means we must share Christ more than the scheduled two hours a week. In fact, sharing Jesus must become a part of our lifestyle if we are to be true Great Commission Christians.

You will be encouraged to grow as a life witness during *Sharing a Living Faith* through the following expectations.

1. The ____**Growing**____ as a ____**Life**____ ____**Witness**____ portion of your Home Study Assignments will remind you of your responsibility to witness and minister to others during the week, besides during FAITH visits.

2. In addition to your prayer partners in your Sunday School class or department, you will have an _____**accountability**_____ ____**partner**____ throughout the semester who will—
   - ____**ask**____ whether you have had witnessing and ministry opportunities during the past week, other than FAITH visits;

Step 8 (10 mins.)

Explain what it means to be a life witness and the importance of looking for opportunities to witness and minister in daily life. Ask participants to fill in the blanks on pages 27–28 in their Journals as you point out ways this study will emphasize growing as a life witness.

Assist in selecting accountability partners and explain the responsibilities throughout the course. Facilitate the exchange of phone numbers. If you have an odd number of participants, you will need to serve as someone's accountability partner.

SAY IT

Step 9 (5 mins.)

Ask accountability partners to practice sharing the **Preparation** portion of the FAITH Visit Outline with each other.

HEAR IT

Step 10 (10 mins.)

Ask participants to fill in the blanks on pages 28–29 in their Journals as you review basic guidelines for responding to questions. Use the computer diskette or the overhead cels. State that suggestions for addressing specific questions will be presented in the appropriate sessions but that these general ones can also be applied as needed.

Basic
Guidelines
for
Responding
to Questions

- **pray** for specific persons you identify, for your participation in FAITH Discipleship training, for your effectiveness as a Team Leader, and for your use by God in divine appointments;
- **discuss** problems or questions you may have in witnessing encounters or in completing other Home Study Assignments;
- periodically **practice** the FAITH Visit Outline and ways new concepts in this course can be applied in witnessing situations.

My accountability partner is _____

Phone number(s): _____

Responding to Questions

In addition to the guidance you will receive during each session of this study for responding to questions about specific areas of the Christian faith, here are some general guidelines to apply, no matter what topic the question relates to. However, not every principle will apply in every situation. Always pray that the Holy Spirit will guide you to an appropriate response that meets the person's need.

1. **Pray** for the person and for the Team member who is sharing.
2. Remember that you are on someone else's turf. You must **establish** **rapport** before a person will trust you or hear what you have to say.
3. **Never** **argue** with the person. Do not argue the rightness of your belief or antagonize the person. **Gently** **probe** for more information that would allow you to share the gospel and to identify the core need behind the question or comment.
4. Take the question seriously. Sensitively **listen** to the objection and **respond** in **love**.
5. **Delay**. In some cases, it is appropriate to ask permission to answer a question at a later time. For example, in response to a question that may not be relevant at that point of the presentation, ask permission to answer it later. Encourage the person to remind you later and then answer the question to the best of your ability.
6. **Answer** **now**. If the person's question is relevant and can be handled at that point in the presentation, go ahead and do so. Make the answer brief and get back to the presentation. Do not get into a debate.
7. **Admit** that you don't know the answer. If you cannot

answer the person's question, say so. Ask for permission to continue sharing.

8. Try to _____**discern**_____ whether the person genuinely wants to know the truth or wants to distract or frustrate you. If the question reveals an obstacle to the person's coming to Christ and the person is willing to discuss it in-depth, explore it from a biblical standpoint, using the evidence you will examine in this study. Try to return to the FAITH presentation, but if this is not possible, you may need to ask permission to visit again for further conversations after the person's issues have been resolved.

9. Keep in mind that you represent Christ and His church. Demonstrating _____**Christlikeness**_____ increases the possibility that the person will respect you and your message.

10. Be _____**concise**_____ and _____**clear**_____. You do not need to explain everything about the topic or about the Christian faith. FAITH is a simple tool to help you and others remember the gospel. Some points will need to be clarified; be prepared to do so as needed or requested.

Remember that you are on holy ground when a person allows you to discuss matters of the soul. Your responsibility is to share what God is doing in your life and to offer a short, easy-to-remember explanation of God's good news. Without compromising the truth of Scripture, you are appropriately asking a person to share his or her understanding of several spiritual matters. You can explain and clarify without arguing.

STUDY IT

Step 11 (5 mins.)

If you have not already done so, describe the nature of Home Study Assignments in FAITH Discipleship.

- Your Discipleship Journey focuses on participants' development as disciples.
- Growing as a Life Witness encourages accountability for witnessing and ministering to others during the week.
- Your Weekly Sunday School Leadership Team Meeting allows participants who are elected Sunday School leaders to report to the Sunday School leadership team.
- Discipling Your Team Members helps Team Leaders disciple Team members as they prepare to lead Team Time at the beginning of the next session and support Team members during the week. They will find reminders about the things the Learners have studied, as well as some tips to help them be better Team Leaders.
- For Further Growth is used to challenge participants with additional reading or discipleship activities.

Overview Home Study Assignments for session 1.

Remind the group that home visits will begin in session 2. Close by asking accountability partners to pray with each other, asking for God's strength and guidance as they seek to grow as His disciples and to enhance their witnessing skills.

Home Study Assignments

Home Study Assignments reinforce this session by helping you apply what you have learned.

Your Discipleship Journey

Journaling activities in Your Discipleship Journey are an important part of your development as a Great Commission Christian through FAITH training.

1. One purpose of FAITH Discipleship is to help you grow in your relationship with God. Start by assessing your personal discipleship habits, using the following scale.

1 = never	4 = usually
2 = seldom	5 = always
3 = sometimes	

I have a daily quiet time.	1	2	3	4	5
I make Christ number one in my life.	1	2	3	4	5
I stay close to the Lord throughout the day.	1	2	3	4	5
I read my Bible daily.	1	2	3	4	5
I study my Bible in depth.	1	2	3	4	5
I memorize a Scripture verse each week.	1	2	3	4	5
I keep a prayer list and pray for those concerns.	1	2	3	4	5
I recognize answers to my prayers.	1	2	3	4	5
I include praise, thanksgiving, confession, petition, and intercession in my prayers.	1	2	3	4	5
I live in harmony with my family and other believers.	1	2	3	4	5
I seek reconciliation when it is needed.	1	2	3	4	5
I attend worship services.	1	2	3	4	5
I attend Bible study.	1	2	3	4	5
I pray for lost persons by name.	1	2	3	4	5
I share my testimony with others.	1	2	3	4	5
I share the plan of salvation with others.	1	2	3	4	5
I witness each week.	1	2	3	4	5
I follow up on persons I have led to Christ.	1	2	3	4	5
I serve in my church.	1	2	3	4	5
I give at least a tithe through my church.	1	2	3	4	5
I minister to others.[3]	1	2	3	4	5

Examine your responses to the inventory and determine where you need to improve. Write one action you will commit to take to grow in discipleship.

_____

_____

2. Record goals you have for this semester of FAITH Discipleship.

A goal for your personal discipleship: _____

_____

_____

A goal for witnessing: _____

_____

_____

A goal for discipling Team members and Sunday School members:

_____

_____

Growing as a Life Witness

Growing as a Life Witness reminds you of your responsibility to witness and minister to others during the week.

1. Contact your accountability partner and plan the way you will communicate each week during the semester.
2. Discuss any persons you are cultivating through ministry or witness.
3. Pray for each other's growth as disciples, as Team Leaders, and as witnesses.

Prayer Concerns	Answers to Prayer
_____	_____
_____	_____
_____	_____
_____	_____
_____	_____
_____	_____
_____	_____

Your Weekly Sunday School Leadership Team Meeting

A FAITH participant is an important member of Sunday School. Encourage Team members who are elected Sunday School workers to attend this weekly meeting. Use this section to record ways your FAITH Team influences the work of your Sunday School class or department. Use the information to report during weekly Sunday School leadership team meetings. Identify actions that need to be taken through Sunday School as a result of prayer concerns, needs identified, visits made by the Team, and decisions made by the persons visited. Also identify ways you can disciple others in your Sunday School class or department and in your church.

1. Think back to your first day of FAITH training and recall as much as you can about your Sunday School class then. Who else from your class was in FAITH training?

_____

2. Think about your class now. How has it changed? How many of the people in your class are new believers or new members of your church? Who has joined you in FAITH training? What role has FAITH played in these changes?

_____

3. A new semester of FAITH is under way. How does the team's preparation for every Sunday through this weekly leadership meeting need to consider the needs of individuals or families visited through FAITH?

_____

4. This time together each week also can facilitate your growth as a disciple. Does your continuing commitment to FAITH training include a commitment to attend this important weekly meeting?

Discipling Your Team Members

This weekly feature suggests actions the Team Leader can take to support Team members, prepare for Team Time, and consider ways to improve visits. This work becomes part of the Team Leader's Home Study Assignments. Add any actions suggested by your church's FAITH strategy.

Support Team Members

❑ Contact Team members during the week. Explain to them that you will pray for them during this semester of FAITH. Discuss their orientation to

FAITH. Emphasize the importance of being on time for Team Time. Briefly remind them of their role during Team Time.

❑ As you talk with Learners this week—
- find out whether they understood their Home Study Assignments, especially the writing of their Sunday School testimonies;
- ask whether they have a prayer partner from their Sunday School class;
- suggest that they preview the FAITH Tip for session 2, "Helpful Visitation Tips," in *A Journey in FAITH Journal*.

❑ Remind members to bring a small Bible with them to take on visits. Teams will make visits after session 2, then return for Celebration Time.

❑ Record specific needs and concerns shared by Team members on the lines provided at the end of Your Discipleship Journey.

Prepare to Lead Team Time
❑ Review Team members' Home Study Assignments.
❑ Overview Leading Team Time for session 2.

Prepare to Lead Visits
❑ Review the FAITH Visit Outline.
❑ Be prepared to explain the contents of the visitation folder.
❑ Be ready to model a visit in which Team members are asked to share their Sunday School testimonies.

Link with Sunday School
❑ Prepare to share with other Sunday School workers a brief summary of what you will study during this semester of FAITH Discipleship. Ask that they pray for you as you continue to learn and grow in your witnessing skills.

For Further Growth

For Further Growth may include additional reading or activities that will enhance your growth as a disciple and a discipler of others. These assignments are intended to be long-term projects and do not have to be completed during this semester of study.

1. Read Matthew 11:1-6; 21:23-27; 22:23-33 to observe the way Jesus handled difficult questions. What did you learn from Jesus' responses that you can apply in witnessing situations?

2. A mentoring relationship is at the heart of being an effective FAITH Team Leader. Read "How to Build Mentoring Relationships" (pp. 262–63) in *Building Bridges Through FAITH Journal*.

---

[1] Avery T. Willis, Jr., *MasterLife 1: The Disciple's Cross* (Nashville: LifeWay Press, 1996), 5.
[2] *Believe* magazine is available by writing to Customer Service Center, MSN 113; 127 Ninth Avenue, North; Nashville, TN 37234-0113; by calling toll free (800) 458-2772; by faxing (615) 251-5933; by ordering online at *www.lifeway.com*; or by emailing *customerservice@lifeway.com*.
[3] Willis, *MasterLife 1*, 29–30.

FAITH AT WORK

I have arrived home in Centralia, Washington, after attending a FAITH training clinic in faraway Tucson, Arizona. Already the people of my church have responded to the call to begin the FAITH training process. Immediately, three members approached me about beginning the training. By the end of the Sunday-evening service, there were five! God is already moving in our midst to begin evangelizing and discipling the people of Centralia.

It's true, I was very reluctant to go to Arizona for the FAITH training clinic. I have more books, tapes, and videos on evangelism and church growth than I need, and one more to add to the stack was too much! But I was desperately searching for a tool that would involve the church in reaching our community for Christ and then keeping new believers in church. I had been approached about attending a FAITH training clinic some time ago but had dismissed the idea as just another program to make busier those who were too busy already.

However, I researched some churches that were involved in or had heard of FAITH. No one told me it had failed. In fact, the reports I heard were astonishing! Pastors told me that people were coming to Christ and then staying in the church to be discipled. I felt that God was showing me that what I had been looking for was right in front of my face.

I approached two other men in my church, Mike and Tim, about attending and prayed that if they were willing to go, then I would take it as an open door from the Lord. They were not only willing but eager! Together we prayed that the Lord would provide the financing for the trip, because without it we wouldn't be able to go. As all of the pieces fell into place, the anticipation of what God would be doing grew. Still I was a bit skeptical, wondering whether we would be sitting through four days of product promotion.

To make a long story short, at the clinic the three of us caught a vision from God! Through the training process we discovered an opportunity and optimism sent by God. Even Tim, who admitted that he struggles with sharing his faith, said that he has finally broken out of his shell forever! I am convinced that God has delivered to us a tool that will be used to bring multitudes to Christ in the Centralia area. The 1,600 miles we traveled to find it was not too far.

Michael Duncan
Pastor, Alder Street Baptist Church
Centralia, Washington

How Do I Know the Bible Is True?

In this session you will—

CHECK IT by engaging in Team Time activities;

KNOW IT by reviewing distinctives of this course from session 1;

HEAR IT by affirming what the Bible says about the truth of God's Word;

SEE IT by viewing a video segment;

SAY IT by discussing possible applications of what you have learned;

STUDY IT by overviewing Home Study Assignments;

DO IT by leading your Team in making visits;

SHARE IT by celebrating.

In Advance

- Overview content.
- Preview teaching suggestions. Prepare key points. Decide whether to use the session 2 computer slides or the overhead cels.
- Enlist participants to read aloud selected Scripture passages to be discussed during the session, if desired.
- Prepare the room for teaching.
- Cue the videotape to the session 2 segment, Digging for the Truth.
- Pray for participants and for Teams as they prepare for their first home visits.
- As Teaching Time begins, direct participants to open their Journals to page 38.

TEAM TIME

CHECK IT (15 mins.)

If the computer diskette is used, display the agenda frame for your Team Time, as desired. Add other points as needed.

CHECK IT agenda:
✔ FAITH Visit Outline
✔ Sunday School Testimony
✔ Other Home Study Assignments
✔ Session 1 Debriefing
✔ Help for Strengthening a Visit

Leading Team Time

All Team members participate in Team Time. They are primarily responsible for reciting the assigned portion of the FAITH Visit Outline and for discussing other Home Study Assignments.

As you direct this important time of CHECK IT activities with your Team, keep in mind that Learners look to you as a role model, motivator, mentor, and friend. Team Time activities can continue in the car as the Team travels to and from visits.

Lead CHECK IT Activities

Since this is the first time for Team Time activities, provide any additional explanation that is needed. Make good use of the 15 minutes that begin each session.

✔ *FAITH Visit Outline*

❑ Team members should be ready to recite all aspects of *Preparation* up to INQUIRY and the key words in *Presentation* (FORGIVENESS, AVAILABLE, IMPOSSIBLE, TURN, HEAVEN) and *Invitation* (INQUIRE, INVITE, INSURE).

❑ Indicate your approval by signing or initialing Journals. Encourage Learners.

✔ *Sunday School Testimony Due*

❑ Ask Team members for their written Sunday School testimonies, due this session. Help evaluate each testimony to make sure it includes one or two of the following aspects: friendship/support received, assistance received during a crisis, personal benefits of Bible study through the class, or ways they have grown as a Christian through experiences in or through the Sunday School class. Discuss how benefits can and do change, reflecting different experiences.

❑ If the written testimony is acceptable, make sure each Team member understands the importance of learning to share it naturally, in his or her own words. Ask for permission to print the testimony in any church materials that publicize FAITH and/or that encourage persons to share their testimonies.

✔ *Other Home Study Assignments*

❑ Are Learners on track with Home Study Assignments? Provide any feedback or help they may need.

✔ *Session 1 Debriefing*

❑ Make sure major concepts from session 1 are understood, since this session provides an orientation to the course.

✔ Help for Strengthening a Visit

❑ This is the first session in which Teams will make home visits. Encourage members and try to allay any concerns. Explain that the Team leader will take the lead in the INTRODUCTION portion of the visit(s) following this session.

❑ Identify a Team member(s) who would be prepared to share a Sunday School testimony at the Team Leader's prompting during a visit. Be sensitive to persons who are ready to share.

Notes

_____

_____

_____

_____

_____

_____

_____

Actions I Need to Take with Learners During the Week

_____

_____

_____

_____

_____

_____

_____

Transition to classrooms for instruction on the session's content. (5 mins.)

TEACHING TIME

KNOW IT

Step 1 (5 mins.)

Direct participants to locate A Quick Review on page 38 in their Journals and to check the correct goals of FAITH Discipleship. Then give the answers, using the computer diskette or the overhead cel.

Goals of
FAITH
Discipleship

Review the three purposes of *Sharing a Living Faith,* using the computer diskette or the overhead cel.

Purposes of
*Sharing a
Living Faith*

State that the three purposes of this course are supported by the process followed in each session's Teaching Time. Review the process, using the computer diskette or the overhead cel.

A New
Process

A Quick Review

Goals of FAITH Discipleship

FAITH Discipleship is the next step in your journey in FAITH, following your semesters of FAITH Basic and Advanced training. FAITH Discipleship will further equip you as a Great Commission witness. Check the ways FAITH Discipleship will do this.

- ☑ 1. By teaching you important biblical truths you need to understand and exemplify as a growing disciple
- ☐ 2. By giving you an overview of the Old Testament
- ☐ 3. By guiding you through a process to deal with past hurts
- ☑ 4. By equipping you to respond to difficult questions you may encounter in witnessing
- ☑ 5. By helping you develop as a life witness for Christ, taking advantage of daily opportunities to share God's love
- ☐ 6. By helping you discover your spiritual gifts
- ☑ 7. By giving you opportunities to practice what you have learned in witnessing situations
- ☑ 8. By helping you develop as a Team Leader
- ☐ 9. By suggesting ways to make lost persons feel guilty
- ☑ 10. By suggesting ways you can disciple others

Purposes of *Sharing a Living Faith*

The first stop on your FAITH Discipleship journey is this course, *Sharing a Living Faith.* This course has three purposes:

1. To help you develop a biblical ____**belief**____ ____**system**____
2. To help you become a more effective ____**witness**____
3. To help you explore ways you can ____**disciple**____ ____**others**____

    The biblical beliefs you will explore in this course are framed as difficult questions you may encounter while making witnessing visits or in everyday witnessing situations that may arise. You will find on the Contents page (p. 3) a list of the questions we will address.

A New Process

Here is the process we will use to explore each question.

1. Defining the ____**Question**____
2. The Bible ____**Speaks**____
3. ____**Entry**____ ____**Points**____ in FAITH Visits
4. How You Can ____**Respond**____

    In addition, your Home Study Assignments will help you apply to your own life what you have learned in each session. Your personal growth as a disciple is one of the primary goals of FAITH Discipleship courses.

Defining the Question: How Do I Know the Bible Is True?

This question is one that has been asked by millions of people in various ways since the Lord gave us His Word. When individuals question the truthfulness of the Bible, we should not be offended. This is a fair question, even a good one. Although some may ask questions to distract you or argue, others may genuinely want to know the truth. We live in an age of relativism in which people have been taught that there is no ultimate truth. It is difficult for many to accept our claim that the Bible contains God's absolute truth.

Here are some ways you might anticipate being questioned or challenged about the truth of the Bible.

- "How do you know the Bible is true?"
- "How can you believe something written so long ago?"
- "What do you mean when you say that the Bible is God's Word?"
- "How can the Bible be God's Word if human beings wrote it?"
- "The Bible is out-of-date, without relevance for today."
- "The Bible has been disproved by scientific and historical discoveries."
- "The Bible is a book of fantasy. How can you believe those things really happened?"

People view the Bible in many different ways. Some see it as—

- the __exact__ __words__ of God;
- a type of __good-luck__ __charm__ to ward off evil;
- an important piece of __literature__ of equal significance with other literary classics;
- containing __some__ __truth__ about God but not all;
- a collection of __stories__ and __fables__;
- a restrictive book of __rules__ that will be used to __hurt__ them or __limit__ their __freedom__.

The truthfulness of the Bible can never be proved to the complete satisfaction of every person you encounter. However, it is important for Christian disciples to know what they believe about the truth of God's Word and to be ready to share their beliefs in ways that will draw others to the God of the Bible.

HEAR IT

Step 2 (5 mins.)

Introduce the content of this session by summarizing Defining the Question. Use the computer diskette or the overhead cel to illustrate questions and comments about the Bible. Ask participants to fill in the blanks in their Journals on page 39.

Defining the Question

Ask participants to fill in the blanks on page 39 in their Journals as you list different views of the Bible. Use the computer diskette or the overhead cel.

Views of the Bible

Step 3 (10 mins.)

Direct participants to turn to page 40 in their Journals and to fill in the blanks as you present the key points in The Bible Speaks. Use the computer diskette or the overhead cels.

The Bible Speaks

The Bible Speaks

The Bible gives many solid reasons we can know it is true and reliable.

1. Jesus treated the Old Testament as ___authoritative___ and ___true___.
- He treated it as ___true___ and ___eternal___ (see John 17:17; Luke 16:17).
- He referred to it as the ___Word___ of ___God___ (see Mark 7:11-13; John 10:34-38).
- He relied on it when facing ___temptation___ (see Matt. 4:4,7,10).
- He denounced those who did not ___believe___ it (see Luke 24:25).
- He used it to convince people of His ___identity___ (see Mark 14:21; Luke 24:44; John 5:39).
  Jesus held what we call the Old Testament in highest regard. He never tried to prove the Old Testament's reliability. He took its truthfulness for granted and encouraged others through His example to do the same.

2. Jesus considered His words to be ___authoritative___ and ___true___ for all time.
- Their source is the ___Father___ (see John 14:24-26).
- Their nature is ___eternal___ (see Matt. 24:35).
- His words are ___life___ (see John 6:63).
- His words should be ___heard___ and ___obeyed___ (see Matt. 7:24-27; John 8:31-32).

3. The disciples and the early believers accepted the Bible as ___authoritative___ and ___true___.
The disciples and the early believers considered the Bible, including the letters and other writings now found in the New Testament, as being from God (see 1 Cor. 2:13; 2 Pet. 1:20-21; 3:16).

4. The New Testament provides ___eyewitness___ accounts of events in the life of Jesus and the early church.
Those who view an event firsthand have the most credibility in describing what actually happened. Many who knew Jesus—who had seen Him, touched Him, and heard Him—were still alive at the time the writings we find in the New Testament were circulated. What the New Testament writers recorded could have easily been challenged or dismissed as fiction. However, we find no evidence from that time that questions the truthfulness of these writings. Not only did their

contemporaries accept the writings as truth, but also many of them laid down their lives for the One of whom the writings testified.

5. Historical ____records____ verify the accuracy of many events and places spoken of in the Bible.

The Bible stands up very well under investigation into the facts it reports. The Bible's content can be confirmed as actual history.

- William F. Albright, a world-famous archaeologist, says: "There is no doubt that archaeology has confirmed the substantial historicity of Old Testament tradition. As critical study of the Bible is more and more influenced by the rich new material from the ancient Near East we shall see a steady rise in respect for the historical significance of now neglected or despised passages and details in the Old and New Testaments."[1]
- Millar Burrows, a Yale archeologist reports: "On the whole, ... archeological work has unquestionably strengthened confidence in the reliability of the Scriptural record. More than one archeologist has found his respect for the Bible increased by the experience of excavation in Palestine."[2]
- Nelson Glueck, a Jewish archaeologist, writes, "It may be stated categorically that no archaeological discovery has ever controverted a Biblical reference."[3]

6. The Bible is ____realistic____ in the way it depicts people and life.

In the Bible we find God's dealings with real people. Their stories are not cleaned up, but rather we see both sides of their lives—their successes and their failures. This gives the Bible the feel of real life, of truthfulness. Here are a few examples of Bible characters whose successes and failures are realistically recorded in the pages of Scripture.

- Moses (see Num. 12:3; 20:7-12)
- David (see 2 Sam. 11:1-4,14; Acts 13:22)
- Peter (see Matt. 26:33-35,69-75; Acts 2:14-39)

Briefly remind members of these successes and failures. You will not have time to go in depth.

7. The Bible offers practical ____answers____ to real-life problems and needs.

The Ten Commandments have formed the basis of many civil laws by which society functions. The Bible also gives individuals guidance for living a successful life. Here are only two reminders of this truth.

- " 'Do not let this Book of the Law depart from your mouth; meditate on it day and night, so that you may be careful to do everything written in it. Then you will be prosperous and successful' " (Josh. 1:8).
- "All Scripture is God-breathed and is useful for teaching, rebuking, correcting and training in righteousness, so that the

If time allows, ask participants to brainstorm Bible promises.

man of God may be thoroughly equipped for every good work" (2 Tim. 3:16-17).

For thousands of years people from every walk of life have relied on the Bible as a guide for living. Many have looked to it for strength, comfort, and direction. Those whose lives have been changed by following the Bible's teachings can say wholeheartedly, "This is the Word of God."

Entry Points in FAITH Visits

Several occasions in FAITH visits offer a person an opportunity to consider the question, How do I know the Bible is true?

1. During an __**Opinion**__ __**Poll**__ visit, persons are asked if they think people should read the Bible more often than they presently do. This may lead the person to ask questions about the truth of God's Word.

2. When __**making**__ __**introductions**__, your Team identifies yourselves as being from a church. Most people will associate your Team with persons who understand and love God's Word. Occasionally, persons will make statements about the Bible to raise an excuse for not talking with you.

3. While sharing a __**Sunday**__ __**School**__ __**testimony**__, you have an opportunity to introduce the impact of Bible study on your life. Often, persons have not considered the need for personal understanding and application of the Bible.

4. As you ask the __**Key**__ __**Question**__, persons will often think about whether they believe or disbelieve the Bible.

5. You will have several opportunities to encourage persons to enroll in or attend __**Sunday**__ __**School**__, where they can study the Bible for themselves. These opportunities may occur in evangelistic, ministry, follow-up, or Opinion Poll visits.

Step 4 (5 mins.)

Direct participants to turn to page 42 in their Journals and to fill in the blanks as you summarize Entry Points in FAITH Visits. Use the computer diskette or the overhead cel.

Entry Points in FAITH Visits

How You Can Respond

Here are possible ways you can respond to the question, How do I know the Bible is true? during witnessing encounters. Your response will depend on the person, the situation, and the Holy Spirit's direction in this circumstance. Always keep in mind the general principles outlined on pages 28–29 in session 1.

1. People are very observant in listening to both what you say and how you say it. Many can sense whether you believe what you are saying. As you are talking about your church or your Sunday School class or as you give the FAITH gospel presentation, speak with the conviction that God's Word has changed your life.

2. Determine whether you need to proceed in sharing the FAITH gospel presentation or whether the concerns raised give you an opportunity to build a relationship so that further ministry and evangelism can take place. It is important to look for opportunities to share the FAITH gospel presentation, but it is also important not to close doors if a relationship needs to be built.

3. Remember that God's Word can stand on its own; it will not return to Him void (see Isa. 55:11). You allow God's Word to speak for itself when you present Scriptures like the ones in the FAITH Visit Outline. Also remember that it is the work of the Holy Spirit to convince people of truth. He calls us to be faithful in believing and sharing the message of God's Word with others. He knows we will encounter persons who have difficulty believing any or all of the simple truth of the Scriptures.

4. Realize that many people ask challenging questions because God is working in their lives. Realize that some people say things that are difficult for us to hear because they have been hurt or have never had relationships with persons who have genuinely been influenced by God's Word. Many people have never read or studied God's Word for themselves. Be prepared to give a copy of the Scriptures to someone who does not have a copy.

5. Learn from the problems and questions people have about God's Word. Many people have been taught from childhood to disregard the Word and to consider Bible believers as extremists. As you hear ways some people question and resist God's Word, become more sensitive to Christ's compassion for those who have been deceived to reject His love and forgiveness.

SEE IT

Step 5 (10 mins.)

To focus on ways witnesses can respond to questions about the Bible, show the session 2 video segment, Digging for the Truth. Ask participants to make notes in the margins of their Journals.

SAY IT

Step 6 (5 mins.)

Ask accountability partners to discuss ways they would respond to a challenge or question about the Bible's validity, using the ideas in the video and in How You Can Respond.

If you are leading students, have accountability partners role-play a situation in which one partner asks a question about the Bible's validity and the other partner responds.

STUDY IT

Step 7 (5 mins.)

Overview Home Study Assignments for session 2.

Transition to assemble with FAITH Teams to prepare for home visits. (5 mins.)

DO IT (110 mins.)

SHARE IT (30 mins.)

Visitation Time

Do It

1. The Team Leader guides preparation for all visits.
2. A game plan should be in place before visits. This means alerting Team members in advance if they are to do Sunday School or evangelistic testimonies.
3. The Team Leader always has not only the option to change the game plan but also the responsibility to state the reason changes were made.
4. Keep in mind the visitation tips Learners have been asked to review (p. 35, A *Journey in FAITH Journal*). Highlight any you feel are especially helpful or needed.
5. Most of all, encourage Team members as they make their first home visits. Be prepared to take the lead in all visits. Model a visit and debrief what happened so that Team members can learn.

Celebration Time

Share It

1. Explain the purpose and importance of Celebration Time and encourage members to stay for this time each week.
2. Encourage Team members to listen carefully as reports are shared, especially about decisions made in visits; the information can be helpful in follow-up.
3. Take the lead in sharing reports.
4. Complete the necessary forms:
   - Evaluation Cards
   - Participation Cards
   - Visitation forms updated with results of visits

Home Study Assignments

Home Study Assignments reinforce this session by helping you apply what you have learned.

Your Discipleship Journey

Journaling activities in Your Discipleship Journey are an important part of your development as a Great Commission Christian through FAITH training.

1. Identify some real-life problems and needs the Bible addresses by matching the following verses with the correct topics.

   ___ 1. Psalm 119:165   a. Anger

   ___ 2. Proverbs 28:13   b. Worry

   ___ 3. Matthew 6:34   c. Anxiety

   ___ 4. 1 Corinthians 13:4-8 d. Patience

   ___ 5. Ephesians 4:2   e. Peace

   ___ 6. Ephesians 6:1-4   f. Guilt

   ___ 7. Philippians 4:6   g. Forgiveness

   ___ 8. Colossians 3:13   h. Parent-child relationships

   ___ 9. James 1:19-20   i. Love

2. Read Deuteronomy 31:12-13. This passage says that we are to hear, learn, apply, and teach God's Word to others. Consider how you identify with each of these assignments. For example:

   • What are you doing to learn God's Word? Are you reading it daily? ❏ Yes ❏ No Memorizing verses? ❏ Yes ❏ No Meditating on the truth of Scripture? ❏ Yes ❏ No

   • What are you doing to put God's Word to practice in your life?

   _____

   _____

   • People are drawn to lives that are being transformed by God's Word. In what ways are you seeking to share with other persons what you are learning from God's Word?

   _____

   _____

3. Be prepared to share what God's Word means to you personally. Practice sharing this with persons in your Sunday School class or with your accountability partner.

4. Ask God to give you a deep love for the Scriptures. Ask God to help you understand and apply His Word so that you might not sin against God (see Ps. 119:11).
5. If someone asked you the most important thing you have recently learned from Scripture, what would you tell that person?

_____

_____

Growing as a Life Witness

Growing as a Life Witness reminds you of your responsibility to witness and minister to others during the week.
1. Talk or meet with your accountability partner and share ways you have cultivated a lost person or have witnessed or ministered on occasions other than FAITH visits.
2. Discuss ways you can apply the session 2 content in witnessing.
3. Pray for lost persons by name and for each other.

Prayer Concerns	Answers to Prayer
_____	_____
_____	_____
_____	_____
_____	_____
_____	_____
_____	_____
_____	_____
_____	_____
_____	_____

Your Weekly Sunday School Leadership Team Meeting

A FAITH participant is an important member of Sunday School. Encourage Team members who are elected Sunday School workers to attend this weekly meeting. Use this section to record ways your FAITH Team influences the work of your Sunday School class or department. Use the information to report during weekly Sunday School leadership team meetings. Identify actions that need to be taken through Sunday School as a result of prayer concerns, needs identified, visits made by the Team, and decisions made by the persons visited. Also identify ways you can disciple others in your Sunday School class or department and in your church.

1. FAITH Teams made or will make visits for the first time this week. If visits have been made, share reports and list any needs that affect your class or department.

   _____

   _____

2. Indicate any individuals/families who are expected to attend on Sunday and whether a FAITH Team member will greet them. Make specific plans to involve other class members in making guests feel comfortable when they attend, such as sitting with guests in the worship service, introducing guests to other class members, and so forth.

   _____

   _____

3. Discuss ways Sunday's Bible-study lesson can involve members and guests in transformational Bible study and discipleship.

   _____

   _____

4. Pray for FAITH Team members, teachers, and department directors.

Discipling Your Team Members

This weekly feature suggests actions the Team Leader can take to support Team members, prepare for Team Time, and improve visits. This work is part of the Team Leader's Home Study Assignments. Add any actions suggested by your church's FAITH strategy.

Support Team Members

❑ Call Team members and encourage them about their participation during the first home visits.

Prepare to Lead Team Time

❑ Overview Leading Team Time at the beginning of session 3.

Prepare to Lead Visits

❑ Review the FAITH Visit Outline to be able to model the entire process for Team members.

❑ Be prepared to explain the procedures in the car as you travel to and from the church, as well as the role of the Team Leader in making visits.

❑ Be prepared to model a visit in which Team member(s) are asked to lead in sharing a Sunday School testimony.

❑ Be prepared to model the use of the Opinion Poll in making visits.

❑ Be prepared to lead the Team to participate during Celebration Time.

Link with Sunday School

❑ Participate in your weekly Sunday School leadership team meeting. Share pertinent information in this meeting, using Your Weekly Sunday School Leadership Team Meeting (p. 47) and FAITH-visit results.

❑ Consider ways your Sunday School can lead members to deepen their commitment to studying and applying God's Word.

For Further Growth

For Further Growth may include additional reading or activities that will enhance your growth as a disciple and a discipler of others. These assignments are intended to be long-term projects and do not have to be completed during this semester of study.

1. Study what the Bible teaches about God's Word.
2. Read Acts 2:22; 1 John 1:1-4; and 2 Peter 1:16 and state how these New Testament writers viewed themselves, their hearers, and their purpose.
3. Read the FAITH Tip on pages 49–50.

---

[1]William F. Albright, as quoted by Josh McDowell, A Ready Defense (Nashville: Thomas Nelson, 1993), 92–93.
[2]Millar Burrows, What Mean These Stones? (New York: Meridian Books, 1941), 1.
[3]Nelson Glueck, Rivers in the Desert: A History of the Negev (New York: Grove, 1959), 31.

Answers to matching activity on page 45: 1. e, 2. f, 3. b, 4. i, 5. d, 6. h, 7 c, 8. g, 9. a

FAITH TIP

The Reliability of the Biblical Documents

Both the quantity and the quality of the manuscripts of the Scriptures give us confidence in the Bible's accuracy. The reliability of these manuscripts points to the Bible's uniqueness.

The Old Testament

As far as anyone knows, no original manuscripts of the Old Testament books now exist. The early copies of the Old Testament were written on leather or papyrus from the time of Moses to the time of Malachi. As they wore out, copies of the manuscripts had to be made by hand. Several thousands of these copies have been found and are available for study. We are largely dependent on these ancient manuscript copies, along with translations and quotations in early Christian writings, for our information about the original writings.

One example of these manuscript copies is the well-known Masoretic text. It was preserved by traditionalists known as Masoretes, who devised extremely complex methods to safeguard the making of copies, around A.D. 600 to 950. They carefully checked each copy by counting from the middle letter of pages, books, and sections. Everything countable was counted by the Masoretes. Their efforts illustrate the care that was taken to preserve the accuracy of the original Old Testament texts generation after generation.

The Dead Sea Scrolls, discovered in 1947, provided us a Hebrew text dating from the second century B.C. Until that time we did not possess copies of the Old Testament dated earlier than A.D. 895. The Dead Sea Scrolls include all Old Testament books except Esther. This discovery has confirmed the reliability of the Masoretic text and other ancient manuscript copies of the Old Testament.

Historical research and archaeological findings have led to the discovery of other important copies of translations of the Old Testament. The most important of all the translations of the Old Testament is the pre-Christian Greek version called the Septuagint. Tradition claims that this version was produced from about 285 to 270 B.C. by 72 Jewish elders at the request of Ptolemy II, king of Egypt, for use by the Greek-speaking Jewish community in Alexandria, Egypt.

The Septuagint is frequently quoted in the New Testament, since it served as the Bible of Greek-speaking Christians in the apostolic period. Many important theological terms in the New Testament derive their meanings from their use in the Septuagint. Although the Septuagint is not considered a completely trustworthy rendering of the Hebrew, it still permits us to compare the Greek with our Hebrew versions. These archaeological discoveries assure us of having a faithful text of the Old Testament.[1]

The New Testament

With over 5,000 Greek manuscripts and 8,000 Latin manuscripts, no other book in ancient literature can compare with the New Testament in documentary support.[2] In addition, hundreds of parchment copies survive, 2,000 church worship books containing many Scripture passages, and more than 80,000 New Testament quotations or allusions in writings of the church fathers.[3] We have only 7 ancient copies of Plato's writings, 5 of Aristotle's, and 643 of Homer's.[4]

Not only are there many more copies of the New Testament, but many of them are also quite early. Approximately 75 papyri fragments can be dated from the early second to the mid-eighth century, covering 25 of the 27 New Testament books. In contrast, the oldest manuscript of Caesar's *Gallic War*, composed between 58 and 56 B.C., dates from about nine hundred years after Caesar's day. The same is true of many classical manuscripts that scholars nevertheless accept as authentic.[5]

Moreover, the quality of the various New Testament manuscripts is without parallel in the ancient world. Because of the great reverence the early Christians had for the Scriptures, they exercised extreme care in accurately copying and preserving the authentic text. Because we have thousands of manuscripts, readings may vary in places; but these usually resulted from visual or auditory errors in copying. Most relate to spellings. Only a minute number would affect the understanding of the text. None call into question a major doctrine or factual teaching.[6]

From these early copies and translations scholars have tried to recapture the original Greek text. The work has been successful, and today we possess a very accurate and reliable New Testament text.

Although it is true that we do not have the first written texts of the Old or the New Testament, sufficient evidence exists that our English versions are trustworthy translations of reliable Hebrew and Greek texts, which faithfully represent the originals.[7]

[1]David S. Dockery, *The Doctrine of the Bible* (Nashville: Convention, 1991), 98–99.
[2]Ken Hemphill, *LifeAnswers: Making Sense of Your World* (LifeWay, 1993), 39.
[3]Dockery, *The Doctrine of the Bible*, 100.
[4]Hemphill, *LifeAnswers*, 39.
[5]Dockery, *The Doctrine of the Bible*, 100.
[6]Hemphill, *LifeAnswers*, 39.
[7]Dockery, *The Doctrine of the Bible*, 100.

SESSION 3

Does God Exist?

In this session you will—

CHECK IT by engaging in Team Time activities;

KNOW IT by reviewing content from session 2;

HEAR IT by affirming what the Bible says about God's existence;

SAY IT by discussing possible applications of what you have learned

in this session;

STUDY IT by overviewing Home Study Assignments;

DO IT by leading your Team in making visits;

SHARE IT by celebrating.

In Advance
- Overview content.
- Preview teaching suggestions. Prepare key points. Decide whether to use the session 3 computer slides or the overhead cels.
- Prepare the room for teaching.
- Pray for participants and for Teams as they prepare to visit.
- As Teaching Time begins, direct participants to open their Journals to page 54.

TEAM TIME

CHECK IT (15 MINS.)

If the computer diskette is used, display the agenda frame for your Team Time, as desired. Add other points as needed.

CHECK IT agenda:

✔ FAITH Visit Outline
✔ Other Home Study Assignments
✔ Session 2 Debriefing
✔ Help for Strengthening a Visit

Leading Team Time

All Team members participate in Team Time. They are primarily responsible for reciting the assigned portion of the FAITH Visit Outline and for discussing other Home Study Assignments.

As you direct this important time of CHECK IT activities with your Team, keep in mind that Learners look to you as a role model, motivator, mentor, and friend. Team Time activities can continue in the car as the Team travels to and from visits.

Lead CHECK IT Activities

✔ FAITH Visit Outline

❑ Be prepared to check off each Learner's memorization of all of **Preparation** (through Transition Statement) and the key words in **Presentation** and **Invitation**.

❑ Indicate your approval by signing or initialing each Learner's Journal. Encourage Learners as you do and indicate any notes you have jotted down that might be helpful.

✔ Other Home Study Assignments

❑ Give as much time as needed to helping Learners understand different responses people might make to the Key Question and ways to answer those responses in love. Indicate that such answers will become clearer throughout FAITH training/visits.

❑ Discuss how FAITH Tips and/or other readings can provide specific help or answer some questions from sessions.

❑ Indicate specific content areas that may appear again on the session 16 written review.

✔ Session 2 Debriefing

❑ Answer any questions that remain from session 2. Emphasize the importance of a good beginning in building trust that can ultimately result in the gospel's being shared. Highlight ways the Sunday School testimony helps build bridges to people.

❑ Review Learners' written Sunday School testimonies.

❑ Indicate specific content areas that may appear again on the session 16 written review.

✔ Help for Strengthening a Visit

❑ Answer any questions that emerged from home visits following session 2.

❑ Review ways to begin a visit.

❑ Identify actions Team members took during last week's visits that were particularly effective and others that might need to be changed.

❑ Suggest ways Team members can improve sharing their Sunday School testimonies.

❑ Call attention to the evangelistic testimony you shared during last week's visit(s). Mention that Team Learners will be introduced during this session to ways to share their testimonies during a visit.

Notes

_____

_____

_____

_____

_____

_____

_____

Actions I Need to Take with Learners During the Week

_____

_____

_____

_____

_____

_____

Transition to classrooms for instruction on the session's content. (5 mins.)

TEACHING TIME

KNOW IT

Step 1 (5 mins.)

Direct participants to locate A Quick Review on page 54 in their Journals and to complete the activities. Then give the answers, using the computer diskette or the overhead cel. Possible answers to question:
1. Opinion Poll visit
2. When making introductions
3. Sunday School testimony
4. When asking the Key Question
5. When encouraging the person to attend Sunday School

A Quick
Review

A Quick Review

In last week's study you examined several reasons we know the Bible is true. Test your recall by marking each statement T for *true* or F for *false*.

__F__ 1. Jesus rejected the Old Testament as no longer relevant.

__T__ 2. Jesus considered His words to be authoritative and true.

__T__ 3. The disciples and the early believers accepted the Bible, including the letters and other writings now found in the New Testament, as from God and therefore authoritative and true.

__F__ 4. The New Testament accounts of events in the life of Jesus and the early church, though inspiring, have been proved to be unreliable secondhand reports.

__F__ 5. For the most part, historical records contradict biblical accounts of events and places.

__F__ 6. The Bible is idealistic in the way it depicts people and life.

__T__ 7. The Bible offers practical answers to real-life problems and needs.

What are two places in FAITH visits when questions about or challenges to the truth of the Bible might arise?

1. _____

2. _____

Check appropriate ways to respond to the question, How do I know the Bible is true?

❑ 1. Tell the person that God will punish him for questioning the Bible's authority.

☑ 2. Speak with the conviction that God's Word has changed your life.

☑ 3. Take time to build a relationship.

☑ 4. Allow God's Word to speak through Scriptures like the ones in the FAITH Visit Outline.

❑ 5. Read to the person from the Book of Leviticus.

❑ 6. Quickly get up and leave before the lightning bolt strikes.

☑ 7. Give the person a copy of the Scriptures.

☑ 8. Realize Christ's compassion for those who have been deceived to reject His love and forgiveness.

Defining the Question: Does God Exist?

This is perhaps one of the first questions you may be asked as you begin to penetrate secular society with the gospel. Many people, having been influenced by an increasingly atheistic society, do not believe that God exists. Many others have a distorted view of God, and they need to be introduced to the God of the Bible, coming to terms with the claim He has on their lives and discovering the joy of living in relationship with Him.

Here are some ways you might anticipate being questioned or challenged about the existence of God.

- "Many gods exist. Which one are you talking about?"
- "I believe that the universe is God."
- "God is an invention of somebody's imagination."
- "God created the world, but He isn't involved in our lives today."
- "How can you believe in something that can't be proved?"
- "I believe that God is found within every person, and we only need to discover our divinity."

In addition to those who hold unbiblical views of God, other persons you encounter may use a variation of this question to distract you or to discourage you from continuing the gospel presentation. Although it is a challenging topic, it is one every believer needs to be ready to answer.

The Bible Speaks

The Bible gives four approaches you will find useful in answering the question, Does God exist?

The ____Universe____ Reveals the Creator

We wonder at the vastness of the universe and marvel at the beauty and intricacies of plants and animals. Much of the way we respond to the question, Does God exist? can be answered by the facts of creation.

1. *Consider the ____vastness____ of our universe.*
- It takes a beam of light, which travels about 700 million miles per hour, more than 100,000 years just to cover the distance of our galaxy, the Milky Way, which is only one among billions of galaxies in the known universe.[1]
- To grasp the size of our universe, pretend that the thickness of one

HEAR IT

Step 2 (5 mins.)

Introduce the content of this session by summarizing Defining the Question. Use the computer diskette or the overhead cel to illustrate questions and comments about God.

Defining the Question

Step 3 (20 mins.)

Direct participants to turn to page 55 in their Journals and to fill in the blanks as you present the key points in The Bible Speaks. Use the computer diskette or the overhead cel. Don't let the details in this section slow you down. Quickly overview them and state that they are provided to communicate the vastness and intricacy of the universe God created.

The Bible Speaks

sheet of paper represents the distance from the earth to the sun, which is about 93 million miles. To depict the distance to the nearest star, we would need a 71-foot-high stack of paper. To cover the diameter of our Milky Way galaxy would require a 310-mile-high stack. To reach the edge of the known universe would require a pile of paper sheets 31 million miles high.[2]

- If the sun were hollow, 1.3 million earths could fit inside it. A star named Antares (if it were hollow) could hold 64 million of our sun. In the constellation Hercules is a star that could contain 100 million of Antares. The largest known star, Epsilon, could easily swallow up several million stars the size of the one in Hercules.[3]

- Our earth is traveling around its own axis at 1,000 miles per hour. It moves around the sun at 67,000 miles per hour and is carried by the sun across our galaxy at 64,000 miles per hour. Every 24 hours we cover 57,360,000 miles. Each year we travel 20,936,400,000 miles across empty space.[4]

2. Consider the ___energy___ in our universe.

- "The protons and neutrons within the nucleus of an atom are held together with a density of one billion tons per cubic inch. This is around forty pounds of energy between each proton."[5]

- This energy force is 1 followed by 38 zeroes times stronger than regular gravitational forces. That number is more than 100 trillion times the number of all the grains of sand on earth's seashores.[6]

- "Albert Einstein estimated that the total amount of energy released from one ounce of water could easily lift 200 million tons of steel one mile above the earth."[7]

3. Consider the ___complexity___ of our universe.

- An atom is almost too small for us to imagine. "On the tip of a ball point pen are so many atoms that if they were carried by an army, marching four abreast, an atom to a man, it would take over 20,000 years for a march-past."[8]

- "It would take 25 trillion protons laid side by side to span a linear inch."[9]

- "There are as many protons in a cubic inch of copper as there are drops of water in the oceans of the world, or grains of sand on the seashores of the earth."[10]

- "The size of an electron is to a dust speck as the dust speck is to the entire earth."[11]

- The smallest insect on this earth is made up of millions of living cells. There are about 75 trillion such cells in the body of an average person. But each individual cell is unbelievably complex. It is vastly more complicated than the most sophisticated giant computer on earth.[12]

- "Each cell is a world brimming with as many as 200 trillion tiny groups of atoms called protein molecules. It is a micro-universe in itself."[13]

The probability that a universe of this vastness and complexity happened by chance has been compared to the possibility that a tornado could sweep through a junkyard and create a functional 747 jet.[14] The Bible tells us that God created the universe and all that is in it:

- "In the beginning God created the heavens and the earth" (Gen. 1:1).
- "By faith we understand that the universe was formed at God's command, so that what is seen was not made out of what was visible" (Heb. 11:3).

Observing the grand scheme of design and order in the universe, from the intricacy of the individual cell to the precise movement of the planets through the unfathomable depths of space, we can conclude that behind creation stands a great Designer who set everything in motion and holds all things together (see Col. 1:15-17).

Human   Beings
Reflect Their Maker

The same sense of order and purposeful design can be observed in human beings.

- The largest molecule in all living things is called deoxyribonucleic acid (DNA). The DNA strand carries the hereditary information from the parent to the offspring. The total length of the DNA strand in one cell is six feet. If all the DNA strands in the human body were bunched together, they could fit into a box the size of an ice cube. But if unwound and joined together, the string could stretch from the earth to the sun and back more than four hundred times.[15]
- If the coded DNA instructions of a single human cell were translated into English, they would fill a one-thousand-volume encyclopedia.[16]
- Consider the way your body functions through voluntary and involuntary muscles, simultaneously controlled by the command center of your brain via the central nervous system.
- Think about the complex processes that take place to allow your senses of touch, smell, taste, hearing, and sight to operate.
- Your soul, encompassing your mind, will, and emotions, is direct evidence that you were created in God's image. And your spirit gives you the capacity to relate personally to God.[17]

Could such a complex being have evolved by accident? The odds that a one-cell animal emerged by pure chance, as evolutionists believe, has been estimated at 1 in 10 to the 40,000th power.[18] Obviously, the odds that a creature with the complexity of a human being developed by chance are infinitely higher.

Genesis 1:26-31 gives the account of the creation of humans.

Other passages talk about how intimately God knows us.

- "You created my inmost being;

    you knit me together in my mother's womb.

  I praise you because I am fearfully and wonderfully made"
  (Ps. 139:13-14).
- "This is what the Lord says—your Redeemer, who formed you in the womb: I am the Lord, who has made all things, who alone stretched out the heavens, who spread out the earth by myself" (Isa. 44:24)
- " 'Even the very hairs of your head are all numbered' " (Matt. 10:30).

God has known each of us since we were in our mother's womb. He created us lovingly, with precision and purpose. Human beings did not just happen. We are part of God's purposeful creation.

Moral   Values
Point to a Just God

We can argue for God's existence on the basis of an objective moral order in the world. In all cultures and periods of history, people have been conscious of an objective standard of right and wrong. People seem to have a built-in sense of what ought and ought not to take place in society, and they universally appeal to some pattern of accepted behavior.

This is the argument adopted by C. S. Lewis in *Mere Christianity*: "My argument against God was that the universe seemed so cruel and unjust. But how had I got this idea of just and unjust? A man does not call a line crooked unless he has some idea of a straight line."[19] You may hear an unbeliever argue that the presence of evil in the world proves that God does not exist. C. S. Lewis's response was, How do I know there is evil unless I know there is good?

Our sense of right and wrong originates from a just, or righteous, God:

- "Righteousness and justice are the foundation of your throne" (Ps. 89:14).
- "The Lord within her is righteous;

    he does no wrong" (Zeph. 3:5).

God upholds right and opposes wrong. Each of His actions is right, and He has provided guidelines, such as commandments, for people to follow so that we too can be righteous. God's righteousness demands that He punish unrepentant evil, but He has also provided a way for unrighteous people to be redeemed through the blood of Christ.

The fact that good and evil are universally recognized points to the Source of all good, our Heavenly Father. Believers enjoy the additional blessing of experiencing God's righteousness firsthand as they are made righteous through faith in Jesus Christ.

We Can _____Experience_____ God

Many have argued that God must exist by definition. Because the idea of God exists in our minds, He must exist objectively outside the mind. Millions throughout the ages have known that He exists because they discovered that only He could fill the void in their hearts. From the time humans were first created, God has chosen to reveal Himself to us in two primary ways.

1. *We experience God through* _____general_____ *revelation.*
God reveals Himself through creation (see Rom. 1:20) and through the human conscience (see Rom 1:19; 2:14-15).

2. *We experience God through* _____special_____ *revelation.*
God reveals Himself through Jesus (see Heb. 1:1-2) and the Bible (see 2 Tim. 3:16; 2 Pet. 1:21).

James 4:8 says, "Come near to God and he will come near to you." Your personal experience with God confirms your belief that God exists. Remember the conversation Moses had with God at the burning bush (see Ex. 3)? God declared that He is to be known as " 'I AM' " (Ex. 3:14). God exists, and we have the privilege of knowing Him and declaring evidence of His presence and power. You know that God exists because you personally experience Him. That is evidence no one can ever deny.

Entry Points in FAITH Visits

Several occasions in FAITH visits offer a person an opportunity to consider the question, Does God exist?
1. As you make _____**evangelistic**_____ or _____**Opinion**_____ _____**Poll**_____ _____**visits**_____, you will encounter many persons who are searching for meaning in life or issuing a cry for help. Many people have been reared to think that God does not care about them. Many really want to believe that Someone is in charge who can bring meaning and purpose to their lives.
2. Conversation will be directed at the beginning of a _____**FAITH**_____ _____**Visit**_____ to a person's INVOLVEMENT in church. This opens the door for a person to begin thinking of his understanding of God.
3. A brief _____**Sunday**_____ _____**School**_____ or _____**evangelistic**_____ _____**testimony**_____ or _____**ministry**_____ _____**visit**_____ provides a forum for considering ways God shows His love for us and can be experienced through a personal relationship with Him.

Remind participants that a personal experience with God is difficult to refute.

Step 4 (5 mins.)

Direct participants to turn to page 59 in their Journals and to fill in the blanks as you summarize Entry Points in FAITH Visits. Use the computer diskette or the overhead cel.

Entry Points
in FAITH
Visits

4. The __**Key**__ __**Question**__ introduces the subject of heaven, which most people will automatically associate with God.
5. The __**FAITH**__ __**gospel**__ __**presentation**__ intentionally points a person to consider God's work in our lives: God's forgiveness is available through the redemption of Christ's blood. God's love is available to all. God is love and judges sin. It is impossible for a person to go to heaven on his own, where God allows no sin. The person will be invited to have the assurance of heaven, the presence of God, and a relationship with God.

How You Can Respond

Here are possible ways you can respond to the question, Does God exist? during witnessing encounters. Your response will depend on the person, the situation, and the Holy Spirit's direction in this circumstance. Always keep in mind the general principles outlined on pages 28–29 in session 1.

1. Focus on the step of faith every person must take to believe in God. Although you have never seen God, you have experienced God's work in your life, and the same God is working in the life of the person you are visiting. This session gives concrete evidence that God exists, which you can share if the person genuinely wants to know. But first and foremost, God wants you to believe and to share with others what you are learning about your relationship with Him.
2. Keep your purpose in mind. You are not actively pressing for a discussion of theological details during a FAITH visit. You are there to minister and share the good news by representing your Sunday School class. Invite persons who have questions and concerns to join your Bible-study class, where they can further examine faith in God.
3. Look for every opportunity to ask permission to share how the Bible answers the Key Question. Let God's Holy Spirit work in the person's life to draw him or her to God's love and mercy.
4. Be sensitive to every opportunity for follow-up by persons in a Sunday School class. Be aware of opportunities to develop a relationship, answer questions, provide resources, or involve the person in other specific ministry or fellowship options.
5. Remain in an attitude of prayer throughout each visit. Pray that God will make Himself known in the life of the person visited. He may use the Team to merely plant a seed as they express their faith in the living God, but He is the One who makes seeds grow and bear fruit.

SAY IT

Step 5 (5 mins.)

Ask accountability partners to discuss ways they would respond to a challenge or question about the existence of God, using the ideas in How You Can Respond.

If you are leading students, have accountability partners role-play a situation in which one partner asks a question about the existence of God and the other partner responds.

STUDY IT

Step 6 (5 mins.)

Overview Home Study Assignments for session 3.

Transition to assemble with FAITH Teams to prepare for home visits. (5 mins.)

Visitation Time

Do It

1. Assign specific responsibilities to your Team Learners. Ask one to share a Sunday School or evangelistic testimony. Ask one to be the navigator to arrange the visitation schedule. Suggest that this person start with the prospect's home that is farthest away. Then work your way back toward the church. Assign another Team Learner to gather age-appropriate materials for your visit. This procedure will save time and will provide good training for Learners.
2. Pray before you go.
3. Use the time in the car to review, allowing Learners to ask questions.
4. Debrief each visit. Facilitate by asking specific questions.

Celebration Time

Share It

1. Hear reports and testimonies.
2. Complete Evaluation Cards.
3. Complete Participation Cards.
4. Update visitation forms with the results of visits.

DO IT (110 MINS.)

SHARE IT (30 MINS.)

Home Study Assignments

Home Study Assignments reinforce this session by helping you apply what you have learned.

Your Discipleship Journey

Journaling activities in Your Discipleship Journey are an important part of your development as a Great Commission Christian through FAITH training.

1. "Be still, and know that I am God" (Ps. 46:10). Spend time talking in prayer with the One who made you and wants to have fellowship with you. Also spend time being quiet in His presence. As you read His Word, hear what He is saying to you. Cultivate a lifestyle of sensitivity to the still, small voice of God.

2. Take a walk and carefully look at things God made, such as rocks, plants, animals, insects, and birds. What do you learn about the One who made these things?

3. There is only one God! Read Deuteronomy 32:39; Isaiah 43:10; Hosea 13:4; 1 Corinthians 8:6; and Ephesians 4:6 to discover why.

4. Read these passages of Scripture and summarize what the Bible says about God's eternal existence.

   Exodus 3:14: _____

   _____

   Job 36:26: _____

   _____

   Psalm 90:2: _____

   _____

   Isaiah 57:15: _____

   _____

5. Recall the four ways you studied that a person can know God exists.

   • The universe reveals the Creator.   • Moral values point to a just God.
   • Human beings reflect their Maker.   • We can experience God.

Select one of these approaches and write the way you would respond to a person who believes that God does not exist.

_____

_____

_____

_____

_____

_____

_____

Growing as a Life Witness

Growing as a Life Witness reminds you of your responsibility to witness and minister to others during the week.

1. Talk or meet with your accountability partner and share ways you have cultivated a lost person or have witnessed or ministered on occasions other than FAITH visits.
2. Discuss ways you can apply the session 3 content in witnessing.
3. Pray for lost persons by name and for each other.

Prayer Concerns	Answers to Prayer
_____	_____
_____	_____
_____	_____
_____	_____
_____	_____
_____	_____
_____	_____
_____	_____

Your Weekly Sunday School Leadership Team Meeting

A FAITH participant is an important member of Sunday School. Encourage Team members who are elected Sunday School workers to attend this weekly meeting. Use this section to record ways your FAITH Team influences the work of your Sunday School class or department. Use the information to report during weekly Sunday School leadership team meetings. Identify actions that need to be taken through Sunday School as a result of prayer concerns, needs identified, visits made by the Team, and decisions made by the persons visited.

1. Share results of visits. Suggest opportunities to minister to persons who were visited.

2. List ways your class or department can minister to or assimilate new members.

_____

_____

3. Evaluate last week's Bible-study session. Discuss ways to make Sunday's lesson applicable to life. Indicate anyone visited by a FAITH Team who is likely to attend on Sunday.

_____

_____

4. Periodically consider actually making follow-up phone calls to prospects and new members during this meeting. (If this is not possible, make assignments.) In the calls communicate excitement about guests' participation in Sunday School.

5. In receiving the new list of absentees, share any information that can help in follow-up. Does this member need a Sunday School ministry visit? If so, by what date and by which FAITH Team?

_____

_____

6. Pray specifically for Sunday School plans and leaders this week.

Discipling Your Team Members

This weekly feature suggests actions the Team Leader can take to support
Team members, prepare for Team Time, and improve visits. This work is part
of the Team Leader's Home Study Assignments. Add any actions suggested by
your church's FAITH strategy.

Support Team Members

❑ Call Team members and talk with them about their participation during
   the class training and visits. Discuss any observations they made during the
   visits and particularly about sharing their Sunday School testimonies.
❑ Discuss ways to prepare and share their evangelism testimonies without
   revealing the answer to the Key Question.
❑ Encourage them as they memorize all of *Preparation* in the FAITH Visit
   Outline.

Prepare to Lead Team Time

❑ Overview Leading Team Time at the beginning of session 4.

Prepare to Lead Visits

❑ Review the FAITH Visit Outline in order to model the entire process for
   Team members.
❑ Be prepared to model a visit in which Team member(s) are asked to lead in
   sharing Sunday School and evangelistic testimonies.
❑ Be prepared to model the use of the Opinion Poll in making visits.
❑ Be prepared to lead your Team to participate during Celebration Time.

Link with Sunday School

❑ Participate in your weekly Sunday School leadership team meeting. Share
   pertinent information in this meeting, using Your Weekly Sunday School
   Leadership Team Meeting (p. 64) and FAITH-visit results.
❑ Does every member of your Team, including yourself, have a prayer partner
   in the Sunday School class? If not, present the need to your class on
   Sunday.

For Further Growth

For Further Growth may include additional reading or activities that will
enhance your growth as a disciple and a discipler of others. These assignments are intended to be long-term projects and do not have to be completed
during this semester of study.

1. Talk with several persons whose lives have been changed because of their
   relationships with God. Listen for ways they came to understand that
   God's work was evident through a life transition, illness, time of decision,
   or crisis, as well as during times of victory.
2. "Come near to God and he will come near to you" (Jas. 4:8). Seek

a growing and life-changing relationship with God through daily habits of Bible study and prayer. He will show evidence of His presence in all areas of your life. Pray that your life will reflect His glory in a way that draws others to Him.

3. Read the FAITH Tip on page 68.

---

[1]H. L. Willmington, *Willmington's Guide to the Bible* (Wheaton: Tyndale House, 1981), 13.
[2]Ibid.
[3]Ibid.
[4]Ibid.
[5]Ibid., 14.
[6]Ibid.
[7]Ibid.
[8]Ibid.
[9]Ibid.
[10]Ibid.
[11]Ibid.
[12]Ibid., 15.
[13]Ibid.
[14]Fred Hoyle, *The Intelligent Universe* (London: Michael Joseph, 1983), 19.
[15]Willmington, *Willmington's Guide to the Bible*, 15.
[16]Ibid.
[17]Avery T. Willis, Jr., *MasterLife 2: The Disciple's Personality* (Nashville: LifeWay Press, 1996), 134.
[18]Normal L. Geisler and Ronald M. Brooks, *When Skeptics Ask* (Wheaton: Victor Books, 1990), 22.
[19]C. S. Lewis, *Mere Christianity* (New York: MacMillan, 1952), 31.

FAITH AT WORK

It was our first semester of FAITH. We had received the assignment to visit a woman from China who had visited our worship services. When we knocked on their door, her husband answered. As we talked through broken English, he told us that he was a research assistant in the chemistry department at the local university. He knew of his wife's attendance at church and her belief in Jesus Christ. As the conversation continued, we asked the Key Question. The man responded with no and stated his unbelief in one God, although he thought Christianity was a good religion and Christians were very polite people.

We then asked the man why he did not believe, and he responded that the Bible left too many questions unanswered. As we talked on about his training and education as a chemist, I asked him whether he understood all of the chemistry formulas and whether they made sense to him. He responded that he did not understand all of the formulas and why they worked. When I asked why he nonetheless accepted them as truth, he responded with a smile, which communicated that he understood the point I was trying to make.

Before we left, we prayed for the man, and we looked for ways our church's international department could minister to him. Nearly a year later he prayed to receive Christ and followed in believer's baptism. God convicted this man of the truth and through love brought him to a saving knowledge of Jesus. God exists!

Steve Stege
Associate Pastor
for Education and Administration
First Baptist Church
Lubbock, Texas

FAITH TIP

A Love Relationship with God

God created you for a love relationship with Himself. That is the very purpose of your life. When this love relationship is real and personal to you, you can share convincing evidence of God's existence and love.

The message of the entire Old Testament can be summarized in Deuteronomy 6:4-5: " 'Hear, O Israel: The Lord our God, the Lord is one. Love the Lord your God with all your heart and with all your soul and with all your strength.' " Jesus identified this as the greatest commandment. Everything in your Christian life, everything about knowing and experiencing God, everything about knowing His will depends on the quality of your love relationship with God. God wants you to love Him with all your being.

God always takes the initiative in this love relationship. We do not naturally seek God on our own initiative. Jeremiah 31:3 says that God loves you with an everlasting love. He drew you to Himself when you were His enemy, and He gave His own Son to die for you. God chose you and loved you. When you responded to His invitation, He brought you into a love relationship with Himself. You cannot know God's activity unless He takes the initiative to reveal it to you.

Your relationship with God can be real and personal. From Genesis to Revelation you see God relating to people in real and intimate ways. Your relationship with God can be real and personal as you respond to His work in your life. A love relationship with God takes place between two real beings. He expends His effort to make your relationship with Him real and personal, and He pours His life into yours.

A relationship with God is also practical. In Scripture you see Him providing manna, quail, and water for the children of Israel. Jesus fed five thousand people to meet their physical needs. You can trust God to be practical in your life, too. Often, we assign God a limited place in our lives, calling on Him only when we need help. In reality, His constant presence is the most practical part of your life. God is the One who is working in our world. He invites you to relate to Him so that He can accomplish His work through you. His whole plan for the advance of the Kingdom depends on His working in real and practical ways through His personal relationships with His people.[1]

---

[1]Henry T. Blackaby and Claude V. King, *Experiencing God* (Nashville: LifeWay, 1990), 43–55.

Is Jesus Really God's Son?

In this session you will—

CHECK IT by engaging in Team Time activities;

KNOW IT by reviewing content from session 3;

HEAR IT by affirming what the Bible says about Jesus' identity;

SEE IT by viewing a video vignette;

SAY IT by discussing possible applications of what you have learned

in this session;

STUDY IT by overviewing Home Study Assignments;

DO IT by leading your Team in making visits;

SHARE IT by celebrating.

In Advance

- Overview content.
- Preview teaching suggestions. Prepare key points. Decide whether to use the session 4 computer slides or the overhead cels.
- Prepare the room for teaching.
- Cue the videotape to the session 4 segment, Who Is Jesus?
- Pray for participants and for Teams as they prepare to visit.
- As Teaching Time begins, direct participants to open their Journals to page 72.

TEAM TIME

CHECK IT (15 MINS.)

If the computer diskette is used, display the agenda frame for Team Time, as desired. Add other points as needed.

CHECK IT agenda:
- ✔ FAITH Visit Outline
- ✔ Evangelistic Testimony
- ✔ Sunday School Testimony
- ✔ Other Home Study Assignments/Session 3 Debriefing
- ✔ Help for Strengthening a Visit

Leading Team Time

All Team members participate in Team Time. They are primarily responsible for reciting the assigned portion of the FAITH Visit Outline and for discussing other Home Study Assignments.

As you direct this important time of CHECK IT activities with your Team, keep in mind that Learners look to you as a role model, motivator, mentor, and friend. Team Time activities can continue in the car as the Team travels to and from visits.

Lead CHECK IT Activities

✔ FAITH Visit Outline

❑ Listen as each Learner recites the appropriate portion of the FAITH Visit Outline (all of **Preparation,** adding the Key Question and Transition Statement, plus key words for **Presentation** and **Invitation**).

❑ Indicate your approval by signing each Learner's Journal.

❑ Involve an Assistant Team Leader in this part of Team Time, if you have this Team member.

✔ Evangelistic Testimony

❑ Review the first draft of written evangelistic testimonies, due this session. Use the criteria from the session 3 FAITH Tip in *A Journey in FAITH Journal.* Explain why you are making your suggestions. Indicate that most testimonies undergo revisions. Be sensitive in helping Team members develop their testimonies, keeping their stories intact. As a reminder, these are the criteria Learners have used to develop their testimonies:

- Define a specific event before (preconversion) and after your conversion (benefits).
- Do not answer the Key Question in your testimony.
- Keep your testimony brief (three minutes or less).
- Do not give too many unnecessary details; instead, concisely reflect your experience.
- Conclude your testimony with the assurance that you are going to heaven.

✔ Sunday School Testimony

❑ If possible, provide time for Team members to practice their Sunday School testimonies. Review of the evangelistic testimony, however, should be your priority.

✔ *Other Home Study Assignments/Session 3 Debriefing*
❑ Answer other questions Learners may have from session 3 or as a result of their Home Study Assignments.

✔ *Help for Strengthening a Visit*
❑ Identify ways Team members can improve sharing their evangelistic testimonies in a visit.
❑ Help your Team, especially Learners, know how to handle the following issues.
  • Dialogue with someone who answers the Key Question with a faith answer by discussing his or her journey of faith in Christ.
  • Briefly explain to a person who answers the Key Question with a works answer that many people feel that doing good things gets them into heaven. Discuss the various ways such a response might be verbalized.
  • Look for opportunities to ask permission to share what the Bible says about how a person goes to heaven.
  • Look for ways to get clarification or explanation if someone shares an unclear response to the Key Question.
  • Prayerfully look for ways to talk with a person who indicates no opinion about the Key Question.

Notes

_____

_____

_____

_____

Actions I Need to Take with Learners During the Week

_____

_____

_____

_____

Transition to classrooms for instruction on the content of the session. (5 mins.)

TEACHING TIME

KNOW IT

Step 1 (5 mins.)

Direct participants to locate A Quick Review on page 72 in their Journals and to complete the activities. Then give the answers, using the computer diskette or the overhead cel. Possible answers to question:

1. Evangelistic or Opinion Poll visits
2. At the beginning of a visit
3. Sunday School or evangelistic testimony or ministry visit
4. When asking the Key Question
5. Throughout the FAITH gospel presentation

A Quick Review

A Quick Review

Last week you learned four ways the Bible addresses the question, Does God exist? Check the statements that identify the four ways.

❑ 1. We know there is a God because every person He created is basically good.
☑ 2. The universe reveals the Creator.
❑ 3. Astronauts have seen God in outer space.
☑ 4. Human beings reflect their Maker.
❑ 5. Many people who have died and been brought back to life have seen God face to face.
❑ 6. God's Word promises that people who keep His commandments will experience a divine visitation.
☑ 7. Moral values point to a just God.
☑ 8. We can experience God.

What are two places in FAITH visits when questions about or challenges to God's existence might arise?

1. _____

2. _____

Check appropriate ways to respond to the question, Does God exist?

☑ 1. Share what you are experiencing in your relationship with God.
❑ 2. Berate the person for his unbelief.
❑ 3. Use every means at your disposal to convince an unbeliever that he is wrong.
☑ 4. Invite the person to Sunday School.
☑ 5. Ask permission to share how the Bible answers the Key Question.
☑ 6. Develop a relationship, answer questions, provide resources, or involve the person in ministry or fellowship options.
☑ 7. Pray that God will use the Team to plant a seed and that He will make the seed grow and bear fruit in the person's life.
❑ 8. Immediately change the subject.

Defining the Question: Is Jesus Really God's Son?

As Christians, we believe that Jesus Christ is the central Person of history and the Ruler of the universe from the foundation of the world. Yet many people we encounter or associate with each day don't recognize His existence. Many who know the name Jesus identify Him only as a historical figure but don't acknowledge that He is the living Son of God and the Savior of all who call on Him in faith.

Here are some ways you might anticipate being questioned or challenged about the deity of Christ.

- "Jesus was a great teacher, but that was long ago."
- "What do you mean? How can God have a son?"
- "Jesus was a good man who healed people and helped others."
- "Jesus died long ago. Why do you talk as if He were alive?"
- "Jesus attained heaven by living a moral life, just as we can."
- "I think of Jesus as the divinity we can all discover in ourselves."

You will find that Jesus has name recognition among certain unbelievers but that their ideas of who He is are greatly distorted. You have the privilege of sharing the good news of life, hope, and purpose that Jesus offers to everyone who believes. To do that, you need a good understanding of what the Bible says about our living Savior and Lord, Jesus Christ.

The Bible Speaks

The Bible presents convincing, life-changing evidence that Jesus is indeed God's Son.

1. Jesus was the promised ____Messiah____.

- Many Old Testament prophets predicted the Messiah's coming (see Isa. 7:14; 9:6-7; 52:13—53; 60:1-3; 63:1-3; Zech. 9:9-10).
- John the Baptist prepared the way for the Messiah's coming (see Luke 3:1-20).
- Jesus identified Himself and was recognized by others as the Messiah (see Matt. 26:63-64; Mark 8:29; Luke 1:67-75; 2:38; John 1:41-42; 4:25-29; 7:25-44; Acts 5:42; 9:22; 17:2-4).

2. Jesus was ____God____ in the flesh.

- Jesus was born to a virgin through the Holy Spirit (see Matt. 1:18-25).

Step 2 (5 mins.)

Introduce the content of this session by summarizing Defining the Question. Use the computer diskette or the overhead cel to illustrate questions and comments about Jesus.

Defining the Question

Step 3 (10 mins.)

Direct participants to turn to page 73 in their Journals and to fill in the blanks as you present the key points in The Bible Speaks. Use the computer diskette or overhead cel. You won't have time to examine all of the Scriptures referenced. Select key verses and be ready in advance to read them or to have enlisted participants read them when called on. Encourage participants to read the other passages on their own.

The Bible Speaks

- Jesus was holy and sinless (see Luke 18:18-19; John 8:46; 2 Cor. 5:21; Heb. 4:14-15).
- Jesus performed God's miracles (see Matt. 8:5-17; 9:18-22; 14:13-36).
- Jesus displayed divine authority (see Matt. 7:28-29; 28:18-20; Luke 7:48-50; John 10:17-18; Col. 2:9-10).
- Jesus identified Himself and was recognized by others as the Son of God (see Matt. 12:50; 14:33; 16:15-16; Mark 1:1,9-11; Rom 1:3-4; Gal. 4:4-6; 1 John 2:22-23; 5:11).
- Jesus is the eternal Word of God (see John 1:1-5,14; Col. 1:15-17).
- Jesus is God (see John 5:17-27; 8:58; 12:44-45; 13:19-20; 14:6-10; Rom. 9:5; 2 Cor. 4:4; Col. 1:15-20; 2:9; Heb. 1:1-13; Rev. 22:13).

3. Jesus fulfilled God's ____purposes____.
- Jesus came to proclaim freedom, bring healing, and release the oppressed (see Luke 4:18).
- Jesus came to introduce the kingdom of God (see Matt. 4:17; 22:1-14; Luke 4:43; 6:20-23; 9:60-62; 22:28-30).
- Jesus came to give abundant life (see John 10:10).
- Jesus came to fulfill the law (see Matt. 5:17-20).
- Jesus came to save us from sin through His death on the cross (see Matt. 20:28; Luke 19:10; John 1:29; 4:42; 10:9; Acts 4:12; 13:23; 1 Cor. 15:3-4; 1 Thess. 5:9-10; 1 John 4:14).
- Jesus came to give us eternal life (see John 3:16; 4:13-14; 6:27,33,35,40; 10:28-30; 11:25-26; Rom. 8:35-39).

4. Jesus ____lives____ today.
- Jesus rose from the dead (see Acts 2:22-36; Rom. 1:3-4; 1 Cor. 15:4-6).
- Jesus offers salvation for those who believe (see Acts 4:12; Rom. 5:10; 10:9; 2 Cor. 5:18-21; Gal. 3:13-14; Eph. 1:7-8; Col. 1:20-22; 1 Thess. 5:9-10; 1 Tim. 2:5-6; Titus 2:14).
- Jesus gives purpose and victory to life (see Matt. 5:3-12; John 1:4-5; 6:35; 8:12; Rom. 6:11-14; 8:36-37; 2 Cor. 4:6; 5:17; Eph. 2:10; Phil. 3:7-11; Col. 1:21-23; 1 John 4:9).
- Jesus ministers in heaven (see Luke 24:50-51; John 14:2; 1 Cor. 1:17; Eph. 4:7-13; 2 Tim. 4:17-18).
- Jesus intercedes for us (see Luke 21:15; John 14:14-17; John 17:6-26; 2 Cor. 12:9-10; Heb. 7:25; 1 John 2:1-2).

5. Jesus will rule His ____kingdom____ for eternity.
- Jesus will return (see John 14:3; Col. 3:1-4; Titus 2:13; Rev. 22:7,12,20).
- Jesus will judge in the final judgment (see John 5:27-30; Acts 17:30-31; Jas. 2:13; Rev. 11:18).
- Jesus is King (see Eph. 1:9-10,20-23; Phil. 2:9-11; Rev. 3:21; 11:15-17; 15:3-4; 17:14; 19:6).

The central person in the Bible is Jesus Christ. Like a majestic hymn of praise, all Scripture testifies to the deity of the One—

- whose miraculous birth split time;
- whose sinless life demonstrated unparalleled love and compassion for others;
- whose sacrificial death demonstrated total submission to the will of His Heavenly Father so that we could be reconciled with Him;
- whose glorious resurrection shattered the bonds of death, making eternal life possible for all who accept Him in faith.

As you have opportunities to share your beliefs about Jesus Christ, you will find that the Bible powerfully speaks to convince others that He is indeed God's Son. But in addition to the testimony of the biblical record, you have further evidence: the fact that Jesus lives in your heart. There is no more persuasive evidence of Jesus' deity than the miracle of a changed life. Always be prepared to share with enthusiasm and gratitude what the living Savior means to you.

Entry Points in FAITH Visits

Several occasions in FAITH visits offer a person an opportunity to consider the question, Is Jesus really God's Son?

1. If you are visiting someone who is already a believer, such as in a **ministry** or **follow-up** **visit**, it will be natural to talk about Jesus as God's Son.
2. During your **Sunday** **School** **testimony** you can relate ways you are learning to trust Christ through your class's ministry and teaching, and you can celebrate ways you are learning to love and follow Christ.
3. The message that Jesus is God's Son is central to Scripture and is the heartbeat of the gospel. As you briefly call attention to each of the following important truths in the **FAITH** **gospel** **presentation**, you emphasize Jesus' role as God's Son.
   - When you introduce the fact that "in him [Jesus] we have redemption through his blood" (Eph. 1:7), you make a bold statement that calls the person to think of who Jesus is.
   - You declare on two occasions that God so loved the world that He gave His only Son (see John 3:16).
   - You announce that a person must turn from sin and self and turn to Christ.
   - You explain the simplicity of the gospel by sharing "that Christ died for our sins according to the Scriptures" (1 Cor. 15:3).
   - You state that a person will be saved if he believes and confesses that Jesus is Lord (see Rom. 10:9).
4. You will have opportunity to share and interpret the picture on the

Emphasize the biblical testimony and a believer's personal testimony that Jesus is God's Son.

Step 4 (5 mins.)

Direct participants to turn to page 75 in their Journals and to fill in the blanks as you summarize Entry Points in FAITH Visits. Use the computer diskette or overhead cel.

Entry Points in FAITH Visits

After presenting point 3, remind participants of the tendency for a Team member to share how she came to know Jesus when sharing the evangelistic testimony. Reinforce the importance of allowing the FAITH gospel presentation to share the impact of the life-changing experience rather than sharing about Jesus during the evangelistic testimony.

SEE IT

Step 5 (10 mins.)

To focus on ways witnesses can respond to questions about Jesus' deity, show the session 4 video segment, Who Is Jesus? Ask participants to make notes in the margins of their Journals. Explain that the video vignette does not present a model that can be used in all witnessing situations. Rather, it is an example of the type of situation that can arise and the type of responses that may be suitable in this situation.

SAY IT

Step 6 (5 mins.)

Ask accountability partners to discuss ways they would respond to a challenge or question about Jesus' deity, using the ideas in the video and in How You Can Respond. If you are leading students, have partners role-play a situation about this topic.

STUDY IT

Step 7 (5 mins.)

Overview Home Study Assignments for session 4.

Transition to assemble with FAITH Teams to prepare for home visits. (5 mins.)

cover of ___**A**___ ___**Step**___ ___**of**___ ___**Faith**___. This will likely help a person think about her relationship with Jesus and to consider what He has done to save us.

5. After sharing the gospel, you will ask the ___**Key**___ ___**Question**___, "Understanding what we have shared, would you like to receive this forgiveness by trusting in Christ as your personal Savior and Lord?" Occasionally at this point a person will raise a question about Jesus' divinity or humanity.

6. During the ___**Invitation**___ portion of the visit you have an opportunity to clarify the message of the gospel by reviewing what Jesus did on our behalf and the importance of committing to Him.

How You Can Respond

Here are possible ways you can respond to the question, Is Jesus really God's Son? during witnessing encounters. Your response will depend on the person, the situation, and the Holy Spirit's direction in this circumstance. Always keep in mind the general principles outlined on pages 28–29 in session 1.

1. We receive assurance that Jesus is God's Son by reading the Scriptures and believing by faith. Let God use the simplicity of John 3:16 to explain the fact that Jesus is God's Son.

2. Acknowledge that certain declarations of Scripture are hard to believe when seeing them through the eyes of the flesh. It seems impossible that Jesus could be born of a virgin or that all prophecies about Jesus would be fulfilled. Yet when we look through the eyes of faith, not only do they begin to make sense, but they also hint at the miraculous nature of God's relationship with and work through Jesus.

3. The picture on the cover of A Step of Faith is a powerful reminder of the unconditional love God has for us. He sent His own Son, Jesus, to die on our behalf. Review that picture now. Think of what goes through the mind of someone who sees that picture for the first time. Be sure to help the person understand how you relate to the persons in the picture gazing into the face of Christ. As you discuss your impressions with the person, explain that you are still learning the personal impact of what Christ has done for you.

4. Prayerfully anticipate that many people struggle with the fact that God loves them more than they can comprehend and that Jesus died because of His love for us. Encourage persons to ask questions and share their concerns, but resist trying to explain everything about the Kingdom. Encourage each person to participate in Sunday School, where they can investigate what Scripture teaches and can explore how it influences lives.

Visitation Time

Do It

1. Your visitation assignments will include evangelistic prospects, recent guests who visited the church and are already believers, and absentees from Sunday School. Approach evangelistic visits with the expectation that you will ask the Key Question. If the person gives a strong faith answer, your Team will have an opportunity for practice. If the prospect does not respond in faith, you as the Team Leader will have an opportunity to demonstrate how to make an evangelistic visit. Remember that you are there to fulfill God's divine purpose, whether in an evangelistic or a ministry role. Remember 2 Timothy 2:2.
2. Pray before you go.
3. Use the time in the car to review, allowing Learners to ask questions.
4. After each visit allow Learners to debrief it. Facilitate the debriefing by asking specific questions.

Celebration Time

Share It

It is important that everyone attend Celebration Time. Emphasize this as an important part of the FAITH process. This is an opportunity to rejoice for decisions that were made. Demonstrate for your Team Learners how to do the following.
1. Hear reports and testimonies.
2. Complete Evaluation Cards.
3. Complete Participation Cards.
4. Update visitation forms with the results of visits.

DO IT (110 MINS.)

SHARE IT (30 MINS.)

Home Study Assignments

Home Study Assignments reinforce this session by helping you apply what you have learned.

Your Discipleship Journey

Journaling activities in Your Discipleship Journey are an important part of your development as a Great Commission Christian through FAITH training.

1. Identify what the Scriptures convey about Jesus' identity as God's Son.

   Matthew 6:9: _____

   Luke 23:34: _____

   John 6:44-46: _____

   John 10:30: _____

   John 14:6-9: _____

   John 17:1: _____

   Romans 8:29-32: _____

   1 John 1:7: _____

   1 John 4:9: _____

   1 John 5:5: _____

2. Identify points in the FAITH Visit Outline that present Jesus as God's Son.

   _____

   _____

   _____

3. Examine the picture on the cover of A *Step of Faith*. Reflect on who Jesus is as you imagine gazing into His eyes as He hangs on the cross for you. Spend time in worship and recommitment to follow Him as the living and victorious Son of God.

4. If someone questioned that Jesus is God's Son, write evidence you could give from your personal experience with Him.

_____

_____

_____

_____

_____

Growing as a Life Witness

Growing as a Life Witness reminds you of your responsibility to witness and minister to others during the week.

1. Talk or meet with your accountability partner and share ways you have cultivated a lost person or have witnessed or ministered on occasions other than FAITH visits.
2. Discuss ways you can apply the session 4 content in witnessing.
3. Pray for lost persons by name and for each other.

Prayer Concerns	Answers to Prayer

Your Weekly Sunday School Leadership Team Meeting

A FAITH participant is an important member of Sunday School. Encourage Team members who are elected Sunday School workers to attend this weekly meeting. Use this section to record ways your FAITH Team influences the work of your Sunday School class or department. Use the information to report during weekly Sunday School leadership team meetings. Identify actions that need to be taken through Sunday School as a result of prayer concerns, needs identified, visits made by the Team, and decisions made by the persons visited.

1. Share results of witnessing and ministry visits. Have Teams made Opinion Poll visits yet? Suggest opportunities to minister to persons who were visited.

   _____

   _____

2. Give or receive information appropriate for future FAITH Team assignments. Are additional prospect-discovery activities needed to keep FAITH assignments up-to-date?

   _____

   _____

3. Pray specifically for Sunday School plans this week. As a team, evaluate the previous session and discuss ways Sunday's Bible-study lesson can involve members and guests in transformational Bible study and discipleship.

   _____

   _____

4. Plan ways your Sunday School class can exalt Jesus and highlight who He is. Emphasize the importance of dealing with the simple and basic truths of the Scripture in clear ways, particularly when unsaved persons or new believers attend.

   _____

   _____

Discipling Your Team Members

This weekly feature suggests actions the Team Leader can take to support Team members, prepare for Team Time, and improve visits. This work is part of the Team Leader's Home Study Assignments. Add any actions suggested by your church's FAITH strategy.

Support Team Members

❑ Call Team members and talk with them about their participation in class training and visits. Discuss any observations they made during the visits and particularly about sharing their Sunday School testimonies.

❑ Discuss ways to prepare and share their evangelism testimonies without revealing the answer to the Key Question.

❑ Encourage them as they memorize all of *Preparation* in the FAITH Visit Outline.

Prepare to Lead Team Time

❑ Overview Leading Team Time at the beginning of session 5.

❑ Be prepared to evaluate Team members' written evangelistic testimonies, using these criteria:
- Define a specific event before (preconversion) and after your conversion (benefits).
- Do not answer the Key Question.
- Keep your testimony brief (three minutes or less).
- Do not give unnecessary details; instead, concisely relate your experience.
- Conclude your testimony with the assurance that you are going to heaven.

Prepare to Lead Visits

❑ Review the FAITH Visit Outline in order to model the entire process for Team members.

❑ Be prepared to model visits in which Team member(s) are asked to lead in sharing Sunday School and/or evangelistic testimonies.

❑ Be prepared to model the use of the Opinion Poll in making visits.

❑ Be prepared to lead your Team to participate during Celebration Time.

Link with Sunday School

❑ Participate in your weekly Sunday School leadership team meeting. Share pertinent information in the meeting, using Your Weekly Sunday School Leadership Team Meeting (p. 80) and FAITH-visit results.

❑ As you participate in Sunday School and in your leadership team meeting, look for ways your class or department can exalt Jesus Christ through praise times, through Bible study, and through application of the Word to life.

For Further Growth

For Further Growth may include additional reading or activities that will enhance your growth as a disciple and a discipler of others. These assignments are intended to be long-term projects and do not have to be completed during this semester of study.

1. Complete a personal scriptural study of Jesus. Read the four Gospel accounts, paying particular attention to Jesus' words.

2. Identify prophecies from the Old Testament that have been fulfilled in Jesus' life and redemptive work. If you have a copy of Handel's *Messiah*, study the passages he memorialized in music. These passages focus on Jesus as the chosen One of God.

3. Study the Scripture passages referenced in the section The Bible Speaks in this session.

Who Is the Holy Spirit?

In this session you will—

CHECK IT by engaging in Team Time activities;

KNOW IT by reviewing content from session 4;

HEAR IT by affirming what the Bible says about the Holy Spirit;

SAY IT by practicing the *Presentation* portion of the FAITH Visit Outline;

STUDY IT by overviewing Home Study Assignments;

DO IT by leading your Team in making visits;

SHARE IT by celebrating.

In Advance
- Overview content.
- Preview teaching suggestions. Prepare key points. Decide whether to use the session 5 computer slides or the overhead cels.
- Prepare the room for teaching.
- Pray for participants and for Teams as they prepare to visit.
- As Teaching Time begins, direct participants to open their Journals to page 86.

CHECK IT (15 MINS.)

If the computer diskette is used, display the agenda frame for Team Time, as desired. Add other points as needed.

CHECK IT agenda:
- ✔ FAITH Visit Outline
- ✔ Evangelistic Testimony
- ✔ Key Question/Transition Statement
- ✔ Other Home Study Assignments
- ✔ Session 4 Debriefing
- ✔ Help for Strengthening a Visit

Leading Team Time

All Team members participate in Team Time. They are primarily responsible for reciting the assigned portion of the FAITH Visit Outline and for discussing other Home Study Assignments.

As you direct this important time of CHECK IT activities with your Team, keep in mind that Learners look to you as a role model, motivator, mentor, and friend. Team Time activities can continue in the car as the Team travels to and from visits.

Lead CHECK IT Activities

✔ FAITH Visit Outline
❑ Call on each Learner to recite the assigned portion of the FAITH Visit Outline (all of **Preparation,** plus key words in **Presentation** and **Invitation**).
❑ Indicate your approval by signing each Learner's Journal. Be prepared to answer any questions Learners may have. Make suggestions for improvement.

✔ Evangelistic Testimony
❑ Call for final written copies of Learners' evangelistic testimonies. Congratulate Team members for achieving another important milestone.
❑ Make sure any revisions include criteria discussed in sessions 3 and 4. Ask for permission to print these testimonies in church materials that publicize the FAITH strategy or that encourage persons to share their faith.
❑ Emphasize to Team members the importance of sharing their testimonies naturally, in their own words, in actual visits.

✔ Key Question/Transition Statement
❑ Practice the Key Question/Transition Statement, helping Learners comfortably use their hands to spell the word *FAITH*.

✔ Other Home Study Assignments
❑ Look over Learners' Home Study Assignments. Are Learners on track? Clarify or emphasize key points from FAITH Tips and/or *Evangelism Through the Sunday School: A Journey of FAITH* as needed.

✔ Session 4 Debriefing
❑ Review the importance of and approach for making Sunday School ministry visits. Help Team members understand how such visits reconnect many inactive members to church life. Highlight ministry

visitation assignments and indicate why certain comments are made during different types of ministry visits (to absentees, nonattenders, members with ministry needs). As inactive members return to Sunday School or church, remind Team members they had a part.

❏ Ask any questions you feel would solidify Learners' understanding of session 4, including questions that will appear on the final written review (ses. 16).

✔ Help for Strengthening a Visit

❏ Be prepared to discuss ways to strengthen a visit, based on what has been discovered in previous sessions.

❏ Be prepared to model an Opinion Poll visit during Visitation Time.

❏ Identify which Team member(s) will take the lead in sharing a Sunday School testimony. Ask another Team member to be prepared to share his or her evangelistic testimony. With sensitivity to Learners and person(s) being visited, be prepared to resume the visit after Team members have shared.

Notes

_____

_____

_____

_____

_____

_____

Actions I Need to Take with Learners During the Week

_____

_____

_____

_____

_____

Transition to classrooms for instruction on the content of the session. (5 mins.)

TEACHING TIME

KNOW IT

Step 1 (5 mins.)

Direct participants to locate A Quick Review on page 86 in their Journals and to complete the activities. Then give the answers, using the computer diskette or the overhead cel. Possible answers to question:

1. Ministry or follow-up visit
2. Sunday School testimony
3. Throughout the FAITH gospel presentation
4. *A Step of Faith*
5. Key Question
6. ***Invitation***

A Quick Review

A Quick Review

The goal of the FAITH evangelism strategy is to introduce people to Jesus Christ. As we continue to penetrate secular society with a Christian witness, we may encounter persons who ask, Is Jesus really God's Son? Last week we examined five reasons we know that Jesus is God's Son. Mark each statement *T* for *true* or *F* for *false*.

F 1. Jesus claimed to be the promised Messiah, but we can't really be sure He was.

F 2. Jesus is one of many gods.

T 3. Jesus fulfilled God's purposes.

F 4. Jesus lived a good life, but now He is dead.

F 5. Jesus will rule His kingdom until God raises up another leader sometime in the future.

What are two places in FAITH visits when questions about or challenges to Jesus' deity might arise?

1. _____

2. _____

Check appropriate ways to respond to the question, Is Jesus really God's Son?

❑ 1. Say something like "No one knows for sure, but Christians certainly hope so."

❑ 2. Explain that the person can receive salvation without accepting Jesus as God's Son.

☑ 3. Use John 3:16 to explain that Jesus is God's Son.

☑ 4. Encourage the person to see the truth through the eyes of faith.

☑ 5. Explain how you relate to the persons on the cover of *A Step of Faith*.

❑ 6. Tell the person not to interrupt your presentation by asking questions.

☑ 7. Encourage the person to attend Sunday School.

Defining the Question: Who Is the Holy Spirit?

Unlike the previous topics in this study—the Bible, God, and Jesus—the Holy Spirit is a subject most unbelievers are completely unfamiliar with. Consequently, it is unlikely that they will ask questions about Him in a witnessing situation. Because many Christians do not understand the work of the Holy Spirit, this session will focus on equipping you with a greater understanding of the Holy Spirit's role in your own life and in God's redemptive plan.

Here are some ways you might anticipate being questioned or challenged about the Holy Spirit.
- "Do all believers have the Holy Spirit?"
- "How does the Holy Spirit work in a believer's life?"
- "Can I be aware of the Holy Spirit's presence?"
- "Is the Holy Spirit the same as Jesus Christ living in me?"
- "What part does the Holy Spirit play in bringing the lost to Christ?"

The Holy Spirit has a very important role in leading lost persons to Christ, so He is present and active when you present the good news or minister to someone. The Holy Spirit also helps you, as a growing disciple, overcome sin and grow in Christlikeness. As both a witness and a growing disciple, you need to understand the identity of the Holy Spirit and His vital work in your own life and in the lives of those He is leading to repentance and salvation.

The Bible Speaks

The Bible teaches that the Holy Spirit is the third Person of the Godhead, or the Trinity, the three Persons being God the Father, God the Son, and God the Holy Spirit. Like God and Jesus, the Holy Spirit has always existed, for Genesis 1:1-3 tells us that the Spirit was present at the creation of the world.

Although many believers are unfamiliar with the work of the Holy Spirit, He is equal in every way to the Father and the Son: "The Spirit searches all things, even the deep things of God. … No one knows the thoughts of God except the Spirit of God" (1 Cor. 2:10-11). Yet the Spirit has a unique role and distinct functions in the work of the Kingdom. Let's examine several of these.

1. The Holy Spirit brings conviction of _____sin_____.
- When lost persons hear the gospel, the Holy Spirit brings

HEAR IT

Step 2 (5 mins.)

Introduce the content of this session by summarizing Defining the Question. Use the computer diskette or the overhead cel to illustrate questions about the Holy Spirit.

Defining the Question

Step 3 (15 mins.)

Direct participants to page 87 in their Journals and to fill in the blanks as you present the key points in The Bible Speaks. Use the computer diskette or overhead cels.

The Bible Speaks

conviction that this message is the truth. As they begin to realize that they can receive eternal life by repenting of their sin and accepting Jesus Christ as Savior, it is the Holy Spirit who reveals this truth to them (see John 16:8-11).

• The Holy Spirit works in believers' lives to convict us of sin. Sin mars fellowship with our Father and prevents us from having a Spirit-filled life. When you feel guilt or sorrow, the Holy Spirit is convicting you of sin. Ask God to forgive you of your sin and to restore a right fellowship with Him (see 1 John 1:9).

2. The Holy Spirit assures us of _____salvation_____.

He witnesses in a believer's heart to make us certain we are spiritually secure (see Rom. 8:16; 2 Cor. 1:22; 5:5; Eph. 1:14). Christ guaranteed our salvation; the Spirit confirms that truth in our hearts.

3. The Holy Spirit indwells individual _____believers_____.

Every believer is indwelled by the Holy Spirit at the moment of conversion (see Rom. 8:9; 1 Cor. 12:3). The Spirit's indwelling—

• provides _____power_____ and _____direction_____ for life;
• provides _____motivation_____ and _____guidance_____ for growing as a disciple;
• results in _____Christlike_____ _____living_____.[1]

4. The Holy Spirit indwells the _____church_____.

The Spirit baptizes each believer into the body of Christ (see 1 Cor. 12:13). The Book of Acts vividly portrays the dramatic way the Holy Spirit came in power on the early church and gave direction to its work. The Holy Spirit is an administrator whose work is to build up the body of Christ. When we as a church open ourselves to His guidance and power, He reveals to us—

• what _____gifts_____ and _____ministries_____ are needed to do God's work;
• what _____fields_____ of _____service_____ to enter;
• how to develop our _____gifts_____ and _____ministries_____ to prepare to enter those fields.[2]

5. The Holy Spirit is our _____counselor_____.

When Jesus explained to His disciples the coming of the Holy Spirit, He spoke of the Spirit as counselor (see John 14:16,26). The Greek word for *counselor* means *one who walks alongside*. Jesus said that He would not leave us as orphans but that He would send us the Holy Spirit, who would walk alongside us forever. The Holy Spirit is constantly with us, comforting us and encouraging us in times of difficulty and helping us make decisions. Herschel H. Hobbs has written that Jesus is our advocate with God, while the Holy Spirit is God's advocate with us.[3]

6. The Holy Spirit is our _____teacher_____.
Jesus called the Holy Spirit the " 'Spirit of truth' " (John 16:13). The Spirit always guides us into the truth, that is, the truth of Jesus Christ. The Spirit does not teach us of Himself but always glorifies Christ (see John 16:14; 1 Cor. 12:3). As we read Scripture, pray, and listen to His direction, the Spirit teaches us in these ways.

- The Spirit helps us understand __who__ Christ is, the _____nature_____ of His ministry, and His __plans__ for the world (see 1 Cor. 2:12).
- The Spirit teaches us how to _____live_____ as _____Christ_____ wants us to live and develops _____Christlike_____ _____qualities_____ in our lives (see Gal. 5:22-23).[4]

7. The Holy Spirit _____intercedes_____ for us.
Have you ever found yourself at a point when you didn't know how to pray or couldn't find adequate words to express yourself to God? Romans 8:26-27 tells us that the Holy Spirit intercedes for us and expresses our needs to our Heavenly Father, according to God's will.

8. The Holy Spirit empowers us to do God's _____work_____.
God does not expect us to do His work in our own strength. The Holy Spirit provides power for Christian life and service.

- The Spirit gives one or more _____spiritual_____ _____gifts_____ to every believer to use in Kingdom ministry and to build up the body of Christ (see Rom. 12:1-8; 1 Cor. 12; Eph. 4).
- The Spirit empowers us to _____witness_____ (see Acts 1:8; 1 Thess. 1:5). We cannot be effective witnesses if we go in our own strength. When we prepare ourselves spiritually and submit to Him, the Holy Spirit gives us strength, boldness, and clear expression as we witness (see 1 Cor. 2:12-13). Remember that it is our responsibility to be obedient in sharing the good news; it is the Holy Spirit's role to bring conviction and lead the lost person to accept the truth of Jesus Christ.

The Scriptures admonish believers to be filled with the Spirit (see Eph. 5:18) and to live a Spirit-filled life (see Rom. 8:1-17). Living in the Holy Spirit's power is essential for a disciple of Jesus Christ. As you have seen, the Spirit works in your heart to help you—

- build a strong relationship with God;
- keep your focus on Jesus Christ and to submit to His control;
- develop Christlike purposes, desires, and character;
- discover God's will and obey Him;
- work for God's kingdom and witness as He wants you to.

The greatest privilege you can have as a witness is to be available

State that divine appointments are an important part of witnessing and ministry. If time allows, share a divine appointment you have experienced or ask a participant to share one.

Step 4 (5 mins.)

Direct participants to turn to page 90 in their Journals and to fill in the blanks as you summarize Entry Points in FAITH Visits. Use the computer diskette or overhead cel.

Entry Points in FAITH Visits

---

for the Holy Spirit's use in a divine appointment. You can praise God that this has resulted because the Holy Spirit has worked in your life as a Christian disciple and has also worked in the lost person's life to produce an openness to God's truth.

Entry Points in FAITH Visits

There are several occasions in FAITH visits when the Holy Spirit plays a vital role in leading the lost to repentance and in directing and empowering the witness.

1. The Holy Spirit of God has been at work in the process of making specific _____**assignments**_____ to FAITH Teams. He is working in the _____**lives**_____ of persons He wants your Team to encounter. Sometimes the visitation assignment will _____**sharpen**_____ you as a disciple of Christ. Often, the Holy Spirit works to _____**minister**_____ to the person through you.

2. The Holy Spirit has worked to _____**match**_____ Team members' unique _____**gifts**_____ and _____**personalities**_____ with the _____**needs**_____ of persons who need Christ.

3. God's Spirit _____**protects**_____ and _____**guides**_____ as you study, practice, travel, and enter communities where you may or may not be welcome. Realize that a spiritual battle is being waged as the adversary tries to deceive and discourage persons from believing and embracing the truth of Jesus Christ.

4. The Holy Spirit _____**uses**_____ your _____**experiences**_____ to draw others to Christ. He uses your Sunday School, evangelism, and baptism testimonies to encourage and instruct.

5. As you briefly declare the message of the gospel and identify God's Word that reinforces each point of that message, God's Spirit _____**convinces**_____ of _____**truth**_____ and _____**convicts**_____ of _____**sin**_____. Occasionally, you will be the person the Spirit uses to reap the harvest. On many other occasions He will use you to plant a seed or cultivate the gospel message in the person's life.

6. The Holy Spirit is present and at work when a person is confronted with the _____**Invitation**_____. Many persons immediately experience evidence of the release from sin when they pray to receive Christ. Others visibly resist the Spirit's ministry.

7. God's Spirit works in the lives of _____**believers**_____ you visit. You will experience the Holy Spirit's ministry as He _____**comforts**_____, _____**guides**_____, and _____**reclaims**_____.

8. The Holy Spirit is at work when you look for and discover _____**divine**_____ _____**appointments**_____. When God chooses to work through you, every encounter is a divine appointment.

9. _____**Celebration**_____ _____**Time**_____ is more than merely reporting results of visits. The Holy Spirit brings _____**renewal**_____ as believers glorify God for His work in the midst of His people.

How You Can Respond

Here are possible ways you can respond to the Holy Spirit's work before, during, and after witnessing encounters.

1. Be a _____**clean**_____ and _____**available**_____ vessel willing to be tested and used by the Holy Spirit. Many times you realize that God seems to be working as much in your life as in the lives of persons you visit.

2. _____**Listen**_____ to the still, small but convincing voice of the Spirit as He tells you what to say and how to respond. The more comfortable you are in using the FAITH Visit Outline, the more flexible you can be in following the Holy Spirit's guidance as He directs through specific situations.

3. Make sure Team members practice an attitude of _____**prayer**_____ throughout each visit. Make sure the person(s) who are not leading in conversation are praying for the person being visited.

4. Carefully and humbly yet _____**straightforwardly**_____ share God's Word. Through the Spirit's work, God's Word is indeed sharper than a double-edged sword (see Heb. 4:12).

5. Be mindful of and receptive to _____**divine**_____ _____**appointments**_____. God will draw people to Christ through your availability.

6. In a follow-up or ministry visit tell the person how the Holy Spirit has ministered to you to develop _____**Christlikeness**_____ or to _____**comfort**_____ and _____**strengthen**_____ you.

7. The goal of the Holy Spirit's work is always to bring glory to Jesus Christ. Be careful to give ____**glory**____ to God for all He is doing as persons learn to minister and share the gospel. You do not have the right to claim that you have done anything. You are not the soul-winner; the Holy Spirit is! He has merely allowed you to be part of His ministry.

Step 5 (5 mins.)

Remind participants that it is not likely that unbelievers will ask questions about the Holy Spirit in witnessing situations. However, the Holy Spirit plays a very active role in winning the lost to Christ. It is also appropriate during a follow-up or ministry visit to testify to the Holy Spirit's work in the witness's life. Present ways participants can respond to the Holy Spirit's work before, during, and after witnessing encounters, using the ideas in How You Can Respond. Ask participants to fill in the blanks on page 91 in their Journals. Use the computer diskette or the overhead cel.

How You Can Respond

SAY IT

Step 6 (5 mins.)

Ask accountability partners to practice sharing the *Presentation* portion of the FAITH Visit Outline with each other.

STUDY IT

Step 7 (5 mins.)

Overview Home Study Assignments for session 5.

Transition to assemble with FAITH Teams to prepare for home visits. (5 mins.)

Visitation Time

Do It

1. Pray for God to lead your Team to a divine appointment. If someone is not home, go next door. It just may be God's divine appointment.
2. Use the time in the car to review, allowing Learners to ask questions.
3. After each visit allow Learners to debrief it. Facilitate the debriefing by asking specific questions.

Celebration Time

Share It

1. Share a divine appointment.
2. Not every Opinion Poll results in a profession of faith, but celebrate all attempts made. Highlight decisions made, prospects discovered, and other outcomes that would encourage and motivate other Teams.
3. Rejoice with other reports.
4. Complete Evaluation Cards.
5. Complete Participation Cards.
6. Update Visitation Forms with the results of visits.

Home Study Assignments

Home Study Assignments reinforce this session by helping you apply what you have learned.

Your Discipleship Journey

Journaling activities in Your Discipleship Journey are an important part of your development as a Great Commission Christian through FAITH training.

1. Read Romans 8:1-17 and describe what it means to live in the Spirit.

   _____

   _____

2. When we are filled with the Holy Spirit, we will produce the fruit of the Spirit. Read Galatians 5:22-23 and list the fruit.

   _____

   _____

   Read through the list again and ask yourself what your personal life, your family life, and your working environment would be like if they were characterized by these attributes.

3. How is the Holy Spirit evident now in your life as a growing disciple?

   _____

   _____

   As a witness? _____

   _____

4. Examine your heart before God and ask Him to reveal obstacles keeping you from living in the Spirit. Is there unconfessed sin? Are you holding a grudge? Have you been disobedient to God's leadership? Do you need to spend more time with Him to grow in the knowledge of His Word and in your relationship with Him through prayer? On the following page, describe any obstacles and changes you will commit to make. You might want to renew your commitment to pray with your accountability partner as you study, serve as a Team Leader, and celebrate what God is doing through FAITH.

_____

_____

_____

Spend time in prayer in which you submit to God's Spirit, allowing Him to minister to, discipline, and transform you through the process of FAITH. Your life will never be the same as you seek to embrace the work of the Great Commission.

Growing as a Life Witness

Growing as a Life Witness reminds you of your responsibility to witness and minister to others during the week.
1. Talk or meet with your accountability partner and share ways you have cultivated a lost person or have witnessed or ministered on occasions other than FAITH visits.
2. Share any commitments you made in activity 4 of Your Discipleship Journey.
3. Pray for lost persons by name and for each other.

Prayer Concerns	Answers to Prayer
_____	_____
_____	_____
_____	_____
_____	_____
_____	_____
_____	_____
_____	_____
_____	_____
_____	_____
_____	_____

Your Weekly Sunday School Leadership Team Meeting

A FAITH participant is an important member of Sunday School. Encourage Team members who are elected Sunday School workers to attend this weekly meeting. Use this section to record ways your FAITH Team influences the work of your Sunday School class or department. Use the information to report during weekly Sunday School leadership team meetings. Identify actions that need to be taken through Sunday School as a result of prayer concerns, needs identified, visits made by the Team, and decisions made by the persons visited.

1. If you do not have a weekly meeting, meet with your class or department. Consider inviting the Sunday School Leadership Team from your class or department to your home after church on a Sunday evening. Excitedly share with the leadership team the results of weekly FAITH visits. Ask for additional names of persons you will need to make a ministry or evangelistic visit. Close with prayer. Consider conducting these meetings regularly until a weekly team prayer meeting is begun.

2. Discuss ways Sunday's Bible-study lesson can involve members and guests in transformational Bible study and discipleship.

   _____

   _____

3. Make assignments for follow-up phone calls to prospects and new members, communicating excitement about their participation in Sunday School. Share and receive information about absentees and make assignments to follow up.

   _____

   _____

4. Share highlights that reflect the Holy Spirit's leadership and presence in FAITH visits thus far. Include actual visit results, an extraordinary sense of God's presence during visits, divine appointments, and so forth.

   _____

   _____

5. Pray for FAITH Teams, the pastor and church staff, and Sunday School department directors and teachers.

Discipling Your Team Members

This weekly feature suggests actions the Team Leader can take to support Team members, prepare for Team Time, and improve visits. This work is part of the Team Leader's Home Study Assignments. Add any actions suggested by your church's FAITH strategy.

Support Team Members

❏ Pray for and personally follow up on any Learner who may need personal encouragement.

❏ Contact Team members during the week to remind them that you are praying for them and to discuss their participation in FAITH. Seek to encourage Learners.

❏ Remember, Learners have overviewed the entire gospel presentation in session 5 and may have questions about their role in making a visit. Record specific needs and concerns in your Journal margin.

❏ Think of appropriate ways to involve an Assistant Team Leader, if assigned to your Team.

Prepare to Lead Team Time

❏ Overview Leading Team Time for session 6.

❏ In a review of session 5 be prepared to overview the entire gospel presentation.

Prepare to Lead Visits

❏ Review the FAITH Visit Outline.

❏ Think about: Do you need to begin gently pushing some Learners out of their comfort zones during evangelistic visits? Some may be hesitant to participate fully without some encouragement.

❏ Be prepared to model a visit in which a Team member is asked to lead in a visit up to asking the Key Question. Think about who might be ready for this opportunity or to share an evangelistic or Sunday School testimony.

❏ Pray for sensitivity as you involve different members in visits and pick up your part of the presentation appropriately and naturally.

❏ Prepare to lead your Team during Celebration Time.

Link with Sunday School

❏ Participate in your weekly Sunday School leadership team meeting. Share pertinent information in this meeting, using Your Weekly Sunday School Leadership Team Meeting (p. 95) and FAITH-visit results.

❏ As you think about new believers in your Sunday School, consider the work of the Holy Spirit in drawing them to Christ. Look for ways your Sunday School can clarify their understanding of the Holy Spirit's role in teaching and discipling believers to grow in Christ.

For Further Growth

For Further Growth may include additional reading or activities that will enhance your growth as a disciple and a discipler of others. These assignments are intended to be long-term projects and do not have to be completed during this semester of study.

1. Keep a journal of ways you see the Holy Spirit at work in your life, in the lives of Team members and Sunday School members, and persons you encounter in FAITH visits. Begin by reviewing notes you have taken in your FAITH resources about ways God's Spirit has been at work.
2. Study the Book of Acts and identify specific actions of the Holy Spirit in the lives of the early believers. Pay particular attention to the Holy Spirit's impact on a pagan world that had sought to destroy Christ's influence.
3. One of the Holy Spirit's roles is to convict you of sin. Read the FAITH Tip on pages 99–100 to learn how to confess your sin and seek forgiveness.

[1]Roy T. Edgemon, *The Doctrines Baptists Believe* (Nashville: Convention, 1988), 101.
[2]Ibid.
[3]Herschel H. Hobbs, *Fundamentals of Our Faith* (Nashville: Broadman Press, 1960), 61.
[4]Edgemon, *The Doctrines Baptists Believe*, 102.

FAITH AT WORK

One evening at the start of Visitation Time we received the names of chronic absentees. Before we left to visit, we were challenged to look for God's divine appointment. If the assigned person was not at home, we were instructed to knock on the neighbor's door on either side. When we arrived at our assigned home, no one was at home, so we left literature and proceeded to the home of one of the neighbors. When a man answered the door and we introduced ourselves, a big smile came across his face. He explained that he had been praying for someone to come to his house that night. The previous evening he had prayed to receive Christ, and today Satan had been attacking him. With Bible in hand, the man said he had a number of questions for which he needed answers and asked us to help him.

Our team sat down and shared with the man the truth of the Scripture, giving him assurance of his salvation. When we prayed with the man and left the house, each of us knew that we had experienced God's divine appointment.

Our team had a sense of joy and thankfulness that evening to know that we were led by the Holy Spirit to do God's work. As we reported during Celebration Time, everyone rejoiced together at the way God had moved to accomplish His will.

Steve Stege
Associate Pastor
for Education and Administration
First Baptist Church
Lubbock, Texas

FAITH TIP

Guide to Confession and Forgiveness

Use these guidelines to walk in the light and to remain in fellowship with God and with other Christians (see 1 John 1:5-10).

Ask the Holy Spirit to Convict You of Sins
See John 16:8-11.
1. Ask God to search your heart, thoughts, and ways (see Ps. 139: 23-24).
2. Let the Holy Spirit use the Word to show you how God views your heart, thoughts, and ways (see Rom. 8:26-27; Heb. 4:12-13).
   - Read your Bible daily.
   - Read special passages as you feel the need.

Agree with God About the Seriousness of Your Sins
1. To confess, agree with God. The word *confess* means *to agree with or admit*. Do not try to excuse your behavior, but accept what God convicts you of (see 1 John 1:8-10).
2. To confess, walk in the light of His holiness (see 1 John 1:7). Do not compare yourself to someone else to try walking in his or her light.
3. To confess, be honest with God (see 1 John 1:8-10). Do not hide anything from God or from yourself.

Acknowledge Christ as the Atoning Sacrifice for Your Sins
See 1 John 2:1-2.
1. Express your sorrow and repentance to God (see Ps. 51).
2. Ask for forgiveness based on the blood of Christ, which cleanses us from all sin (1 John 1:7; 2:2). Do not base your request on past or future works of righteousness (see Titus 3:5).
3. Turn over your sins to your advocate, Christ (see Heb. 4:14,16; 7:25; 9:24-26; 10:19,22; 1 John 2:2). Do not consider your sins again. Because God has forgiven you, consider those sins to be history.

Walk in the Light with Other Christians
See 1 John 1:7.
1. Be honest with other Christians about your sins. To walk in the light is to be open and honest (see 1 John 1:7).
2. Confess your sins to other understanding Christians as needed (see Jas. 5:16).
   - Confess during prayer with other believers.

- Confess only to those who can help bear your burden in the spirit of humility (see Gal. 6:1). They should be persons who can keep a confidence and can help you overcome temptation.
- Tell others only what is necessary. On some occasions you need to confess only that you have sinned and that God has forgiven you. At other times you may confess the sin but not the details. (If your confession relates to sexual impurity, do not go into detail. If you need to discuss details, do so with your pastor or a trained counselor.) If your sin is known or affects the church, ask others to forgive you as God has.
- Confess only your sin, not someone else's. Do not blame anyone for your sin. Accept your responsibility. Do not implicate others.

3. Renounce your sin and make restitution if possible (see Luke 19:8). Any restitution is not to be considered penance, not payment for your sin. It is not done to relieve any guilt feelings, because Christ has already forgiven you. Yet restitution helps restore anything you have taken from another person and may witness to that person.

Walk in the Light with Christ
See 1 John 1:7.

1. When you sin again, immediately confess and ask God to forgive you.
2. Do not give up your struggle to be free from a sin you repeatedly commit. Satan will try to convince you that God will not forgive you for committing the same sin again. Of course, genuine repentance and turning from sin are necessary for you to receive forgiveness. However, sometimes you sin again in spite of your good intentions. If you seek forgiveness in genuine repentance, God will forgive you again.
   - Be careful that you do not sin because you know that you can ask to be forgiven. God does not play games. If you willfully sin, you treat lightly Christ's sacrifice for you.
   - If you continually commit the same sin, counsel with your pastor or a trained Christian counselor.
   - Sin in a Christian's life does not change the person's relationship as a child of God, but it creates a barrier to fellowship with Him.

Forgiveness is God's gift. Confession and repentance are the God-ordained ways to free you from sin's penalty, presence, and power. Although you never reach perfection in this world, through Christ you can continually walk in the light with our holy God.[1]

1Avery T. Willis, Jr., *MasterLife 3: The Disciple's Victory* (Nashville: LifeWay, 1996), 54–55.

Why Does Evil Exist?

In this session you will—

CHECK IT by engaging in Team Time activities;

KNOW IT by reviewing content from session 5;

HEAR IT by affirming what the Bible says about the evil in the world;

SAY IT by discussing possible applications of what you have learned in this session;

STUDY IT by overviewing Home Study Assignments;

DO IT by leading your Team in making visits;

SHARE IT by celebrating.

In Advance
- Overview content.
- Preview teaching suggestions. Prepare key points. Decide whether to use the session 6 computer slides or the overhead cels.
- Prepare the room for teaching.
- Pray for participants and for Teams as they prepare to visit.
- As Teaching Time begins, direct participants to open their Journals to page 104.

CHECK IT (15 MINS.)

If the computer diskette is used, display the agenda frame for Team Time, as desired. Add other points as needed.

CHECK IT agenda:
✔ FAITH Visit Outline
✔ Other Home Study Assignments
✔ Session 5 Debriefing
✔ Help for Strengthening a Visit

Leading Team Time

All Team members participate in Team Time. They are primarily responsible for reciting the assigned portion of the FAITH Visit Outline and for discussing other Home Study Assignments.

As you direct this important time of CHECK IT activities with your Team, keep in mind that Learners look to you as a role model, motivator, mentor, and friend. Team Time activities can continue in the car as the Team travels to and from visits.

Lead CHECK IT Activities

✔ FAITH Visit Outline
❑ Listen while each Learner recites all of *Preparation, Presentation* through the FORGIVENESS statement and verse (Eph. 1:7a), as well as other key words in *Presentation* and *Invitation.*
❑ Indicate your approval by signing or initialing Journals. Encourage Learners.

✔ Other Home Study Assignments
❑ Check to see whether Learners shared their evangelistic testimonies with two different believers. Briefly discuss how these two believers responded to the testimonies.
❑ Discuss benefits Learners are discovering from assigned reading material in *Evangelism Through the Sunday School* and in the FAITH Tip "Nurturing a New Christian" in *A Journey in FAITH Journal.*
❑ Make sure Learners are writing in Your Journey in Faith (their journaling section).

✔ Session 5 Debriefing
❑ Learners have heard the entire gospel presentation by viewing the videotape, hearing the presentation during visits, and overviewing it in session 5. Ask Learners to share how comfortable they are becoming with understanding the significance of sharing the complete gospel presentation.
❑ Remind Learners that although the gospel presentation is built on the letters in *FAITH, A Step of Faith* is used to help lead a person to make a commitment to Christ and enroll in Sunday School. Indicate that each of the following six sessions will focus on a letter of the gospel presentation and on how to use the leaflet in leading a person to make a decision to follow Christ.

✔ Help for Strengthening a Visit
❑ Encourage Learners to be constantly in prayer for one another and for persons being visited. Emphasize the importance of looking for

opportunities to build bridges that allow us to share the gospel while, at the same time, being sensitive to the needs of the person being visited. Call attention to the fact that many times a Team might inadvertently close a door to receptivity to the gospel because they come across as pushy.

❑ Remind Team members of the importance of being available to the Holy Spirit and of relying on Him to prepare someone for the gospel. We are to be prepared to share and to know how to compassionately lead someone to make the commitments that will change his or her life forever.

Notes

_____

_____

_____

_____

_____

_____

_____

Actions I Need to Take with Learners During the Week

_____

_____

_____

_____

_____

Transition to classrooms for instruction on the content of the session. (5 mins.)

TEACHING TIME

KNOW IT

Step 1 (5 mins.)

Direct participants to locate A Quick Review on page 104 in their Journals and to complete the activities. Then give the answers, using the computer diskette or the overhead cel. Possible answers to question:

1. Visitation assignments
2. Matching Team members' gifts and personalities with lost persons' needs
3. Protecting and guiding the witness
4. Sunday School, evangelism, and baptism testimonies
5. Convincing of truth, convicting of sin
6. Comforting, guiding, and reclaiming believers
7. *Invitation*
8. Divine appointments
9. Renewing believers in Celebration Time

A Quick Review

HEAR IT

Step 2 (5 mins.)

Introduce the content of this session by summarizing Defining the Question. Use the computer diskette or the overhead cel to illustrate questions and comments about evil.

A Quick Review

Last week you studied the role of the Holy Spirit in leading the lost to Christ and in helping you grow as a believer. Mark each of the following statements T for *true* or F for *false*.

__F__ 1. The Holy Spirit is the second Person of the Godhead.
__T__ 2. Jesus Christ sent the Counselor to us.
__T__ 3. The Holy Spirit came to be our Teacher.
__F__ 4. The Holy Spirit came to bring glory to Himself.
__T__ 5. The Holy Spirit brings conviction of sin.
__F__ 6. The Holy Spirit plays a role in salvation but not in discipleship.

What are two places in FAITH visits when the Holy Spirit plays a vital role in convicting of sin and in guiding the witness?

1. _____   2. _____

Check appropriate ways to respond to the Holy Spirit's work before, during, and after witnessing encounters.
☑ 1. Be a clean and available vessel willing to be used by the Spirit.
☑ 2. Listen to the Spirit's voice as he tells you how to respond.
☐ 3. Warn the person that the Holy Spirit has the power to strike him dead, depending on his response to the gospel presentation.
☑ 4. Make sure Team members pray throughout the visit.
☐ 5. Ask the Spirit to bring dreadful consequences into the life of someone who doesn't accept Christ.
☑ 6. Straightforwardly share God's Word.
☑ 7. Be mindful of and receptive to divine appointments.
☑ 8. Tell the person how the Holy Spirit has helped you develop Christlikeness or has comforted and strengthened you.
☑ 9. Give glory to God for all He is doing.

Defining the Question: Why Does Evil Exist?

All people experience evil to some degree in their personal lives. The experience of evil can be so painful that it becomes a barrier to faith in God. When people are confronted with the claims of the gospel of Jesus Christ, they may question the purpose of evil in the world and why a God who is both good and all-powerful can allow it to exist. They may demand answers about evil before they are willing to make a commitment to Christ in faith.

Here are some ways you might anticipate being questioned or challenged about the existence of evil.

- "If God is good and all-powerful, why does He allow evil to exist?"
- "Does God cause evil things to happen, like natural disasters?"
- "If God cared about us, there would be no evil in the world."
- "Evil exists only in the mind."
- "If God won't stop evil, what hope do we have?"

Many people experience natural evil. Almost every day we hear news stories about natural evils like earthquakes, tornadoes, hurricanes, droughts, deadly and crippling diseases, and winter storms. Natural disasters can destroy everything a family has worked for all of their lives, plus the lives of precious family members and friends. When we share God's love, we frequently encounter the question, If God is good and and all-powerful, why does He allow this kind of evil in His world?

People also experience moral evil, the harmful act of a wicked person or group. Robberies, rapes, murders, assaults, child abuse, wars, and terrorist activities also make the headlines every day. Each of these will leave someone with a devastating memory of how cruel human beings can be to one another. Even worse are cruel acts that are committed by someone who should have been a source of love and protection. Our visitation efforts often bring us into contact with the victims of such evil. Painful memories may be a barrier to personal faith in a loving God. When these victims ask about the existence of evil, we must be prepared to share a biblical response that offers hope and healing.

The Bible Speaks

How does the Bible explain the existence of evil? Like most of the hard questions of life, the Bible does not give us a simple answer. However, it tells us the truth about God and His purpose for His creation so that we can trust Him even when we don't fully understand.

1. Evil exists because we have ____free____ ____will____.
The Book of Genesis tells us that God created the world and all that is in it from nothing. His creation was good (see Gen. 1:31). God created human beings in His image (see Gen. 1:27). One way we resemble God is in our free will, which means that we are free to choose good or evil (see Gen. 2:16-17). People sometimes wonder why God created us with the ability to choose evil. The freedom to choose between good and evil is essential to a moral universe. If we were not free to choose, we would be nothing more than programmed robots, incapable of making truly moral choices. Forced obedience would be foreign to the freely chosen love relationship God wants us to enjoy with Him.

Defining
the Question

Step 3 (20 mins.)

Direct participants to turn to page 105 in their Journals and to fill in the blanks as you present the main points in The Bible Speaks. Use the computer diskette or the overhead cels.

The Bible
Speaks

Some people also wonder why God does not destroy all evil in the world. If God destroyed evil, He would annihilate the entire human race, "for all have sinned and fall short of the glory of God" (Rom. 3:23). God is patient, not wanting anyone to be lost (see 2 Pet. 3:9). He permits evil people to live so that all might have the opportunity to fulfill their eternal destinies by accepting Christ and living in relationship with their Creator.[1]

2. Evil exists because of the intrusion of an evil <u>adversary</u>.

Satan entered God's good creation and deceived Eve by twisting what God had said, by planting doubts in her mind about God's goodness, and by appealing to her fleshly desire for the fruit (see Gen. 3:1-6). The Bible does not fully explain Satan's origin or identity. Apparently, he had been a beautiful angelic being and was therefore a created being. Along with other angelic beings, Satan had chosen to rebel against God (see 2 Pet. 2:4; Jude 6), becoming the enemies of God and humans. He is the deceiver and accuser of human beings (see Rev. 12:9-10). He tempts us to yield to our fleshly desires and then accuses us of our failure.[2] First Peter 5:8 says that Satan "prowls around like a roaring lion looking for someone to devour."

3. The human choice to sin has affected the entire <u>created</u> <u>order</u>.

The natural evil we encounter in the world results from the curse God placed on creation after the sin of Adam and Eve (see Gen. 3:17-18). Their sin apparently caused a disruption in God's good creation. Paul explained that "the creation was subjected to frustration, not by its own choice, but by the will of the one who subjected it" (Rom. 8:20). Today we still see the effect of human sin in the pollution and exploitation of the environment.[3]

Adam and Eve's choice to sin also brought about the fallen state of humankind. Something tragic happened to the human family when Adam and Eve ate the forbidden fruit. Sin resulted in separation from God, shame, guilt, disruption of personal relations, pain and suffering, loss of freedom, bondage to sin, and physical death. As a result of the fall, each person enters the world with a sinful nature, inherently prone to do wrong rather than right (see Rom. 3:9-18).

4. God dealt with the problem of evil by sending His <u>Son</u> to pay the penalty for <u>sin</u>.

"All have sinned" (Rom. 3:23), and "the wages of sin is death" (Rom. 6:23). We all deserve to die (see Luke 13:3). Yet God sent His Son in human flesh to live a sinless life and to die on a cross to pay the penalty for our sin (see John 3:16; 1 Cor. 15:3-4; 2 Cor. 5:21).[4] Jesus' righteousness allows us to relate to a holy God and to dwell in His presence forever (see John 10:10; 14:3). Jesus is the answer to both our personal problem with evil and our inherited inclination to choose evil. That is the heart of the exciting news you share through FAITH!

5. *God will totally and finally* _____**defeat**_____ *evil.*

The Bible makes clear that God is greater than evil and will ultimately destroy it. God is just (see Jas. 2:13), and judgment belongs to Him. Evil will be appropriately rewarded by an almighty and holy God.

- God will deliver the _____**earth**_____ from the natural evil that plagues us. Jesus demonstrated His mastery over nature when He was on earth (see Matt. 8:23-27). Paul noted that at the end of time "the creation itself will be liberated from its bondage to decay and brought into the glorious freedom of the children of God" (Rom. 8:21).
- God will judge evil _____**deeds**_____ and _____**people**_____. While biblical passages on judgment serve as warnings to those who pursue lives of wickedness (see Ex. 14; Isa. 37; Acts 12), they encourage those who have been victimized by evil (see 2 Pet. 2:5-6,9). Everyone will face judgment at the end of time (see Rev. 20:11-15). Our God is the Judge of all the earth.
- God will condemn the evil _____**powers**_____ that operate in our world. Satan and his forces will be cast into "the lake of burning sulfur" (Rev. 20:10).

6. *We can* _____**trust**_____ _____**God**_____ *when we do not understand why evil things happen.*

- God _____**cares**_____ about us (see 1 Pet. 5:7).
- God can bring _____**good**_____ from any situation (see Rom. 8:28).
- God is _____**present**_____ with us (see 1 John 4:4).
- God gives us strength to _____**resist**_____ evil (see Matt. 6:13; Jas. 1:13-16).
- God promises a better _____**future**_____ with Him (see John 14:3; Rev. 21:3-4).

We cannot answer every question that can be raised about the existence of evil. Believers can trust their Heavenly Father to fulfill the biblical promises He has given us about His goodness, love, and care, knowing that the past, present, and future are in His hands. To unbelievers we can offer the promises of God's Word and our living hope for an eternity free of evil in the presence of the One " 'who is, and who was, and who is to come, the Almighty' " (Rev. 1:8).

Direct participants to turn to page 108 in their Journals and to fill in the blanks as you summarize Entry Points in FAITH Visits. Use the computer diskette or the overhead cel.

Entry Points in FAITH Visits

SAY IT

Step 5 (5 mins.)

Ask accountability partners to discuss ways they would respond to a question about the existence of evil, using the ideas in How You Can Respond.

If you are leading students, have accountability partners role-play a situation in which one partner asks a question about the existence of evil and the other partner responds.

Entry Points in FAITH Visits

Several occasions in FAITH visits offer a person an opportunity to consider the question, Why does evil exist?

1. During the **INTRODUCTION** portion of an evangelistic visit you may learn about natural evil the person has experienced. Information on the Visitation Assignment Card may identify issues they have wrestled with.

2. As you share your **Sunday** **School** or **evangelistic** **testimony**, some persons will think of confrontations with evil they have experienced. Briefly relating your experience with evil may be appropriate.

3. Some persons' responses to the **Key** **Question** will reflect their struggle with or the consequences of evil.

4. **AVAILABLE** **FOR** **ALL** can touch a sensitive chord for many persons who are wrestling with the consequences of evil. Many have difficulty accepting that God loves them no matter what they have done or what has happened.

5. The Holy Spirit often works through **IMPOSSIBLE** and **T** **is** **for** **TURN** in the hearts of persons who have been victims of moral evil. God can use these concepts in the heart of someone who has committed evil toward others. The importance of God's judgment against sin is central to the message of FAITH, and persons will wrestle with this truth.

6. The thought of **HEAVEN** **HERE** can be a staggering one for a person whose life has been ravaged by evil.

7. The **Invitation** is a powerful tool in the hands of the Holy Spirit. Some persons will openly question God's willingness to provide salvation and meaning in life when the storms of life have brought devastation.

How You Can Respond

Here are possible ways you can respond to the question, Why does evil exist? during witnessing encounters. Your response will depend on the person, the situation, and the Holy Spirit's direction in this circumstance. Always keep in mind the general principles outlined on pages 28–29 in session 1.

1. When you talk with someone who has committed evil, be compassionate, but also provide scriptural direction and guidance.

2. Emphasize the importance of accepting the forgiveness God provides. God's forgiveness allows a person to accept release from guilt. It also helps a person forgive others.

3. You will know personally of experiences when God's mercy and grace have overcome the consequences of evil. Be straightforward in explaining the redemption and hope we have because of Christ.
4. Do not let your accounts of your personal experiences with evil dominate your testimony. God will use your testimony to convince the person that a new life is possible outside the clutches of evil.
5. Be particularly sensitive to ways Satan uses some persons to threaten those who seek to do God's will. Never place your Team in danger. On the other hand, realize that God will demonstrate great power as you boldly witness to persons gripped by sin.
6. Make sure you have prayer partners who are actively praying that Satan will be bound as your Team makes visits.
7. Emphasize the importance of understanding that God loves the sinner even though the consequences of sin must be paid.
8. Look for opportunities for follow-up by your Team members or Sunday School members.

Visitation Time

Do It

1. As you visit, listen for signs of evil's influence in the lives of those you are visiting. The Lord may give you an opportunity to share some of the biblical insights you have learned.
2. Reflect on the difference your church makes in the community. Is there less moral evil because your church is there? As your church functions as salt, it prevents the spread of evil; as it functions as light, it brings to people a greater understanding of the world in which they live and of God's love.
3. Use the time in the car to review, allowing Learners to ask questions.
4. After each visit allow Learners to debrief it. Facilitate the debriefing by asking specific questions.

Celebration Time

Share It

1. Ask a Team member to take the lead in sharing reports.
2. Hear reports and testimonies.
3. Complete Evaluation Cards.
4. Complete Participation Cards.
5. Update Visitation Forms with the results of visits.

STUDY IT

Step 6 (5 mins.)

Overview Home Study Assignments for session 6.

Transition to assemble with FAITH Teams to prepare for home visits. (5 mins.)

DO IT (110 MINS.)

SHARE IT (30 MINS.)

Home Study Assignments

Home Study Assignments reinforce this session by helping you apply what you have learned.

Your Discipleship Journey

Journaling activities in Your Discipleship Journey are an important part of your development as a Great Commission Christian through FAITH training.

1. Mark the following statements *T* for *true* or *F* for *false*.
___ 1. God is the author of evil.
___ 2. God does not have the power to stop evil.
___ 3. Free choice is a good gift from God.
___ 4. To eliminate evil would necessitate God's removing our free will.
___ 5. Without free will, true love and obedience would not be possible.

2. Read and reflect on Psalm 37. Underline words and phrases that help you relate to ministry for those who are bombarded by evil.

3. In Romans 3 Paul paints a humbling portrait of the human heart without Christ. Write Paul's description in each of the following verses.

Romans 3:10: _____

Romans 3:11a: _____

Romans 3:11b: _____

Romans 3:12a: _____

Romans 3:12b: _____

Romans 3:12c: _____

Romans 3:13: _____

Romans 3:14: _____

Romans 3:15: _____

Romans 3:16: _____

Romans 3:17: _____

Romans 3:18: _____

4. Carefully read Revelation 20—22 to remind yourself of God's final solution for evil and suffering.

Growing as a Life Witness

Growing as a Life Witness reminds you of your responsibility to witness and minister to others during the week.

1. Talk or meet with your accountability partner and share ways you have cultivated a lost person or have witnessed or ministered on occasions other than FAITH visits.
2. Discuss ways you can apply the session 6 content in witnessing.
3. Pray for lost persons by name and for each other.

Prayer Concerns	Answers to Prayer
_____	_____
_____	_____
_____	_____
_____	_____
_____	_____
_____	_____
_____	_____
_____	_____
_____	_____
_____	_____
_____	_____

Your Weekly Sunday School Leadership Team Meeting

A FAITH participant is an important member of Sunday School. Encourage Team members who are elected Sunday School workers to attend this weekly meeting. Use this section to record ways your FAITH Team influences the work of your Sunday School class or department. Use the information to report during weekly Sunday School leadership team meetings. Identify actions that need to be taken through Sunday School as a result of prayer concerns, needs identified, visits made by the Team, and decisions made by the persons visited.

1. Highlight FAITH needs/reports that affect your class/department or age group. Among persons contacted through FAITH this week, who is likely to attend on Sunday? Ask specific class members to take specific actions to make guests feel welcome. For some ministry visits, is follow-up needed by the class/department?

_____

_____

2. Share relevant information about persons who will be the focus of future FAITH assignments so that visits can be especially personal and meaningful. Are some people the focus of continuing cultivation by your FAITH Team? Are additional prospect-discovery activities needed?

_____

_____

3. Participate in evaluating last week's Bible-study session and discuss ways Sunday's lesson can involve members and guests in transformational Bible study and discipleship.

4. Record prayer requests for your teacher and department director.

_____

_____

5. Forgiveness is a significant theme in the gospel and in the FAITH gospel presentation. Is your class/department characterized by a forgiving, loving spirit? List and discuss ways to further cultivate an atmosphere of acceptance and reconciliation.

_____

_____

Discipling Your Team Members

This weekly feature suggests actions the Team Leader can take to support Team members, prepare for Team Time, and improve visits. This work is part of the Team Leader's Home Study Assignments. Add any actions suggested by your church's FAITH strategy.

Support Team Members

❑ Contact Team members during the week. Remind them that you are praying for them. Discuss prayer concerns and answers to prayer.
❑ This week Learners are memorizing the FAITH presentation through FORGIVENESS. Encourage them to meditate on the significance of forgiveness in their personal lives.
❑ Learners have a significant amount of reading this week. Encourage them in this. It is important that they grasp the basic concepts in the reading material.
❑ Record specific needs and concerns shared by Team members on the lines provided.

_____

_____

Prepare to Lead Team Time

❑ Review Team members' Home Study Assignments.
❑ Overview Leading Team Time for session 7.

Prepare to Lead Visits

❑ Review the FAITH Visit Outline.
❑ Be prepared to explain the significance of God's forgiveness.

Link with Sunday School

❑ Participate in your weekly Sunday School leadership team meeting. Share pertinent information in this meeting, using Your Weekly Sunday School Leadership Team Meeting (p. 112) and FAITH-visit results.
❑ Think about ways your Sunday School can help members, especially new Christians, distinguish good and evil in our society. Your teachers may want to use television news stories or newspaper or magazine articles to introduce Sunday School topics that speak to current events.

For Further Growth

For Further Growth may include additional reading or activities that will enhance your growth as a disciple and a discipler of others. These assignments are intended to be long-term projects and do not have to be completed during this semester of study.

1. Build a relationship with someone whose life has been bruised by the consequences of evil. Share the assurance of redemption and grace through a relationship with Christ Jesus.

2. Build a relationship with someone whose life has brought hurt to others. Communicate Christ's compassion for persons who have let evil influence their lives.

3. Study *Making Peace with Your Past* (LifeWay, 1992) to learn how to deal with the consequences of evil and to help others who have been affected.

---

[1] Ken Hemphill, *LifeAnswers: Making Sense of Your World* (Nashville: LifeWay, 1993), 109, 112–13.
[2] Ibid., 110.
[3] Ibid.
[4] Ibid., 113.

Answers to true/false activity on page 110: 1. F, 2. F, 3. T, 4. T, 5. T

Why Does God Permit Suffering?

In this session you will—

CHECK IT by engaging in Team Time activities;

KNOW IT by reviewing content from session 6;

SEE IT by viewing a video vignette;

HEAR IT by affirming what the Bible says about suffering;

STUDY IT by overviewing Home Study Assignments;

DO IT by leading your Team in making visits;

SHARE IT by celebrating.

In Advance

- Overview content.
- Preview teaching suggestions. Prepare key points. Decide whether to use the session 7 computer slides or the overhead cels.
- Prepare the room for teaching.
- Cue the videotape to the session 7 segment, It's Not Fair.
- Pray for participants and for Teams as they prepare to visit.
- As Teaching Time begins, direct participants to open their Journals to page 118.

CHECK IT (15 MINS.)

If the computer diskette is used, display the agenda frame for Team Time, as desired. Add other points as needed.

CHECK IT agenda:

✔ FAITH Visit Outline
✔ Other Home Study Assignments
✔ Session 6 Debriefing
✔ Help for Strengthening a Visit

Leading Team Time

All Team members participate in Team Time. They are primarily responsible for reciting the assigned portion of the FAITH Visit Outline and for discussing other Home Study Assignments.

As you direct this important time of CHECK IT activities with your Team, keep in mind that Learners look to you as a role model, motivator, mentor, and friend. Team Time activities can continue in the car as the Team travels to and from visits.

Lead CHECK IT Activities

✔ FAITH Visit Outline
❑ Listen while each Learner recites all of *Preparation;* all of F and A, *Forgiveness* and *Available;* the key words for I, T, and H in *Presentation;* and the key outline words in *Invitation.*
❑ Indicate your approval by signing or initialing Journals. Encourage Learners.
❑ Give Learners an opportunity to practice reciting the portion of the FAITH Visit Outline they have learned to this point.

✔ Other Home Study Assignments
❑ Check to see whether Learners listed two or three persons who might have a particular interest in knowing that God's forgiveness is available for them. Discuss how your FAITH Team can impact their lives with the gospel and with ministry. Also discuss the assigned reading material. Encourage Learners to continue writing in Your Journey in Faith (their journaling section).

✔ Session 6 Debriefing
❑ Learners are beginning to learn the gospel presentation. God's forgiveness becomes the foundation on which the rest of the gospel is shared. It is vital to understand that God's forgiveness is based on the free gift of grace that God gives because of Jesus' sacrificial death. As part of the gospel presentation, each letter is accompanied by at least one verse.

✔ Help for Strengthening a Visit
❑ Many people will not be aware of the free gift of forgiveness that God offers. Some are living with guilt and remorse because of sin in their lives. Others are insensitive to the fact that they are sinners who reject God's love and rebel against Him. The message of forgiveness may be an unfamiliar one to them. Emphasize the importance of showing compassion and understanding with each person being visited. It helps to remember that your Team is not

going to be judgmental but to share that real hope exists because God provides forgiveness through faith in Jesus.

❑ Have Learners had opportunities to practice parts of the gospel presentation in home visits? When they visit a Sunday School class member or fellow Christian, sometimes practice is a good option.

❑ Have Learners seen someone come to know Christ in a home visit?

Notes

_____

_____

_____

_____

_____

_____

_____

_____

_____

Actions I Need to Take with Learners During the Week

_____

_____

_____

_____

_____

_____

Transition to classrooms for instruction on the content of the session. (5 mins.)

TEACHING TIME

KNOW IT

Step 1 (5 mins.)

Direct participants to locate A Quick Review on page 118 in their Journals and to complete the activities. Then give the answers, using the computer diskette or the overhead cel. Possible answers to question:

1. INTRODUCTION
2. Sunday School or evangelistic testimony
3. Key Question
4. AVAILABLE FOR ALL
5. IMPOSSIBLE, *T* is for TURN
6. HEAVEN HERE
7. *Invitation*

A Quick Review

A Quick Review

Last week you learned a biblical response to the question, Why does evil exist? See if you can fill in the blanks to review what you learned.

1. Evil exists because we have __**free**__ __**will**__.
2. Evil exists because of the intrusion of an evil __**adversary**__.
3. The human choice to sin has affected the entire __**created**__ __**order**__.
4. God dealt with the problem of evil by sending His __**Son**__ to pay the penalty for __**sin**__.
5. God will totally and finally __**defeat**__ evil.
6. We can __**trust**__ __**God**__ when we do not understand why evil things happen.

What are two places in FAITH visits when questions or challenges about a biblical view of evil might arise?

1. _____

2. _____

Check appropriate ways to respond to the question, Why does evil exist?

☑ 1. Provide scriptural direction and guidance for persons who have committed evil acts.

❏ 2. Explain that God will not forgive certain offenses.

❏ 3. Graphically describe your idea of what hell is like.

☑ 4. Emphasize the importance of accepting the forgiveness God provides.

☑ 5. Explain the redemption and hope we have in Christ.

☑ 6. Use your testimony to convince the person that a new life is possible.

☑ 7. Don't place your Team in danger, but let God demonstrate His power through your bold witness.

❏ 8. Declare to the person that people like him are responsible for much of the evil in the world.

☑ 9. Have prayer partners pray that Satan will be bound during the visit.

☑ 10. Emphasize that God loves the sinner even though the consequences of sin must be paid.

Defining the Question: Why Does God Permit Suffering?

Like the existence of evil, the reason for human suffering has been pondered for ages. No one has expressed the questions more eloquently and urgently than God's servant Job. Job voiced his questions because he saw an apparent conflict between his view of God and what he was experiencing in his life. He understood God to be both good and sovereign—having all power. Although Job was a godly man, he had been stripped of his possessions and his children and had been afflicted with a painful physical malady that made every day pure misery. Job could not understand why God had allowed these bad things to enter his life.

Many people have the same questions as Job. Their personal sufferings may be the source of their questions, or the questions may be provoked by the sufferings of others. Because the news media constantly keep before us fresh examples of human suffering, we cannot be surprised by the question.

Here are some ways you might anticipate being questioned or challenged about suffering.

- "Why do bad things happen to good people?"
- "What does God have against me?"
- "What did I do to deserve this?"
- "Why do we have to suffer?"
- "Where is God when we suffer?"

When others suffer, believers can affirm that God exists, that He is good, that He cares for us, that He is all-powerful, and that He has a purpose for our lives. The Bible gives us insight into God's purposes in allowing suffering.

The Bible Speaks

1. Some suffering results from evil _____ **decisions** _____.

We learned last week that our freedom to choose evil over good is part of the human condition. When people choose evil actions like murder, abusive behavior, and lying, they always bring suffering on themselves and others.[1]

2. Some suffering results from the fallen state of _____ **creation** _____.

We also learned last week that when sin entered the world, it profoundly affected the entire created order. God told the man that the

HEAR IT

Step 2 (5 mins.)

Introduce the content of this session by summarizing Defining the Question. Use the computer diskette or the overhead cel to illustrate questions about suffering.

Defining the Question

Step 3 (10 mins.)

Direct participants to turn to page 119 in their Journals and to fill in the blanks as you present the key points in The Bible Speaks. Use the computer diskette or the overhead cel.

The Bible Speaks

fruitful ground had been cursed so that it would bear thorns and thistles (see Gen. 3:18). God told the woman that she would have increased pains in childbirth (see Gen. 3:16). Today we see examples of sin's impact on human beings and nature in the form of genetic defects, disease, and natural disasters.[2]

3. Some suffering results from bad ____choices____.

Suffering is often inherent in the choices we make. If we smoke, we risk cancer. If we drink, we risk cirrhosis of the liver. If we commit sexual sin, we risk disease, unwanted pregnancy, and psychological harm. An angry God does not cause these results. The risks are inherent in the disobedient acts. In Romans 1:27 Paul wrote that those who commit indecent and disobedient sexual acts will receive the due penalty in their own flesh. The sinful act itself opens them to the inherent consequences. God's laws are designed to protect us from such unnecessary suffering. That is why obedience to God's law is so important to abundant living.[3]

4. Some suffering results from the work of ____Satan____.

Recall from last week's study that Satan is the enemy of God and human beings. His desire is to kill, steal, and destroy (see John 10:10). The Gadarene demoniac described in Matthew 8 was suffering because of the acts of a demon. Job's suffering was directly related to the work of the adversary. Satan's forces are also at work today, deceiving people with lies and luring them to destructive pursuits. When we make sinful choices, we open ourselves to Satan's influence in our lives.[4]

5. Some suffering is for the sake of ____righteousness____.

Jesus is the perfect example of a righteous person who suffered at the hands of evildoers.[5] This was the Father's plan for Him. Scripture tells us that Jesus' character matured through suffering and that He learned obedience through suffering (see Heb. 5:8-9). His suffering demonstrated His commitment to be our Savior (see Heb. 2:10).

Christians today are being persecuted for their faith in increasing numbers. In this country Christians can lose their jobs for being honest, be ejected from certain venues for sharing their faith, or be harassed for upholding Christian values. Worldwide many Christians suffer for their faith, being jailed, tortured, or put to death. Each year between two and three hundred thousand believers die for their faith.

When believers suffer for the cause of Christ, they experience fellowship with Christ in His sufferings (see Phil. 1:29-30; 3:10-11; Col. 1:24). Paul, who suffered so much to spread the gospel, wrote, "I want to know Christ and the power of his resurrection and the fellowship of sharing in his sufferings, becoming like him in his death, and so, somehow, to attain to the resurrection from the dead" (Phil. 3:10-11).

When it is necessary to suffer for the cause of Christ, we can remember Jesus' words: " 'Blessed are those who are persecuted because of righteousness, for theirs is the kingdom of heaven' " (Matt. 5:10).

6. Some suffering is a _____mystery_____.
Identifying the why of the suffering may not always be possible. Although we want to understand, some suffering always remains a mystery.[6] The sufferings of God's servant Job fit into this category. He never knew why he suffered.

7. God ___cares___ when we suffer.
- God helps us in our weakness (see Rom. 8:26).
- God gives us His Spirit to intercede for us (see Rom. 8:26-27).
- God works in everything for our good (see Gen. 50:20; Rom. 8:28). God does not cause evil, but He works redemptively in all things. Here are some ways He brings good from suffering.
  —He grows us in the image of His Son (see Rom. 5:3-5; Phil. 3:10-11).
  —Suffering teaches us dependence on God. When Paul prayed for God to remove the thorn from his flesh, the thorn was not removed, but Paul came to a deeper understanding of the sufficiency of God's grace (see 2 Cor. 12:8-9).
  —Suffering purifies our faith (see 1 Pet. 1:6-7).
  —Suffering often provides a platform for witnessing when we testify to God's power to sustain His children.
  —God suffers with us. He has already paid the greatest price to relieve suffering permanently. He sent His Son, who voluntarily suffered the penalty of our sin.
- God promises that nothing can separate us from His love (see Rom. 8:35-39).[7]

It is difficult to explain to an unbeliever why her child died tragically or why she was the victim of abuse. Suffering can be accepted only in the context of trust in a good, loving God who cares for us, has a purpose for our lives, and desires to bring good from any situation. You have the privilege of introducing people to the One whose suffering makes possible that saving faith.

Entry Points in FAITH Visits

Several occasions in FAITH visits offer a person an opportunity to consider the question, Why does God permit suffering?
1. When persons are suffering through crises and life transitions, a Team from a Sunday School class can make _____ministry_____ _____visits_____ to members and prospects for their class.

Step 4 (5 mins.)

Direct participants to turn to page 121 in their Journals and to fill in the blanks as you summarize Entry Points in FAITH Visits. Use the computer diskette or the overhead cel.

Entry Points in FAITH Visits

SEE IT

Step 5 (10 mins.)

To focus on ways witnesses can respond to questions about suffering, show the session 7 video segment, It's Not Fair. Ask participants to make notes in the margins of their Journals.

SAY IT

Step 6 (5 mins.)

Ask accountability partners to discuss ways they would respond to a question about suffering, using the ideas in the video and in How You Can Respond.

If you are leading students, have accountability partners role-play a situation in which one partner asks a question about suffering and the other partner responds.

2. Information may be provided on your Visitation Assignment Card that signals a specific need your Team can address. During the _____**INTRODUCTION**_____ segment you may learn about challenges, crises, or special needs in the person's life or family.

3. As you conduct the _____**Opinion**_____ **Poll**___, you will encounter persons who are hurting. God will amaze you by directing your Team to the right persons at the right time if you are open and sensitive to His leadership.

4. Some persons will question the fact that a God of love (identified in John 3:16 as part of A is for AVAILABLE and I is for IMPOSSIBLE) permits suffering. If so, questions will likely come when you ask the _____**Key**_____ _____**Question**_____.

5. As persons begin identifying with those who are standing in __**A**__ __**Step**__ __**of**__ _____**Faith**_____ picture holding hammers and mallets, occasionally they will cite a time of crisis through which they have journeyed or are presently experiencing.

6. Occasionally, you will encounter a person who wants to attend Sunday School and church but cannot because of physical needs. This provides a good opportunity for _____**ministry**_____.

How You Can Respond

Here are possible ways you can respond to the question, Why does God permit suffering? during witnessing encounters. Your response will depend on the person, the situation, and the Holy Spirit's direction in this circumstance. Always keep in mind the general principles outlined on pages 28–29 in session 1.

1. God uses times of crisis and suffering to make some people more receptive to the ministry of His Holy Spirit and of believers who are available to be used by Him. Be aware that a time of short-term or long-term crisis may give you and other Christians opportunities to meet needs in Christ's name and to help the person and his family experience God's grace, mercy, and comfort.

2. Be prepared to take care of some ministry needs while you are with the person. Refer other needs to others in the class or in the church. Occasionally refer specific needs to other professional or volunteer groups with the permission of the person in need.

3. Be very sensitive to the fact that during times of crises, some people cry out against those who try to help. Anger, fear, or rejection often accompanies a person's attempt to conceal the hurt. You can listen and offer words of comfort. You can also lead your Team to look for ways to provide ministry during the time of suffering.

4. Remember the power of God's Word and the ministry of the gospel during times of crisis or suffering. Take the opportunity to share a

Sunday School testimony, as well as the FAITH gospel presentation, through which God's Spirit can offer comfort and direction.

5. Make sure you record appropriate information on the Visitation Assignment Card and return it with suggestions for follow-up.

6. Encourage Sunday School leaders to look for ways to target persons with special needs in Sunday School. On many occasions a new class targeting persons with a similar life need or transition can be more successful in reaching and assimilating them than an existing class.

7. Pray with the person and ask permission to include the person's need(s) in reports to prayer networks.

8. Reflect on your personal experiences of suffering. God often places in your life persons with similar experiences. Let God minister to others through the lessons He has taught you.

Visitation Time

Do It

1. Be a good listener. You earn the right to share the good news by listening to the story of the persons you visit. They may share with you some things that make you uncomfortable or may raise some questions you would rather not address—but listen. It is not necessary to be able to answer all of their questions, but it is necessary to care.

2. During INTRODUCTION listen for any signs of suffering, either in their lives or in their extended families. Listen and demonstrate concern. Do not offer easy solutions. Remember Job's friends!

3. If there is a need in the home that you can meet, offer your help or your church's help.

4. All Team members should know the FAITH presentation through A is for AVAILABLE. While visiting, invite Team members to support you up to the letter A.

Celebration Time

Share It

1. Ask a Team member to take the lead in sharing the report.
2. Hear reports and testimonies.
3. Complete Evaluation Cards.
4. Complete Participation Cards.
5. Update visitation forms with the results of visits.

STUDY IT

Step 7 (5 mins.)

Overview Home Study Assignments for session 7.

Transition to assemble with FAITH Teams to prepare for home visits. (5 mins.)

DO IT (110 MINS.)

SHARE IT (30 MINS.)

Home Study Assignments

Home Study Assignments reinforce this session by helping you apply what you have learned.

Your Discipleship Journey

Journaling activities in Your Discipleship Journey are an important part of your development as a Great Commission Christian through FAITH training.

1. Identify what Paul learned about a believer's suffering by reading 2 Corinthians 12:7-10 and matching the following lessons with the correct verses.

   _____ 1. The suffering gave God an opportunity to   a. Verse 7
            demonstrate the sufficiency of His grace.   b. Verse 9
   _____ 2. God refused to remove Paul's suffering.   c. Verse 10
   _____ 3. The suffering was a source of torment from
            Satan.
   _____ 4. Paul's weakness became a source of rejoicing.
   _____ 5. Paul became aware of his weakness.
   _____ 6. God's power is made perfect in human
            weakness.
   _____ 7. Paul's reliance on God's strength made him
            more useful in God's work.

2. Read Philippians 4:4-13. Write in your own words each statement that can be useful in times of suffering.

   _____

   _____

   _____

   _____

   _____

3. If a lost person asked you why he was suffering with a disease and were willing to listen, what approach would you take in talking with him? Write a general outline on the following page.

_____

_____

_____

_____

Growing as a Life Witness

Growing as a Life Witness reminds you of your responsibility to witness and minister to others during the week.

1. Talk or meet with your accountability partner and share ways you have cultivated a lost person or have witnessed or ministered on occasions other than FAITH visits.
2. Discuss ways you can apply the session 7 content in witnessing.
3. Pray for lost persons by name and for each other.

Prayer Concerns	Answers to Prayer
_____	_____
_____	_____
_____	_____
_____	_____
_____	_____
_____	_____
_____	_____
_____	_____
_____	_____
_____	_____

Your Weekly Sunday School Leadership Team Meeting

A FAITH participant is an important member of Sunday School. Encourage Team members who are elected Sunday School workers to attend this weekly meeting. Use this section to record ways your FAITH Team influences the work of your Sunday School class or department. Use the information to report during weekly Sunday School leadership team meetings. Identify actions that need to be taken through Sunday School as a result of prayer concerns, needs identified, visits made by the Team, and decisions made by the persons visited. Also identify ways you can disciple others in your Sunday School class or department and in your church.

1. Highlight needs that surfaced in FAITH visits and discuss ways these reports affect the ministry of your class/department or age group. Especially discuss ways to keep assimilation of newcomers a priority for the group.

   _____

   _____

   _____

2. Consider the extent to which members are becoming increasingly sensitive and responsive to the hurts of people. In what ways can you communicate the truths you discovered in this session with your Sunday School leadership team?

   _____

   _____

   _____

3. How does preparation for Sunday need to consider the varying needs of families/individuals represented by selected FAITH visits?

   _____

   _____

   _____

4. Participate in evaluating last Sunday's Bible-study session. Discuss ways Sunday's lesson can involve members and guests in transformational Bible study and discipleship.

_____

_____

_____

5. Record prayer requests for your teacher and department director.

_____

_____

_____

Discipling Your Team Members

This weekly feature suggests actions the Team Leader can take to support Team members, prepare for Team Time, and improve visits. This work is part of the Team Leader's Home Study Assignments. Add any actions suggested by your church's FAITH strategy.

Support Team Members
❑ Contact Team members during the week. Remind them that you are praying for them. Discuss prayer concerns and answers to prayer.
❑ Record specific needs and concerns of Team members.

_____

Prepare to Lead Team Time
❑ Review Team members' Home Study Assignments.
❑ Review Leading Team Time for session 8.

Prepare to Lead Visits
❑ Review the FAITH Visit Outline.
❑ Be prepared to explain the significance of God's forgiveness being available for all but not automatic.

Link with Sunday School
❑ Participate in your weekly Sunday School leadership team meeting. Share pertinent information in this meeting, using Your Weekly Sunday School Leadership Team Meeting (p. 126) and FAITH-visit results.
❑ Make sure your Sunday School is always sensitive to members and their families and friends who are suffering. Think of ways your class or department can offer hope and alleviate pain when possible.

For Further Growth

For Further Growth may include additional reading or activities that will enhance your growth as a disciple and a discipler of others. These assignments are intended to be long-term projects and do not have to be completed during this semester of study.

1. Read *The Problem of Pain* by C. S. Lewis.
2. Recall incidents of personal crisis and suffering you have encountered in FAITH visits. If you have recorded these as prayer requests in your FAITH Journals, review your notes. Through your experiences, what has God taught you about His compassion for persons who are hurting? In what ways has He used your Team and your Sunday School to minister to those who are suffering?
3. Complete word studies of *suffer* and *compassion* in the Scriptures.

¹Ken Hemphill, *LifeAnswers: Making Sense of Your World* (Nashville: LifeWay, 1993), 117.
²Ibid., 117–18.
³Ibid., 118.
⁴Ibid.
⁵Ibid., 119.
⁶Ibid.
⁷Ibid., 120–24.

Answers to matching activity on page 124: 1. b, 2. b, 3. a, 4. b, c, 5. b, 6. b, 7. c

What Does It Mean to Be Lost?

In this session you will—

CHECK IT by engaging in Team Time activities;

KNOW IT by reviewing content from session 7;

HEAR IT by affirming what the Bible says about what it means to be lost;

SAY IT by discussing possible applications of what you have learned in this session;

STUDY IT by overviewing Home Study Assignments;

DO IT by leading your Team in making visits;

SHARE IT by celebrating.

In Advance
- Overview content.
- Preview teaching suggestions. Prepare key points. Decide whether to use the session 8 computer slides or the overhead cels.
- Prepare the room for teaching.
- Pray for participants and for Teams as they prepare to visit.
- As Teaching Time begins, direct participants to open their Journals to page 132.

CHECK IT (15 MINS.)

If the computer diskette is used, display the agenda frame for Team Time, as desired. Add other points as needed.

CHECK IT agenda:
✔ FAITH Visit Outline
✔ Session 7 Debriefing/Other Home Study Assignments
✔ Help for Strengthening a Visit

Leading Team Time

All Team members participate in Team Time. They are primarily responsible for reciting the assigned portion of the FAITH Visit Outline and for discussing other Home Study Assignments.

As you direct this important time of CHECK IT activities with your Team, keep in mind that Learners look to you as a role model, motivator, mentor, and friend. Team Time activities can continue in the car as the Team travels to and from visits.

Lead CHECK IT Activities

✔ FAITH Visit Outline
❑ Listen while each Learner recites all of **Preparation;** all of the outline points for the letters F (FORGIVENESS), A (AVAILABLE), and I (IMPOSSIBLE); key words for the letters T (TURN) and H (HEAVEN); and key words for the **Invitation.**
❑ Indicate your approval by signing or initialing Journals. Encourage Learners.
❑ Provide an opportunity for Learners to practice reciting the portions of the FAITH Visit Outline they have learned to this point.

✔ Session 7 Debriefing/Other Home Study Assignments
❑ God's forgiveness is available for everyone. Even the most hardened criminal or the most unloving person is the target of God's love and forgiveness. John 3:16 reminds us of the scope of God's love and forgiveness ("God so loved the world … that whoever"). This same verse introduces us to the fact that God's forgiveness is not automatic ("whoever believes in Him"). This passage also focuses on the consequences of not accepting God's forgiveness ("perish"). It is important to remember that many persons you visit will not understand that God's forgiveness is available to them, but it is not automatic.

✔ Help for Strengthening a Visit
❑ Many persons you seek to visit will indicate that they do not have much time for a lengthy visit. Some persons may not allow your Team to enter the house because of time or personal constraints. Your primary jobs are to seek to build relationships with people and to introduce them to the idea of enrolling in your Sunday School class or department. Indeed, you look for opportunities to ask the Key Question, hear responses, and share the FAITH gospel presentation. But also look for opportunities to build bridges with the person through Sunday School enrollment. God may be using you to plant a seed. He may also be using you and your Team members to nurture relationships on His behalf and to prepare the

harvest. Be sensitive to opportunities God is providing for you in the midst of visits.

Notes

_____

_____

_____

_____

_____

_____

_____

_____

Actions I Need to Take with Learners During the Week

_____

_____

_____

_____

_____

_____

Transition to classrooms for instruction on the content of the session. (5 mins.)

TEACHING TIME

KNOW IT

Step 1 (5 mins.)

Direct participants to locate A Quick Review on page 132 in their Journals and to complete the activities. Then give the answers, using the computer diskette or the overhead cel. Participants should have checked source 1 (We can control our own decisions but not those of others), 3 (Our sinful choices have natural consequences), 4 (We cannot control all effects of Satan's work in the world, but avoiding sin will reduce his influence in our lives). Sources 2, 5, and 6 are beyond our control. Possible answers to question:

1. Ministry visits
2. INTRODUCTION
3. Opinion Poll
4. Key Question
5. *A Step of Faith*
6. Ministry actions

A Quick
Review

A Quick Review

Review the key points from session 7 by checking the sources of suffering humans can control.

☑ 1. Some suffering results from evil decisions.
☐ 2. Some suffering results from the fallen state of creation.
☑ 3. Some suffering results from bad choices.
☑ 4. Some suffering results from the work of Satan.
☐ 5. Some suffering is for the sake of righteousness.
☐ 6. Some suffering is a mystery.

Fill in the blank.
Last week you learned that no matter what the source of suffering is, God _____**cares**_____ when we suffer.

What are two places in FAITH visits when questions about or challenges to a biblical view of suffering might arise?

1. _____

2. _____

Check appropriate ways to respond to the question, Why does God permit suffering?

☑ 1. Use crises to meet needs in Christ's name and to offer God's comfort.
☐ 2. Tell persons who are suffering that they deserve it.
☑ 3. Refer ministry needs to others in the class or in the church or to professional or volunteer groups.
☑ 4. Listen to expressions of anger, fear, or rejection and offer comfort.
☑ 5. Use a Sunday School testimony and the FAITH gospel presentation as opportunities for the Holy Spirit to offer comfort and direction.
☐ 6. If someone has lost a loved one, distract them by involving them in an academic discussion of the reasons people suffer.
☑ 7. Suggest ways others can meet a suffering person's needs.
☑ 8. Encourage Sunday School leaders to look for ways to target persons with special needs in Sunday School.
☑ 9. Pray with and for someone who is suffering.
☑ 10. Let God minister to others through the lessons He has taught you.
☐ 11. Explain to someone who is suffering that God is punishing his sin.

Defining the Question: What Does It Mean to Be Lost?

The word *lost* means having gone astray; no longer possessed or known; not capable of being found or recovered. The word conveys the sense of a haunting void, darkness, loneliness, or regret. Most, if not all, parents have either experienced or at least worried about a child's becoming lost or separated from them. The thought is terrifying to any parent.

The horror of physical lostness pales in comparison to the reality of spiritual lostness. People who remain spiritually lost will spend eternity in the torment of hell, separated from God.

Here are some ways you might anticipate being questioned or challenged about spiritual lostness.

- "I'm not lost. I'm on track with my goals for success in life."
- "A loving God wouldn't condemn people to hell."
- "How do you know what a lost person's destiny will be?"
- "If I'm lost, what do I need to do to be saved?"
- "God can't condemn me. I give money to good causes and try to help others."

The essence of lostness is a life without a personal relationship with God through His Son, Jesus Christ. Our Heavenly Father cares for everyone with an intense love and desires that none should be lost but that all should be saved (see 2 Pet. 3:9). As we try to lead lost persons to personal encounters with Jesus Christ, we must realize the awful condition and consequences of lostness as presented in Scripture and embrace our Lord's passion and sense of mission as He sought to find and save the lost (see Luke 19:10).

The Bible Speaks

The Bible clearly defines what it means to be lost.

1. To be trapped in ___sin___

God is holy and is above sin. Between holy God and sinful people is an impenetrable sin barrier that separates the human race from God. Romans 3:10-18 describes the horrible and heartbreaking results of being under sin's power. Under the letter *I* in the FAITH presentation you present the fact that "all have sinned and fall short of the glory of God" (Rom. 3:23, NKJV).

HEAR IT

Step 2 (5 mins.)

Introduce the content of this session by summarizing Defining the Question. Use the computer diskette or the overhead cel to illustrate questions and comments about being lost.

Defining the Question

Step 3 (20 mins.)

Direct participants to turn to page 133 in their Journals and to fill in the blanks as you present the key points in The Bible Speaks. Use the computer diskette or overhead cel.

The Bible Speaks

2. To be spiritually _____dead_____

Without Christ the lost are spiritually dead. Romans 6:23 tells us that "the wages of sin is death." Paul wrote to the Ephesians, "You were dead in your transgressions and sins, in which you used to live when you followed the ways of this world and of the ruler of the kingdom of the air, the spirit who is now at work in those who are disobedient" (Eph. 2:1-2). Spiritual deadness permeates the whole being of people who don't know Christ.

3. To live under God's _____wrath_____

Ephesians 2:3 says that "we were then by nature objects of [God's] wrath *and* heirs of [His] indignation, like the rest of mankind."[1] God's anger against sin will one day come to fruition, and the lost will be swept away even as the people were swept away by the flood in the days of Noah.

4. To be separated from _____Christ_____

Ephesians 2:12 says, "Remember that at that time you were separate from Christ." Can you imagine being totally separated from our loving Savior and Lord with no possibility of having your sin forgiven? Persons who die without accepting Christ will be separated from Him in hell forever. As the FAITH presentation affirms, God's forgiveness can be received only through Jesus Christ (see Eph. 1:7).

5. To live without _____God_____

Many people in our world may say that they believe in God. But Scripture tells us, "You believe that there is one God. Good! Even the demons believe that—and shudder." (Jas. 2:9). Many try to live good, moral lives. However, an intellectual assent to God's existence and a life of goodness and morality do not earn a person heaven and eternal life if the person is living without Christ Jesus.

6. To live without _____hope_____

A most pitiful state of existence in this world is to be without hope. Just look around you in your workplace or daily routine and look into the faces of people. Many are just going through the motions of living. Many have no hope or no joy, no meaning or purpose in this life because they don't know the Source of these treasures. Only Jesus can give them hope both in this world and for the next.

7. To be already _____condemned_____

John 3:18 says, " 'Whoever believes in him is not condemned, but whoever does not believe stands condemned already because he has not believed in the name of God's one and only Son.' " Lost persons have already been judged and found guilty. In the FAITH presentation we hear under *I* that God is just: "Judgment is without mercy" (Jas.

2:13, NKJV). Unbelievers face all consequences of sin themselves, whereas the condemnation is lifted for a believer who has come to Christ in simple faith.

8. To live against _____Jesus_____
Matthew 12:30 tells us that " 'he who is not with me is against me.' " Some people say they love Jesus and believe in him but do not totally trust Him as Savior and Lord; their statement is empty. The verse in the FAITH presentation " 'Not everyone who says to Me, "Lord, Lord," shall enter the kingdom of heaven' " (Matt. 7:21, NKJV) again reminds us that those who have a positive emotion for Jesus but no saving faith do not have true salvation but continue in a state of lostness.

9. To be _____dying_____ in sin
John 8:24 says, " 'I told you that you would die in your sins; if you do not believe that I am the one I claim to be, you will indeed die in your sins.' " If a person refuses to believe that Jesus is the Christ and the only way to God, this choice of not believing is the sin that condemns. Lost people live in the realm of sin. Only Jesus can take away a person's sin.

10. To live as a child of the _____devil_____
John 8:44 tells us that " 'you belong to your father, the devil, and you want to carry out your father's desire.' " These pointed words are very frightening. Lost persons do not realize that they belong to the devil. But this is what our Lord said. When people receive Jesus as Savior and Lord, they become children of God and a part of God's family to live in fellowship with Him.

11. To live as God's _____enemy_____
Romans 5:10 says, "If, when we were God's enemies, we were reconciled to him through the death of his Son, how much more, having been reconciled, shall we be saved through his life." Lost people work against God and His will and plan for their lives. As God's enemies they need to trust Christ and begin to seek to live by God's will and plan.

12. To live without _____peace_____
If asked to name something they want, most people would mention peace. God tells us in Isaiah 57:20-21 that "there is no peace … for the wicked." Lost people can have no peace, only constant inner turmoil that yields a life of insecurity. They are longing for what can be found only in Jesus. Paul wrote in Romans 5:1, "Since we have been justified through faith, we have peace with God through our Lord Jesus Christ."

13. To be spiritually _____blind_____

God's word tells us that "the message of the cross is foolishness to those who are perishing, but to us who are being saved it is the power of God" (1 Cor. 1:18). Unbelievers are actually blinded to the light of the gospel. Their minds cannot comprehend the reality and truth of God. Second Corinthians 4:3-4 gives a good picture of the lost persons: "Even if our gospel is veiled, it is veiled to those who are perishing [the lost]. The god of this age has blinded the minds of unbelievers, so that they cannot see the light of the gospel of the glory of Christ, who is the image of God."

A Christian's sensitivity to lostness is extremely important in sharing Christ meaningfully. Enjoying the light and freedom of living in Christ, many of us may have forgotten what it is like to be lost without Christ. By realizing the hopelessness and fearfulness of those without Christ, we can focus on their need for Him and can be motivated to share His love more intentionally. If we can explain what it means to be lost, we are then ready to share the glorious news of what it means to be saved.

Entry Points in FAITH Visits

Several occasions in FAITH visits offer an opportunity to identify and address a person's spiritual lostness.

1. The FAITH _____**Visitation**_____ _____**Assignment**_____ _____**Card**_____ often indicates a person's spiritual condition. Your Team will often know that the person you are visiting is without Christ. On many other occasions you will be assigned to make a visit where you know little about the person.

2. The _____**INTRODUCTION**_____ and _____**INTERESTS**_____ segments of the visit are crucial in learning about the person's background. During this portion of the visit the person begins feeling comfortable with your Team.

3. The _____**evangelistic**_____ _____**testimony**_____ is an extremely important tool to identify with the person (Preconversion Experience). Likewise, it is important to remember the benefits of sharing that since you had a life-changing experience, you have assurance of heaven and eternal life. Unsaved persons do not always relate to eternal life as a future possibility. They are looking more for what can make a difference in life now.

4. Each point in the _____**FAITH**_____ _____**gospel**_____ _____**presentation**_____ relates directly to a person who has willingly or unknowingly rejected God's love. Many unsaved persons have heard the good news, but few have heard it in a personal way,

Step 4 (5 mins.)

Direct participants to turn to page 136 in their Journals and to fill in the blanks as you summarize Entry Points in FAITH Visits. Use the computer diskette or overhead cel.

Entry Points in FAITH Visits

directed to them by someone who cares for them. Some will hear the gospel for the first time as you share.

5. People have a thousand _____**questions**_____ and _____**excuses**_____ about repentance, God's love and forgiveness, and eternal life. "The message of the cross is foolishness to those who are perishing" (1 Cor. 1:18). Matthew 19:25-26 reminds us that even though salvation seems impossible through our own eyes, with God nothing is impossible!

6. The _____**Invitation**_____ is vital for a lost person. The person needs to know not only the facts of the message but also the heart of the message. The unsaved person needs to know that he has a choice, but he also needs to know what the choices are and the consequences of his choice.

7. Many persons who invite you into their lives will reject the message of the gospel. Many of these persons will need _____**follow-up**_____ _____**opportunities**_____ by your Team and by others in your Sunday School class. Believe that God will use your faithfulness to plant and nurture the seeds of the gospel.

How You Can Respond

Here are possible ways you can respond to the issue of spiritual lostness during witnessing encounters. Your response will depend on the person, the situation, and the Holy Spirit's direction in this circumstance. Always keep in mind the general principles outlined on pages 28–29 in session 1.

1. Don't be judgmental as you dialogue with anyone, particularly an unsaved person. Do everything possible to relate to the person and to guide him in understanding his need for salvation and the fact that God offers salvation and the assurance of eternal life for him through Christ.

2. Just as the message of the FAITH gospel presentation is simple, the gospel itself is staggeringly simple. Do not seek to cloud the issue of eternal life. Recall the way Jesus shared with Nicodemus, who wanted to discuss deep theological issues (see John 3:1-21). Recall the way Jesus confronted a sinful woman looking for meaning in life (see John 4:4-26).

3. Pray fervently before visiting an unsaved person.

4. Remember the struggles you and others have had in accepting the simple truths of the gospel. Remember words of Scripture that helped you. Remember words of encouragement and instruction that guided you to the point of belief. Be sensitive to the struggles people have in questioning and seeking to accept God's forgiveness and assurance of eternal life.

SAY IT

Step 5 (5 mins.)

Ask accountability partners to discuss ways they would respond to a person's spiritual lostness, using the ideas in How You Can Respond.

If you are leading students, have accountability partners role-play a situation in which one partner asks a question about what it means to be lost and the other partner responds.

STUDY IT

Step 6 (5 mins.)

Overview Home Study Assignments for session 8.

Transition to assemble with FAITH Teams to prepare for home visits. (5 mins.)

5. Look for every opportunity to naturally ask the Key Question and get permission to share how the Bible answers that question. On the other hand, be sensitive to ways the Holy Spirit may be using your Team to build a relationship with a person who is beginning to consider the ministry of the gospel.

6. Be prepared to show and dialogue about the picture on the cover of *A Step of Faith*. Many persons who resist the message of the gospel are convicted when they begin seeing themselves before the Christ who died for them. Be sensitive to the Holy Spirit's leadership as you talk with and listen to someone who is lost.

7. Look for opportunities to enroll and involve unsaved persons in Sunday School.

Visitation Time

Do It

1. Are Team members becoming increasingly comfortable with making adjustments as the visit merits? While your Team should plan in advance what is to happen and what responsibilities the various Team members will assume, the best visit is one in which visitors adjust to the needs of the situation.

2. Team Leader, as you make changes in the FAITH Visit Outline, be sure to explain why. Affirm your Team Learners as they show increasing confidence and ease in sharing their testimonies and in using the FAITH Visit Outline.

3. Pray for sensitivity to the situations the Team will encounter in these visits. Always be open to enrolling someone in Sunday School.

4. At the Team Leader's cue, learners should be able to share FORGIVENESS and AVAILABLE.

Celebration Time

Share It

1. Ask a Team Learner to take the lead in sharing your Team's report.
2. Hear reports and testimonies.
3. Complete Evaluation Cards.
4. Complete Participation Cards.
5. Update visitation forms with the results of visits.

Home Study Assignments

Home Study Assignments reinforce this session by helping you apply what you have learned.

Your Discipleship Journey

Journaling activities in Your Discipleship Journey are an important part of your development as a Great Commission Christian through FAITH training.

1. Read Luke 15. Note similarities and differences between physical lostness and spiritual lostness.

   _____

   _____

   _____

   _____

2. In addition to praying for persons you know who have no relationship with Christ, identify actions you and others could take to begin building relationships with these persons.

   _____

   _____

   _____

3. Sometimes lost persons seem to have happy lives and seem to be oblivious to the consequences of sin. Remember that through the eyes of God, these persons are moving toward ruin. Read Psalm 73. Describe the real difference between the saved and the lost.

   _____

   _____

4. Review your evangelistic testimony. Describe what your life was like without knowing Christ.

   _____

   _____

Growing as a Life Witness

Growing as a Life Witness reminds you of your responsibility to witness and minister to others during the week.

1. Talk or meet with your accountability partner and share ways you have cultivated a lost person or have witnessed or ministered on occasions other than FAITH visits.
2. Discuss ways you can apply the session 8 content in witnessing.
3. Pray for lost persons by name and for each other.

Prayer Concerns	Answers to Prayer

Your Weekly Sunday School Leadership Team Meeting

A FAITH participant is an important member of Sunday School. Encourage Team members who are elected Sunday School workers to attend this weekly meeting. Use this section to record ways your FAITH Team influences the work of your Sunday School class or department. Use the information to report during weekly Sunday School leadership team meetings. Identify actions that need to be taken through Sunday School as a result of prayer concerns, needs identified, visits made by the Team, and decisions made by the persons visited. Also identify ways you can disciple others in your Sunday School class or department and in your church.

1. Highlight FAITH needs/reports that affect your class/department or age group.

_____

_____

2. In what ways does the reality that people are lost without Christ permeate your class/department? For example, is a clear explanation of the gospel periodically given in class? Is the teacher consistently ready to give an invitation during class if the session and the Holy Spirit so lead? Is the class a praying and caring body that reaches out to the lost?

_____

_____

3. Participate in evaluating last week's session and discuss ways Sunday's Bible-study lesson can involve members and guests in transformational Bible study and discipleship.

_____

_____

4. Pray for teacher(s) and department director(s).

Discipling Your Team Members

This weekly feature suggests actions the Team Leader can take to support Team members, prepare for Team Time, and improve visits. This work is part of the Team Leader's Home Study Assignments. Add any actions suggested by your church's FAITH strategy.

Support Team Members
❑ Contact Team members during the week. Remind them that you are praying for them. Discuss prayer concerns and answers to prayer.
❑ Record specific needs and concerns of Team members.

_____

_____

Prepare to Lead Team Time
❑ Review Team members' Home Study Assignments.
❑ Preview Leading Team Time for session 9.

Prepare to Lead Visits
❑ Review the FAITH Visit Outline.
❑ Be prepared to explain the significance of God's forgiveness being available for all but not automatic.

Link with Sunday School
❑ Participate in your weekly Sunday School leadership team meeting. Share pertinent information in this meeting, using Your Weekly Sunday School Leadership Team Meeting (p. 141) and FAITH-visit results.
❑ Encourage Sunday School teachers to periodically call on Team members to share reports from their FAITH experiences. Encourage your Team members to give periodic updates in your class.
❑ The goal of FAITH is to reach lost persons with the gospel. That is also a primary purpose of the Sunday School. Make sure this purpose is being carried out through your Sunday School's organization and processes.

For Further Growth
For Further Growth may include additional reading or activities that will enhance your growth as a disciple and a discipler of others. These assignments are intended to be long-term projects and do not have to be completed during this semester of study.
1. Review "Five Frank Facts" (pp. 91–96) in _Evangelism Through the Sunday School_ by Bobby Welch (LifeWay, 1997) to recall facts about lost people and our need to share the gospel intentionally day by day.
2. Read a resource that focuses on the perspective of the unsaved person. Consider _Out of Their Faces and into Their Shoes_ by John Kramp (Broadman & Holman, 1995), _Church for the Unchurched_ by George G. Hunter III (Abingdon, 1996), or _Inside the Mind of Unchurched Harry and Mary_ by Lee Strobel (Zondervan, 1993).

¹From _The Amplified Bible New Testament_ © The Lockman Foundation 1954, 1958, 1987. Used by permission.

What Does It Mean to Be Saved?

In this session you will—

CHECK IT by engaging in Team Time activities;

KNOW IT by reviewing content from session 8;

HEAR IT by affirming what the Bible says about what it means to be saved;

SAY IT by practicing the *Invitation* portion of the FAITH Outline;

STUDY IT by overviewing Home Study Assignments;

DO IT by leading your Team in making visits;

SHARE IT by celebrating.

In Advance
- Overview content.
- Preview teaching suggestions. Prepare key points. Decide whether to use the session 9 computer slides or the overhead cels.
- Prepare the room for teaching.
- Pray for participants and for Teams as they prepare to visit.
- As Teaching Time begins, direct participants to open their Journals to page 146.

TEAM TIME

CHECK IT (15 MINS.)

If the computer diskette is used, display the agenda frame for Team Time, as desired. Add other points as needed.

CHECK IT agenda:
✔ FAITH Visit Outline
✔ Other Home Study Assignments
✔ Session 8 Debriefing
✔ Help for Strengthening a Visit

Leading Team Time

All Team members participate in Team Time. They are primarily responsible for reciting the assigned portion of the FAITH Visit Outline and for discussing other Home Study Assignments.

As you direct this important time of CHECK IT activities with your Team, keep in mind that Learners look to you as a role model, motivator, mentor, and friend. Team Time activities can continue in the car as the Team travels to and from visits.

Lead CHECK IT Activities

✔ FAITH Visit Outline
❑ Listen while each Learner recites the FAITH Visit Outline: all of **Preparation** and all of **Presentation,** adding *T* is for TURN to the gospel presentation, plus the key words for **Invitation.** Be aware of time limits if two Learners are sharing; someone may need to recite in the car going to and from visits.
❑ Initial each Learner's work in his or her Journal.
❑ Practice other parts of the outline as time allows.

✔ Other Home Study Assignments
❑ Emphasize the importance of involving the Sunday School class in FAITH, whether by prayer support, in training, or in follow-up. Explain that in this session Sunday School will be the focus of building bridges to people.
❑ Ask: Do class/department members who are not participating in FAITH still see themselves as a part of this ministry? In what ways? Are you sharing prayer needs and results of visits with fellow class members? Are they praying for you and for people you and your Team will visit? Are your class, department, and church growing spiritually and numerically?
❑ Home Study Assignments and memorization are reaching their maximum. Make a special effort during the week to personally encourage Learners, especially those who may have fallen behind in memory work or home study.

✔ Session 8 Debriefing
❑ Some important theological truths are communicated in this part of the gospel presentation. Are Learners at ease and confident in sharing about both God's love and His justice? About their own sinfulness?
❑ Ask Learners to recall from their personal experience—
  • their need to be saved;
  • their inability to save themselves;

- God's saving initiative in their lives (their life-changing experience).

Doing so will help them continue to identify with the people they visit. All of us are sinners in need of God's grace. Some of us have been fortunate enough to receive and accept it, while others still need to know about God's forgiveness. Letting them know is a big part of what FAITH is all about.

❑ If your group needs it, overview ways to respond to a works answer to the Key Question.

✔ Help for Strengthening a Visit

❑ Have most Team members seen someone accept Christ during a home visit by this time? If so, remind Team members of how such a visit should motivate them to continue in their efforts. If not, remind Team members that God is still working, even if they have not seen specific desired results.

❑ Call on the Assistant Team Leader, if your Team has one, to encourage other Team members; he or she may have had experiences in earlier FAITH training that can motivate others.

❑ As important as practice is, it is not the same as sharing the gospel in a home visit. Acknowledge that even as you encourage your Team to practice with one another and with other believers, as the opportunity allows.

Notes

_____

_____

_____

_____

_____

Actions I Need to Take with Learners During the Week

_____

_____

_____

_____

Transition to classrooms for instruction on the content of the session. (5 mins.)

TEACHING TIME

KNOW IT

Step 1 (5 mins.)

Direct participants to locate A Quick Review on page 146 in their Journals and to complete the activities. Then give the answers, using the computer diskette or the overhead cel. Possible answers to question:

1. Visitation Assignment Card
2. INTRODUCTION and INTERESTS
3. Evangelistic testimony
4. Each point in the FAITH Visit Outline
5. The person's questions and excuses
6. ***Invitation***
7. Follow-up opportunities

A Quick Review

A Quick Review

Last week you studied several biblical answers to the question, What does it mean to be lost?

1. To be trapped in _____ **sin** _____
2. To be spiritually _____ **dead** _____
3. To live under God's _____ **wrath** _____
4. To be separated from _____ **Christ** _____
5. To live without _____ **God** _____
6. To live without _____ **hope** _____
7. To be already _____ **condemned** _____
8. To live against _____ **Jesus** _____
9. To be _____ **dying** _____ in sin
10. To live as a child of the _____ **devil** _____
11. To live as God's _____ **enemy** _____
12. To live without _____ **peace** _____
13. To be spiritually _____ **blind** _____

What are two places in FAITH visits when questions about or challenges to a biblical view of lostness might arise?

1. _____

2. _____

Check appropriate ways to respond to the issue of spiritual lostness.

- ☐ 1. Shout at the person that if he is lost, he is going to hell.
- ☐ 2. Ask a lost person to name all of the sins he has committed.
- ☑ 3. Don't be judgmental, but guide the lost person to understand his need for salvation.
- ☑ 4. Communicate the simplicity of the gospel message.
- ☑ 5. Pray fervently before visiting an unsaved person.
- ☑ 6. Be sensitive to the struggles people have in questioning and seeking to accept God's forgiveness and assurance of eternal life.
- ☑ 7. Look for every opportunity to ask the Key Question, but be sensitive to ways you need to build a relationship.
- ☑ 8. Show and dialogue about the picture on the cover of *A Step of Faith*.
- ☑ 9. Look for opportunities to enroll and involve unsaved persons in Sunday School.
- ☐ 10. Point out to someone that it is obvious he is lost.

Defining the Question: What Does It Mean to Be Saved?

Last week we defined *lostness* as life without a personal relationship with God through His Son, Jesus Christ. The good news for lost people is that Jesus " 'came to seek and to save what was lost' " (Luke 19:10). Only He can fill the void lost people have in their deepest beings. This week we will learn what it means for a person to have that void filled by Jesus Christ.

In our world you will likely encounter misconceptions and confusion about what salvation means and how it is gained. You may hear remarks like these.

- "I know I will be saved because I believe in God, and I do good for others."
- "I'm sure I'm going to heaven because I've never committed a crime or hurt anyone."
- "Why do I need to be saved? There's nothing wrong with me."
- "Salvation means discovering your own divinity, which lies within every person."
- "Salvation is achieved after you are reincarnated through progressively higher states of existence."

The Bible defines *salvation* differently. It is a free gift of God for those who accept Jesus Christ as Savior. Therefore, it cannot be merited by our goodness or earned by our good works. Ephesians 2:8-9 says, "It is by grace you have been saved, through faith—and this not from yourselves, it is the gift of God—not by works, so that no one can boast." You have learned the FAITH gospel presentation to introduce lost people to the Author of salvation, Jesus Christ. You will be blessed by gaining a deeper understanding of what salvation means for you and for those with whom you have opportunities to share.

The Bible Speaks

The Bible tells us what it means to be saved.

1. To trust _____Christ_____ as Savior

Jesus said, " 'I am the way and the truth and the life. No one comes to the Father except through me' " (John 14:6). Your FAITH gospel presentation emphasizes what a person must do to be saved.

- Repent by turning from sin and self (see Luke 13:3).
- Trust Christ alone (see 1 Cor. 15:3-4).
- Confess and believe that Christ is Savior (see Rom. 10:9).

HEAR IT

Step 2 (5 mins.)

Introduce the content of this session by summarizing Defining the Question. Use the computer diskette or the overhead cel to illustrate questions and comments about salvation.

Defining the Question

Step 3 (15 mins.)

Direct participants to turn to page 147 in their Journals and to fill in the blanks as you present the key points in The Bible Speaks. Use the computer diskette or the overhead cel.

The Bible Speaks

2. To be _____ forgiven _____

In the FAITH Gospel Presentation the letter *F* is for Forgiveness: "In Him [meaning Jesus] we have redemption through His blood, the forgiveness of sins" (Eph. 1:7, NKJV). Because we have all sinned (see Rom. 3:23), we all need forgiveness of our sins (see Rom. 6:23). Salvation through Jesus Christ is the only way to have forgiveness for our sin.

3. To be no longer _____ condemned _____

Having been saved through faith in Christ, we are now in Christ Jesus. Romans 8:1 tells us, "There is now no condemnation for those who are in Christ Jesus, because through Christ Jesus the law of the Spirit of life set me free from the law of sin and death."

4. To be in a right _____ relationship _____ with God

Lost persons are separated from God because of their sin. But when we repent of our sin and put our trust in Christ alone for salvation, we can enjoy a relationship with God through Christ's righteousness: "All this is from God, who reconciled us to himself through Christ and gave us the ministry of reconciliation: that God was reconciling the world to himself in Christ, not counting men's sins against them" (2 Cor. 5:18-19).

5. To be _____ born _____ again

In John 3:6 Jesus told the Pharisee Nicodemus: " 'Flesh gives birth to flesh, but the Spirit gives birth to spirit. You should not be surprised at my saying, "You must be born again!" ' " Just as we were born once physically, by being saved, we are born again spiritually into God's kingdom.

6. To be a new _____ creation _____

"If anyone is in Christ, he is a new creation; the old has gone, the new has come!" (2 Cor. 5:17). Having been born again and placed in Christ by the Spirit of God, we are now a new creation. All things become new. We start all over. The past is gone. Each new day is a new creation.

7. To be a _____ child _____ of God

First John 3:1-2 tells those who have been saved: "How great is the love the Father has lavished on us, that we should be called children of God! And that is what we are! The reason the world does not know us is that it did not know him. Dear friends, now we are children of God, and what we will be has not yet been made known." All who believe and trust in Christ are adopted into God's family as His children.

8. To be _____free_____ indeed

Whereas lost persons were enslaved by sin, we are set free when we are saved: " 'If the Son sets you free, you will be free indeed' " (John 8:36). This freedom means that we are no longer charged with our sins but are now cleansed of them by Jesus Christ's sacrifice on the cross.

9. To be a _____disciple_____ of Christ

To those who had believed in Him, Jesus said: " 'If you hold to my teaching, you are really my disciples. Then you will know the truth, and the truth will set you free' " (John 8:32). Once we are saved, a disciple's desire is to grow in a relationship with Him by knowing Him and obeying Him more fully.

10. To have a life of _____peace_____

A great desire among most people is to have peace with God and peace with others. To be saved is to receive a peace that passes all understanding (see Phil. 4:7). Jesus Himself is our personal peace who lives in us, and He is the Prince of Peace for all humankind (see Isa. 9:6).

11. To be assured of _____eternal_____ _____life_____

Jesus said that one great benefit of His salvation is knowing that we will live with him in heaven forever (see John 14:3). First John 5:11-13 also tells us: "God has given us eternal life, and this life is in his Son [Jesus]. He who has the Son [Jesus] has life; he who does not have the Son of God does not have life. I write these things to you who believe in the name of the Son of God so that you may know that you have eternal life." As soon as we are saved, we can rejoice in knowing that we have already begun to spend eternal life with our Heavenly Father and our Savior, Jesus Christ, who died to save us.

In FAITH training you have learned that lost persons must call on the name of the Lord to be saved (see Rom. 10:9). Paul asked some questions that every Christian needs to consider: "How, then, can they call on the one they have not believed in? And how can they believe in the one of whom they have not heard? And how can they hear without someone preaching to them? And how can they preach unless they are sent?" (Rom. 10:14-15). Paul's point is that people cannot be saved unless someone shares Christ with them.

FAITH gives you a wonderful opportunity to share the good news of salvation through intentional visits and daily encounters. Every lost person needs to know that God's intention is for them—
- to enjoy a love relationship with Him;
- to have inner peace with their Creator and to live at peace with others;
- to discover the purpose He created for them to fulfill in this world and through eternity with Him.

Thus, it is important to share and to train Team Learners to share what salvation through Christ means for all who place their trust in Him.

Entry Points in FAITH Visits

Several occasions in FAITH visits offer a person an opportunity to consider the question, What does it mean to be saved?

1. One great privilege you have is to visit persons who already declare faith in Jesus as Savior. You will encounter many persons who are your brothers or sisters in Christ. You may learn of the person's belief in Christ when reviewing the ___**Visitation**___ ___**Assignment**___ ___**Card**___ or during the ___**INVOLVEMENT**___ segment of the visitation. Likewise, you may learn that a person trusts Christ for forgiveness of sin through the response to the ___**Key**___ ___**Question**___.

2. Your visits will certainly lead you to persons who do not know Christ. You will look for opportunities to share your evangelistic testimony particularly during the ___**INVOLVEMENT**___ segment of the visit. Listen to your own words as you share. You are identifying that through a life-changing experience, you now have assurance of eternal life. Even though you do not tell the person about Christ at this point, you are well aware that your acceptance of Christ as your Savior was your life-changing experience. You may relate specifically to several life crises and struggles that other persons experience. Yet you have been saved from the consequences of sin against God.

3. Every point in the ___**FAITH**___ ___**Visit**___ ___**Outline**___ identifies why a person needs to be saved and what a person needs to do to be saved.

4. When you ask the ___**Key**___ ___**Question**___, you give someone an opportunity to be saved by accepting Christ.

5. Often as you share in a ___**ministry**___ ___**visit**___, people who are hurting or rebellious will lash out against you or the church. This is sometimes a signal that the person is desperate to know if salvation truly makes a difference in life.

6. The picture on the cover of _**A**_ _**Step**_ _**of**_ _**Faith**_ brings many persons to realize their need for salvation.

7. The discussion of ___**baptism**___ provides a picture of what happens to persons when they are saved.

Step 4 (5 mins.)

Direct participants to turn to page 150 in their Journals and to fill in the blanks as you summarize Entry Points in FAITH Visits. Use the computer diskette or the overhead cel.

Entry Points
in FAITH
Visits

How You Can Respond

Here are possible ways you can focus on the meaning of salvation during witnessing encounters. Your response will depend on the person, the situation, and the Holy Spirit's direction in this circumstance. Always keep in mind the general principles outlined on pages 28–29 in session 1.

1. __Celebrate__ with those who have already trusted Christ as Savior. Although every Christian is somewhere on the journey of faith, we have something great and eternal in common with each believer. You can talk about how you both came to know Christ as Savior. Talk about what Christ is doing in your lives now. Encourage each other as you both seek to trust and obey Christ.

2. Every Christian needs the fellowship and ministry of the church. As you discover believers who are not involved in Bible study, ministry, fellowship, or worship, look for ways to build bridges to a church or Sunday School class. Always look for opportunities to __enroll__ and __involve__ persons, including new Christians, in Sunday School.

3. Do not hesitate to ask permission to __share__ the FAITH Visit Outline with a person who professes to be a Christian. This can be good practice for a Team member, and God can use this time to encourage the believer in his or her own faith or to convict if the person is not truly saved.

4. When sharing with lost persons, share each point of the FAITH gospel presentation as someone who is authentically __learning__ that point from experience. Be careful never to come across as judgmental. Let the compassion of Christ come across as you speak.

5. Follow the Holy Spirit's __direction__. It is His work to convict and convince. Let Him do what only He can do. He may lead you to explain or clarify one or more points during the *Invitation.* You may also need to share additional words of testimony or Scripture to explain one or more points of the gospel.

6. As you minister to hurting, rebellious, or antagonistic persons, __remember__ ways others have effectively ministered to you. Remember Christ's compassion for those who hurt.

7. If you come across as one who has arrived at the end of the journey of faith, it will be difficult for the lost person to accept what you say. If you seek to relate to the person as someone who is __growing__ in your faith and seeking to follow Christ no matter what the consequences, God will honor your attempts.

Step 5 (5 mins.)

Direct participants to turn to page 151 in their Journals and to fill in the blanks as you summarize How You Can Respond. Use the computer diskette or the overhead cel.

How You Can Respond

SAY IT

Step 6 (5 mins.)

Ask accountability partners to practice the *Invitation* portion of the FAITH Visit Outline.

STUDY IT

Step 7 (5 mins.)

Overview Home Study Assignments for session 9.

Transition to assemble with FAITH Teams to prepare for home visits. (5 mins.)

Visitation Time

Do It

1. Go out in the attitude and Spirit of Christ Jesus, humbling yourself and allowing someone else to see Christ in you.
2. How are you able to serve others through the visits and contacts you make this week? Are there ways you can meet someone's need? Lift someone's load? Hold out Christ's light to someone else? How are you allowing others to serve you during any times of need? Remember, your Sunday School class is there for you, too.
3. As the Team returns to the church from its visits, the Team Leader should guide in an evaluation of what happened and what follow-through should be made by the Team and/or class/department. Discuss how the report should be presented during Celebration Time; be careful not to tell personal or sensitive details that surfaced during visits.
4. At the Team Leader's cue, Learners should be able to share IMPOSSIBLE.

Celebration Time

Share It

1. Highlight the results of ministry visits as you debrief with your Team. Indicate the different types of Sunday School ministry visits and why certain topics were discussed in the different types of visits. What would Team members suggest as actions for follow-up?
2. Hear reports and testimonies.
3. Complete Evaluation Cards.
4. Complete Participation Cards.
5. Update visitation forms with the results of visits.

Home Study Assignments

Home Study Assignments reinforce this session by helping you apply what you have learned.

Your Discipleship Journey

Journaling activities in Your Discipleship Journey are an important part of your development as a Great Commission Christian through FAITH training.

1. Review Scripture passages that clarify for you what it means to be saved. Begin with John 10:9-10; Romans 5:1-11; 2 Corinthians 5:17-21; and 1 Peter 1:3-9.

2. Christ has saved you from the consequences of sin. Make a list of sins from which you know He has released you.

   _____

   _____

3. As you think about your life after you were saved, list benefits of your salvation.

   _____

   _____

   _____

   _____

   Take time to thank God for each of these benefits. Keep them in mind to share with lost persons.

4. Review the point "To be saved is to be a disciple of Christ" (p. 149). Identify ways Christ is leading you to be His disciple and obedient follower.

   _____

   _____

   _____

5. You have been saved in order to serve Christ. List actions you are learning that Christ is calling you to do in order to serve Him.

_____

_____

_____

Growing as a Life Witness

Growing as a Life Witness reminds you of your responsibility to witness and
minister to others during the week.

1. Talk or meet with your accountability partner and share ways you have
   cultivated a lost person or have witnessed or ministered on occasions other
   than FAITH visits.
2. Discuss ways you can apply the session 9 content in witnessing.
3. Pray for lost persons by name and for each other.

Prayer Concerns	Answers to Prayer
_____	_____
_____	_____
_____	_____
_____	_____
_____	_____
_____	_____
_____	_____
_____	_____
_____	_____
_____	_____
_____	_____

Your Weekly Sunday School Leadership Team Meeting

A FAITH participant is an important member of Sunday School. Encourage Team members who are elected Sunday School workers to attend this weekly meeting. Use this section to record ways your FAITH Team influences the work of your Sunday School class or department. Use the information to report during weekly Sunday School leadership team meetings. Identify actions that need to be taken through Sunday School as a result of prayer concerns, needs identified, visits made by the Team, and decisions made by the persons visited. Also identify ways you can disciple others in your Sunday School class or department and in your church.

1. Highlight FAITH needs/reports that affect your class/department or age group.

   _____

   _____

2. The most significant result of being saved is a restored personal relationship with God now and for all eternity. What are ways the department/class can impact persons with the truth that, for believers, heaven is HERE?

   _____

   _____

   That heaven is also HEREAFTER?

   _____

   _____

3. How will the class begin to follow up on persons who received a ministry visit?

   _____

   _____

   On someone who accepted Christ in an evangelistic visit?

   _____

   _____

4. What areas of our Sunday School need to be started or strengthened, based on input from ministry and Opinion Poll visits?

_____

_____

5. Pray now for your teacher(s) and department director(s).

Discipling Your Team Members

This weekly feature suggests actions the Team Leader can take to support Team members, prepare for Team Time, and improve visits. This work is part of the Team Leader's Home Study Assignments. Add any actions suggested by your church's FAITH strategy.

Support Team Members

❑ Pray for and personally follow up on any Learner who may need personal encouragement.

❑ Contact Team members during the week to remind them that you are praying for them and to discuss their participation in FAITH.

❑ Learners are memorizing the gospel presentation through *T* is for TURN. As you discuss this content with Team members, remind them that this is the heart of the gospel.

Prepare to Lead Team Time

❑ Overview Leading Team Time for session 10.

❑ Review the FAITH Visit Outline.

Prepare to Lead Visits

❑ Be prepared to explain the benefits and procedures of making Sunday School ministry visits.

❑ Be prepared to model a visit in which Team members are asked to lead in a visit up to the point of *T* is for TURN.

❑ Be prepared to lead your Team to participate during Celebration Time.

Link with Sunday School

❑ Participate in your weekly Sunday School leadership team meeting. Share pertinent information in this meeting, using Your Weekly Sunday School Leadership Team Meeting (p. 155) and FAITH-visit results.

❑ Be sensitive to times when the subject of salvation arises in Sunday School lessons. Teachers can use these as opportunities to present the plan of salvation for persons attending the class or department who may not be saved. Teachers can also present benefits like the ones in this session to clarify the meaning of salvation when appropriate.

For Further Growth

For Further Growth may include additional reading or activities that will enhance your growth as a disciple and a discipler of others. These assignments are intended to be long-term projects and do not have to be completed during this semester of study.

1. Read "The Person God Uses" (pp. 119–25) in *Evangelism Through the Sunday School* by Bobby Welch (LifeWay, 1997).
2. Read the FAITH Tip "God's Wonderful Work of Salvation" (p. 91) in *A Journey in FAITH Journal*.
3. Read *Jesus by Heart* by Roy Edgemon and Barry Sneed (LifeWay, 1999). Start by reading the excerpt in the FAITH Tip on page 158.

FAITH TIP

A Child of God

Every person's DNA (deoxyribonucleic acid) is different—except that of identical twins. Their perfectly matched internal coding makes them one and the same. Their hearts, their very cells are created as one at conception; they are mirror reflections of each other—inside and out.

The second you repented of your sin and God accepted you as His forgiven child, you were reborn. Immediately, God gave you your birthright—a new spiritual DNA (see 1 Pet. 1:3-4). Your spiritual DNA perfectly matches that of God's Son, Jesus Christ. When God accepted you as His child, you became an entirely new person (see 2 Cor. 5:17). Just as God gives a newborn baby all the DNA code needed to grow to adulthood, He immediately gave you the new spiritual DNA you needed to live a life that glorifies Him; to walk with God; and to live a life of love, trust, and obedience—just as Jesus did. You received the spiritual DNA you need to grow to spiritual maturity. That means that as a child of God, you now have a heart like His Son, Jesus.

You have been given a second chance at life—a second chance to change the world. And with Jesus empowering you, you can do it. Because you are in Jesus and Jesus is in you (see John 14:20), you can do what He has done—bring glory to God. Because the Spirit of Jesus lives in you (see John 3:5-6), you have the ability—and the calling—to glorify God on the outside, just as Jesus did (see Eph. 4:22-23).

Retrace your spiritual path.

1. *God changed you.* The old you has been transformed: "If any man be in Christ, he is a new creature: old things are passed away; behold, all things are become new" (2 Cor. 5:17).

2. *God gave you a new spiritual identity in Christ.* You now have Christ in you, and you are in Him (see John 14:20): "To them God has chosen to make known among the Gentiles the glorious riches of this mystery, which is Christ in you, the hope of glory" (Col. 1:27).

3. *God will use your life for His glory.* Through your heart-to-heart-relationship with Jesus, God has empowered you to love, trust, and obey Him. God's love and power will be revealed to others through your surrendered life. Other people will see Jesus in you, and God will be glorified (see John 13:31; 17:26).[1]

---

[1]Roy Edgemon and Barry Sneed, "Your New Spiritual DNA," *Jesus by Heart* (Nashville: LifeWay, 1999), 23–24.

Why Do I Need the Church?

In this session you will—

CHECK IT by engaging in Team Time activities;

KNOW IT by reviewing content from session 9;

HEAR IT by affirming what the Bible says about the importance of being

involved in church;

SEE IT by viewing a video segment;

SAY IT by discussing possible applications of what you have learned in this

session;

STUDY IT by overviewing Home Study Assignments;

DO IT by leading your Team in making visits;

SHARE IT by celebrating.

In Advance
- Overview content.
- Preview teaching suggestions. Prepare key points. Decide whether to use the session 10 computer slides or the overhead cels.
- Prepare the room for teaching.
- Cue the videotape to the session 10 segment, A Fish Story.
- Pray for participants and for Teams as they prepare to visit.
- As Teaching Time begins, direct participants to open their Journals to page 162.

Leading Team Time

All Team members participate in Team Time. They are primarily responsible for reciting the assigned portion of the FAITH Visit Outline and for discussing other Home Study Assignments.

As you direct this important time of CHECK IT activities with your Team, keep in mind that Learners look to you as a role model, motivator, mentor, and friend. Team Time activities can continue in the car as the Team travels to and from visits.

Lead CHECK IT Activities

✔ FAITH Visit Outline
❑ Listen while each Learner recites all of the *Preparation* and *Presentation* content and key words for *Invitation.*
❑ Give opportunities for Learners to practice reciting the portions of the FAITH Visit Outline they have learned to this point.

✔ Other Home Study Assignments
❑ This may be a good time to discuss the benefits of keeping a weekly journal as part of FAITH training. Discuss some of the truths or understandings gained through the weekly Bible studies. Dialogue about how the reflective questions have influenced Learners' training experience.

✔ Session 9 Debriefing
❑ *T* is for TURN. This is the point in the gospel in which a person makes a significant choice—whether to receive salvation. To be forgiven, a person must turn from his sin and turn to Christ. He must trust Christ and Christ only. The imagery of turning is reinforced with the simple question, If you were driving down the road and someone asked you to turn, what would he or she be asking you to do? (Change direction.) Most people can easily understand the idea of changing from one direction to another. The Bible uses the word *repent* to depict the same thing. The Bible is clear about the need for a person to repent of sin and to live for Christ (change direction) by committing to and trusting Him. Team members will need to remember the significance of the concepts behind the letter *T* to help explain and emphasize the how of the gospel.

✔ Help for Strengthening a Visit
❑ The illustration of changing directions in a car is the only dialogue that is planned as part of the actual gospel presentation. It is important to ask the person to share his or her answer to the question. The response is predictable, but by asking the question,

you call the person's attention to the gospel and increase his or her participation in the discussion. You might be talking with a child, a younger youth, or someone who obviously does not drive. If so, adapt the question to something like, If you were riding down the road and you asked the driver to turn, what would you be wanting the driver to do? Usually, it will be significant to use the word *repent* only after the question has helped you explain what the word means. Using the turning analogy to emphasize faith in Christ also helps clarify the meaning of *repent*. For many unsaved or unchurched people, *repent* is associated with religious or churchy terms; without a relevant, contemporary explanation, this word might lose much of its significance.

❑ Remind Team members to listen during each visit for ministry opportunities, as well as for things a person might say to help you identify with his or her spiritual journey.

❑ Discuss how, as a Team Leader, you communicate follow-up information to the appropriate age group/class/department when you encounter family members of different ages in a home visit.

Notes

_____

_____

_____

_____

_____

Actions I Need to Take with Learners During the Week

_____

_____

_____

_____

Transition to classrooms for instruction on the content of the session. (5 mins.)

TEACHING TIME

KNOW IT

Step 1 (5 mins.)

Direct participants to locate A Quick Review on page 162 in their Journals and to complete the activities. Then give the answers, using the computer diskette or the overhead cel. Possible answers to question:

1. Visitation Assignment Card
2. INVOLVEMENT
3. Key Question
4. Every point in the FAITH Visit Outline
5. Ministry visits
6. *A Step of Faith*
7. Discussion of baptism

A Quick Review

A Quick Review

Last week you studied several biblical answers to the question, What does it mean to be saved?
1. To trust _____**Christ**_____ as Savior
2. To be _____**forgiven**_____
3. To be no longer _____**condemned**_____
4. To be in a right _____**relationship**_____ with God
5. To be _____**born**_____ again
6. To be a new _____**creation**_____
7. To be a _____**child**_____ of God
8. To be _____**free**_____ indeed
9. To be a _____**disciple**_____ of Christ
10. To have a life of _____**peace**_____
11. To be assured of _____**eternal**_____ _____**life**_____

What are two places in FAITH visits when questions about or challenges to a biblical view of salvation might arise?

1. _____

2. _____

Check appropriate ways to focus on the biblical meaning of salvation.
☑ 1. Celebrate with those you discover who have already trusted Christ as Savior.
❑ 2. If someone claims to be saved, ask him to prove it.
❑ 3. Explain that salvation is available only to those who join your church.
☑ 4. Look for opportunities to enroll and involve persons in Sunday School.
☑ 5. Ask to share the FAITH Visit Outline even with a person who professes to be a Christian.
❑ 6. Ask a professing Christian how much he tithes.
☑ 7. Share each point of the FAITH gospel presentation as someone who is authentically learning that point from experience.
☑ 8. Follow the Holy Spirit's direction as you share and let Him convict and convince.
☑ 9. As you minister to hurting, rebellious, or antagonistic persons, remember ways others have effectively ministered to you. Remember Christ's compassion for those who hurt.
☑ 10. Relate to the lost person as someone who is growing in your faith and seeking to follow Christ.

Defining the Question: Why Do I Need the Church?

In intentional visits and in daily life you will encounter questions about church involvement from both Christians and non-Christians. Because of past, perhaps even hurtful, experiences those who are not involved in church will question the importance of participating in its life and ministry.

Here are some ways you might anticipate being questioned or challenged about the importance of the church.

- "I don't need the church. I believe in God, and He's all I need."
- "Church members are a bunch of hypocrites. They're as bad as the rest of us."
- "I'll never go back to church. They had their chance to care for me, and they let me down."
- "I suppose the church has helped people in the past, but I don't see it as relevant for today's society."
- "Why should I sit in church on Sunday? That's my only time to relax."
- "Churches are a blight on society. They consist of narrow-minded bigots who want to restrict our freedom."

When people question the importance of being involved in church, they may ask from a variety of perspectives.

1. One perspective may be _____antagonism_____.

They may have had bad experiences that hurt them. Perhaps someone in their family died, and no one from the church called. They may have been involved in a church fight that turned into personal attacks. They may have trusted a church leader who let them down through immoral behavior. Personal experiences like these leave deep wounds that are slow to heal. They may assume that all churches are like the one where they had the unpleasant experience, and they may be unwilling to let themselves be vulnerable again. Others may disagree with a church's stand on a social issue. As atheists become more open about their disbelief in God, they will more aggressively oppose the church's work and influence in our society.

2. Another perspective may be __no__ _____religious_____ _____heritage_____.

Many people have not grown up going to church regularly. Maybe their parents worked on Sunday or viewed Sunday as a day of leisure. God and church were simply never part of their lives, so they don't feel a

HEAR IT

Step 2 (5 mins.)

Introduce the content of this session by summarizing Defining the Question. Use the computer diskette or the overhead cel to illustrate questions and comments about the church.

Defining the Question

Direct participants to turn to page 163 in their Journals and to fill in the blanks as you present the three perspectives on the church. Use the computer diskette or the overhead cel.

Perspectives on the Church

need for them. Believers will more frequently encounter this attitude as society becomes more secular. Some may genuinely ask what the church has to offer them, since they have no history with the church.

3. A third perspective may be _____indifference_____.
Some people view the church as irrelevant and as not making a difference in society and in individual lives. Seeing the church's services, forms of communication, and activities as entrenched in outdated traditions from a past generation, they feel that the church does not have anything to offer them and their generation. Some indifference may result from a perceived credibility problem. Many unbelievers have known church members whose lives were no different from those of pagans. Disillusioned, they assume that all church members are hypocrites.

   As a Christian, you have quite a different perspective on the church. Perhaps through a ministry visit, your Sunday School testimony, or your personal testimony you can hint at the true nature of the church by sharing ways God has touched you through your church.

The Bible Speaks

A church is a community of believers in Jesus Christ. In the New Testament *church* may refer to a local congregation under the lordship of Christ (see Gal. 1:2) or to the universal church Christ said he would establish (see Matt. 16:18). Several key Bible passages give us ideas of what church life should be and why it is important for every believer.

1. The church is the ___body___ of Christ.
In 1 Corinthians 12:12-27 Paul's comparison of the church to the human body gives us an idea why church life is important.
- Christ is the ___Head___ of the church (see Eph. 4:14-16; Col. 1:18). Because the church is Christ's body, His very presence is in the life of His church. As the Head of the church, Christ gives it purpose and unity. If we want to honor Christ, we will be involved in doing His work through the church.
- The church is a ___unity___ (see 1 Cor. 12:12-13). The Holy Spirit's presence unites every believer in the body of Christ. The whole church body functions as a single unit, just as a human body does. Together we represent Christ and do His work more effectively than we could individually.
- Each church member has a ___purpose___ (see 1 Cor. 12:14-20). Every member of the church plays an important role.

Step 3 (10 mins.)

Direct participants to turn to page 164 in their Journals and to fill in the blanks as you present the key points in The Bible Speaks. Use the computer diskette or the overhead cels.

The Bible Speaks

All members have contributions to make and are missed when they fail to be and do what God has called them to be and do. The Holy Spirit gives spiritual gifts to members of the church body so that each can carry out his part in building up the body of Christ (see 1 Cor. 12:28-30).

- Church members are **_interdependent_** (see 1 Cor. 12:21-27). Each Christian must rely on other Christians. It would be ridiculous for us to claim that we do not need anyone else to help us be all God intends us to be. We rely on one another for strength and encouragement, "as iron sharpens iron" (Prov. 27:17). Hebrews 10:24-25 emphasizes the role of the body of Christ in stimulating one another to service and in encouraging one another to remain true to the faith in spite of difficulty.

2. The church is the **_people_** of God.

First Peter 2:9-10 refers to believers as "a chosen people, a royal priesthood, a holy nation, a people belonging to God, that you may declare the praises of him who called you out of darkness into his wonderful light. Once you were not a people, but now you are the people of God; once you had not received mercy, but now you have received mercy." The church is God's special possession. We are in the world to do His work.[1]

3. The church is a **_family_** of believers.

The New Testament refers to the church as a family or "members of God's household" (see Gal. 6:10; Eph. 2:19). God is our Father (see Gal. 4:6-7), and we are His children (see Rom. 8:16-17). Other believers are our brothers and sisters in Christ, and we are commanded to "love one another" (1 John 3:11).[2] All of the benefits of a loving family are available to every church member.

4. The church is the **_bride_** of Christ.

Jesus referred to Himself as the bridegroom (see Luke 5:34-35), and New Testament writings describe the church as His bride (see 2 Cor. 11:2; Rev. 19:7-9; 21:9; 22:17). At the end of time will be a marriage feast for Christ and the church when we will be united with Him forever. Christ is preparing His church for that day of great victory and joy.[3]

5. The church is an expression of the **_kingdom_** of God.

The kingdom is the rule of Christ in the hearts of people. The church is the kingdom of heaven on earth, because it is made up of people who have yielded their lives to Christ's rule. Church members recognize Jesus as King, and they are His subjects. They realize that they are citizens of a kingdom that is more important, stronger, and more lasting than a secular kingdom or nation (see Col. 1:13). Jesus instructed us to pray for the coming of the kingdom on earth (see Matt. 6:10).[4] Our participation in church can teach us what it means to be citizens of God's kingdom.

6. *The church is responsible for fulfilling God-given* __functions__.

We have seen through a variety of biblical pictures that the church belongs to Jesus, and He expects the church to accomplish His purposes in the world.

Ask participants to fill in the blanks on page 166 in their Journals as you explain the five functions of the church, using the computer diskette or the overhead cel.

**Functions of
the Church**

- Jesus commanded us to be involved in __evangelism__ (see Matt. 28:19-20; Acts 1:8). The church plays a vital role in pointing the way to Jesus Christ.
- The church is also expected to be involved in __discipleship__ (see Matt. 28:19-20; Eph. 4:12-16). Church members are to grow in knowledge of and commitment to their Lord through Bible study and application. A believer's local church offers many ways to be discipled and to disciple others.
- The church is to enjoy Christian __fellowship__ (see Luke 4:16; Acts 2:42-47; Heb. 10:25). Through the Holy Spirit we can have fellowship with one another and with Christ. This is a fellowship that millions of people long for but don't realize is available in the church.
- Like the early church, today's church is to carry out __ministry__ (see Acts 2:45; 4:32,34-35; Eph. 4:11-12). By combining their spiritual gifts and resources, church members can accomplish more in Christ's name than they could individually.
- Through __worship__ the church praises God and hears His voice. Worship involves all we are in praising who God is and what He has done. We were created for worshiping God. Participating in church helps us do this.

God gave us the church to help us become more like Christ and to give us an opportunity to be involved in the work of God's kingdom. By worshiping with other Christians, studying God's Word together, and encouraging one another as we ourselves are encouraged, we can move toward what God desires us to be. The church also serves as the natural vehicle for sharing Jesus with others and for ministering to both Christians and non-Christians. Through the church, believers can work together to make an eternal difference in countless lives.

Entry Points in FAITH Visits

Several occasions in FAITH visits offer a person an opportunity to consider the question, Why do I need the church?

1. When you begin the visit, the **INTRODUCTION** identifies your Team as being from your church. This sets the stage for the person to consider the need for the church.
2. During the **INVOLVEMENT** portion of the visit, you have an opportunity to discuss whether the person has any connection with and involvement in the church. This will reveal much about a person's attitude toward the church.
3. The questions asked during the **Opinion** **Poll** help point to the need for ministries provided by a church. By asking and receiving responses to these questions, you set the stage for future discussion about the church's purpose of ministry.
4. The **Sunday** **School** **testimony** may surprise many people in revealing the benefits of coming together for Bible study, fellowship, and ministry.
5. As you share issues raised in **A** **Step** **of** **Faith**, you point to the need for a person not to be ashamed to follow Christ. Among other things, a person follows Christ by being part of a church's ministry. Some people will raise important questions about the church's role in their lives.
6. As you make **ministry** or **follow-up** **visits**, you will encounter many persons who either have deemphasized their connection with church or are learning what the church and Sunday School can mean in their lives.

How You Can Respond

Here are possible ways you can respond to the question, Why do I need the church? during witnessing encounters. Your response will depend on the person, the situation, and the Holy Spirit's direction in this circumstance. Always keep in mind the general principles outlined on pages 28–29 in session 1.

1. The FAITH Sunday School Evangelism Strategy has given many churches and church members a renewed sense of commitment to doing the work of Christ through the church. You can explain that in some ways your church or Sunday School is once again seeking to represent Christ in your community no matter how ineffectively the person feels that was done in the past.
2. Team members' testimonies will be valuable in explaining the importance of church in people's lives. The Sunday School

Step 4 (5 mins.)

Direct participants to turn to page 167 in their Journals and to fill in the blanks as you summarize Entry Points in FAITH Visits. Use the computer diskette or overhead cel.

Entry Points in FAITH Visits

SEE IT

Step 5 (10 mins.)

To focus on ways witnesses can respond to questions about someone's need for the church, show the session 10 video segment, A Fish Story. Ask participants to make notes in the margins of their Journals. Remind members that the video vignette does not present a model that can be used in all witnessing situations. Rather, it is one example of a situation that can arise and the type of response that may be suitable in this situation.

SAY IT

Step 6 (5 mins.)

Ask accountability partners to discuss ways they would respond to a challenge or question about the need for the church, using the ideas in the video and in How You Can Respond.

If you are leading students, have accountability partners role-play a situation in which one partner asks a question about the need for the church and the other partner responds.

STUDY IT

Step 7 (5 mins.)

Overview Home Study Assignments for session 10.

Transition to assemble with FAITH Teams to prepare for home visits. (5 mins.)

testimony gives a wonderful opportunity to emphasize the benefits of fellowship, ministry, worship, and Bible study, as well as the results of growing in Christ. The baptism testimony provides a direct opportunity to emphasize the role of the church.

3. Because some people will want to criticize certain aspects of your church, be very careful how you seek to represent your church. Do not give in to the temptation to call names of persons who have misrepresented the commission of Christ. Seek to be redemptive as you explain that Christ works through His people.

4. Be prepared to describe some of your church's ministries or special opportunities. If you are given the privilege of completing the entire FAITH Visit Outline, you can present and briefly explain some of these opportunities at the close of the visit. When you identify that yours may be a very brief visit, consider leaving at least one item from your church that interprets the ministries offered.

5. If an unbeliever accepts Christ, help him understand that the church will help him grow and learn more about Christ. If he does not accept Christ at this time, help him understand that by being a part of the church, he can better understand the things you have just shared.

6. Do not hesitate to leave Sunday School literature with the person. Briefly point out the upcoming week's study and what she can do to prepare for the study. Do not just hand the material to the person and imply, "Just read this."

7. Identify appropriate ways to follow up on the visit. Encourage other persons in the Sunday School class or elsewhere in the church to follow up. Surprise the person by proving that your church really cares and that Jesus really makes a difference in your life.

8. If the person is a believer who has withdrawn from fellowship in a church, use passages in this session to point out that the body of Christ needs his gifts to make a difference in others' lives. Also emphasize his need for other believers' support and encouragement.

9. Respond to objections about church members' hypocrisy by emphasizing individual accountability before God and the personal need for salvation and/or fellowship with believers. Point out that the fact that some church members may be hypocrites does not mean that all members are. Point to Jesus' habit, recorded in Luke 4:16, of frequenting the synagogue in spite of the religious leaders' hypocrisy.

Visitation Time

Do It

1. Think about the importance of the church in your life. Think about the impact your church has in your community. You are a part of that impact as you and your FAITH team members visit with others. As you visit, you may encounter persons at the end of their rope who are in need of the encouragement a Sunday School class and a loving fellowship can offer. God may be preparing you for a divine appointment in which He can use you to make a difference in a life.
2. Remember the persons who have accepted Christ and are now a part of your church as a result of FAITH teams that have made visits. These individuals have added their gifts and talents to your church and are enriching your church. Usually, people who have recently accepted Christ know more people who have not accepted Christ.
3. Reflect on the difference you are making through your church as you go.
4. All Team members should know the FAITH presentation through *H* is for HEAVEN. While visiting, invite Team members to support you throughout the presentation.

DO IT (110 MINS.)

Celebration Time

Share It

1. Ask a Team member to take the lead in sharing reports.
2. Hear reports and testimonies.
3. Complete Evaluation Cards.
4. Complete Participation Cards.
5. Update visitation forms with the results of visits.

SHARE IT (30 MINS.)

Home Study Assignments

Home Study Assignments reinforce this session by helping you apply what you have learned.

Your Discipleship Journey

Journaling activities in Your Discipleship Journey are an important part of your development as a Great Commission Christian through FAITH training.

1. Read Acts 2:42-47. In the columns below, write things the early church did as the body of Christ and modern ways your church carries out the same actions.

The Early Church	My Church
_____	_____
_____	_____
_____	_____
_____	_____
_____	_____
_____	_____
_____	_____

2. Evaluate your church's strength in carrying out the primary scriptural purposes listed below. Circle 1 to assign the lowest score and 5 to assign the highest score.

Evangelism	1	2	3	4	5
Discipleship	1	2	3	4	5
Fellowship	1	2	3	4	5
Ministry	1	2	3	4	5
Worship	1	2	3	4	5

3. What benefits have you gained by participating in your church?

_____

_____

Be ready to share these benefits during evangelistic and ministry visits when you have opportunities.

4. Imagine being a non-Christian who is facing a crisis. Think about the person's emotions and needs. If your church knew about the person's situation, how could it encourage and minister to this person?

_____

_____

Check the things your Sunday School could do for the person.

5. One problem some unbelievers have with the church is hypocrisy or a lack of integrity. This criticism highlights the importance of believers' lifestyles. Examine your lifestyle and daily witness. Prayerfully consider and list ways you can be a better representative of Christ in the world.

_____

_____

Growing as a Life Witness

Growing as a Life Witness reminds you of your responsibility to witness and minister to others during the week.

1. Talk or meet with your accountability partner and share ways you have cultivated a lost person or have witnessed or ministered on occasions other than FAITH visits.
2. Discuss your responses to activities 2 and 5 in Your Discipleship Journey.
3. Pray for lost persons by name and for each other.

Prayer Concerns	Answers to Prayer
_____	_____
_____	_____
_____	_____
_____	_____
_____	_____
_____	_____

Your Weekly Sunday School Leadership Team Meeting

A FAITH participant is an important member of Sunday School. Encourage Team members who are elected Sunday School workers to attend this weekly meeting. Use this section to record ways your FAITH Team influences the work of your Sunday School class or department. Use the information to report during weekly Sunday School leadership team meetings. Identify actions that need to be taken through Sunday School as a result of prayer concerns, needs identified, visits made by the Team, and decisions made by the persons visited. Also identify ways you can disciple others in your Sunday School class or department and in your church.

1. Highlight FAITH needs/reports affecting your class/department or age group. Receive and provide information about future visitation assignments. Do records reflect the information that is needed for visits and for follow-up?

   _____

   _____

2. Periodically evaluate the growth of your class/department. Are new Christians consistently becoming part of the group? Are these new believers beginning to grow in their faith and to discover their spiritual gifts? Are mature members leaving the class to accept leadership positions? Is the class reaching out beyond itself, so much so that a new unit or more space may be needed? Is the fellowship inclusive and attractive to all people?

   _____

   _____

3. How should preparation for Sunday consider the needs of individuals or families visited through FAITH? Discuss ways Sunday's Bible-study lesson can involve members and guests in transformational Bible study and discipleship.

   _____

   _____

4. Your class/department has committed to support you throughout FAITH training. FAITH assignments are reaching their peak for many Team members, so it is appropriate to ask your leadership team to pray for you and all FAITH participants at this significant time in training.

5. List prayer requests for your teacher and department director.

_____

_____

Discipling Your Team Members

This weekly feature suggests actions the Team Leader can take to support Team members, prepare for Team Time, and improve visits. This work is part of the Team Leader's Home Study Assignments. Add any actions suggested by your church's FAITH strategy.

Support Team Members

❏ Contact Team members during the week. Remind them that you are praying for them. Discuss prayer concerns and answers to prayer.

❏ This week Learners are memorizing the FAITH presentation through the *Invitation.* As you discuss this content with Team members, remind them that this is when someone has the opportunity to make a life-changing decision.

❏ Learners have a significant amount of reading during home study this week. The information is important to read and understand because it interprets *A Step of Faith.* Encourage Learners to read the FAITH Tips and to be prepared to discuss the significance of this leaflet in preparation for session 11.

❏ Record specific needs and concerns shared by Team members.

_____

_____

Prepare to Lead Team Time

❏ Review Team members' Home Study Assignments.

❏ Overview Leading Team Time for session 11.

Prepare to Lead Visits

❏ Review the FAITH Visit Outline.

Link with Sunday School

❏ Participate in your weekly Sunday School leadership team meeting. Share pertinent information in this meeting, using Your Weekly Sunday School Leadership Team Meeting (p. 172) and FAITH-visit results.

❏ Many benefits of church membership are realized by participating in Sunday School. Evaluate the way your class or department promotes fellowship, Christian love, and a deeper understanding of God's Word. Are the benefits being communicated clearly?

For Further Growth

For Further Growth may include additional reading or activities that will enhance your growth as a disciple and a discipler of others. These assignments are intended to be long-term projects and do not have to be completed during this semester of study.

1. Think of ways your church can stay connected with and minister to persons who are unable to attend every Sunday or who are homebound. Pray about becoming involved in this ministry.

2. Interview your pastor and other church leaders to discover how you can regularly pray for and support the work of the church.

3. Interview one or more church members who were reached through FAITH visits. Discover ways they are learning to grow in Christ as they become involved in various ministries of the church. These can become avenues for assimilating and discipling new Christians who enter your fellowship in the future.

---

[1]Roy T. Edgemon, *The Doctrines Baptists Believe* (Nashville: Convention, 1988), 115–16.
[2]Ibid., 116.
[3]Ibid.
[4]Ibid.

SESSION 11

Why Are Bible Study and Prayer Important?

In this session you will—

CHECK IT by engaging in Team Time activities;

KNOW IT by reviewing content from session 10;

HEAR IT by affirming what the Bible says about the importance of Bible study and prayer;

SAY IT by discussing possible applications of what you have learned in this session;

STUDY IT by overviewing Home Study Assignments;

DO IT by leading your Team in making visits;

SHARE IT by celebrating.

In Advance
- Overview content.
- Preview teaching suggestions. Prepare key points. Decide whether to use the session 11 computer slides or the overhead cels.
- Prepare the room for teaching.
- Pray for participants and for Teams as they prepare to visit.
- As Teaching Time begins, direct participants to open their Journals to page 178.

CHECK IT (15 MINS.)

If the computer diskette is used, display the agenda frame for Team Time, as desired. Add other points as needed.

CHECK IT agenda:
- ✔ FAITH Visit Outline
- ✔ Session 10 Debriefing
- ✔ Help for Strengthening a Visit

Leading Team Time

All Team members participate in Team Time. They are primarily responsible for reciting the assigned portion of the FAITH Visit Outline and for discussing other Home Study Assignments.

As you direct this important time of CHECK IT activities with your Team, keep in mind that Learners look to you as a role model, motivator, mentor, and friend. Team Time activities can continue in the car as the Team travels to and from visits.

Lead CHECK IT Activities

✔ FAITH *Visit Outline*

❑ Listen while each Learner recites the FAITH Visit Outline beginning with HOW and including all of the **Invitation.** Indicate any notes for improvement.

❑ Make sure Team members know the correct sequence in using *A Step of Faith* in making transition from the gospel presentation to leading someone to declare commitments to Christ as Savior and Lord, to enroll in Sunday School, and to publicly acknowledge new faith in Jesus. Since several Home Study Assignments dealt with the use of *A Step of Faith*, you may not need additional review of session 10 assignments.

❑ Make certain Team members are able to lead a person to pray to receive Christ and to pray for Christian growth. Also, be certain Team members are comfortable in leading a person to record commitment(s) they have made and to provide the information the church needs.

✔ *Session 10 Debriefing*

❑ Heaven HERE and Heaven HEREAFTER are fundamental beliefs of the Christian. Do Learners demonstrate a sense of comfort in sharing their joy in Christ and their assurance of eternal life in God's presence?

❑ H also stands for HOW. This becomes the hinge on which a Learner is able to clarify for another person how a person can have God's forgiveness, heaven and eternal life, and Jesus as personal Savior and Lord. Make sure the person is becoming increasingly comfortable in using the picture on the cover of *A Step of Faith* to identify with the need for God's forgiveness. You received earlier training to help your Team know what to do if *A Step of Faith* is not available.

✔ *Help for Strengthening a Visit*

❑ Remind Team members that they are seeing the Holy Spirit at work as they make themselves available for visitation. Recall examples of ways you have seen the Holy Spirit at work when a person has heard the FAITH gospel presentation.

❑ One of the great privileges and responsibilities in FAITH training is to encounter family members of someone you are assigned to visit. Although your Team is focusing on persons from your Sunday School department or class, you quickly learn that there are many opportunities to minister to and share the gospel with persons of other age divisions. Dialogue about ways to meaningfully include in a visit preschoolers, children, youth, and adults who would not be assigned to your department or class.

❑ Indicate that next week's practice session is a good way to improve skills and increase confidence. Share schedule adjustments.

Notes

_____

_____

_____

_____

_____

_____

Actions I Need to Take with Learners During the Week

_____

_____

_____

_____

_____

Transition to classrooms for instruction on the content of the session. (5 mins.)

TEACHING TIME

KNOW IT

Step 1 (5 mins.)

Direct participants to locate A Quick Review on page 178 in their Journals and to complete the activities. Then give the answers, using the computer diskette or the overhead cel. Possible answers to question:
1. INTRODUCTION
2. INVOLVEMENT
3. Opinion Poll
4. Sunday School testimony
5. *A Step of Faith*

A Quick Review

A Quick Review

Last week you learned ways the Bible answers the question, Why do I need the church? Review what you learned by substituting the words below in the correct summary statements.

interdependent • kingdom • unity • Head • people • family
functions • body • bride • purpose

1. The church is the ____**body**____ of Christ.
   • Christ is the ____**Head**____ of the church.
   • The church is a ____**unity**____.
   • Each church member has a ____**purpose**____.
   • Church members are ____**interdependent**____.
2. The church is the ____**people**____ of God.
3. The church is a ____**family**____ of believers.
4. The church is the ____**bride**____ of Christ.
5. The church is an expression of the ____**kingdom**____ of God.
6. The church is responsible for fulfilling God-given ____**functions**____.

How many of the church's five functions can you recall?
1. ____**Evangelism**____
2. ____**Discipleship**____
3. ____**Fellowship**____
4. ____**Ministry**____
5. ____**Worship**____

What are two places in FAITH visits when questions about or challenges to the need for the church might arise?

1. _____

2. _____

Check appropriate ways to respond to the question, Why do I need the church?
- ☑ 1. Point out that your church or Sunday School is seeking to represent Christ in your community.
- ☑ 2. Use Sunday School and baptism testimonies to emphasize the benefits of fellowship, ministry, worship, and Bible study.
- ☑ 3. Do not criticize those who have misrepresented the commission of Christ. Emphasize that God works through His people.
- ☐ 4. State that your church is without problems and sin.
- ☑ 5. Describe some of your church's ministries.

☑ 6. If a person accepts Christ, tell him that the church will help him grow and learn about Christ. If he does not, tell him that he can better understand what you have shared by attending church.

☑ 7. Leave Sunday School literature with the person and point out the upcoming week's study.

❑ 8. Explain that it is all right for church members to sin because they can always receive God's forgiveness.

☑ 9. Encourage Sunday School and other church members to follow up as appropriate.

☑ 10. If the person is a believer who is not in fellowship with a church, point out that the church needs his gifts and that he needs the church's support and encouragement.

☑ 11. Respond to objections about church members' hypocrisy by emphasizing individual accountability before God and the personal need for salvation and/or fellowship with believers.

❑ 12. Point out that accepting Christ without attending church nullifies a person's salvation.

Defining the Question: Why Are Bible Study and Prayer Important?

How healthy would you be if you ate only one meal a week? How close would your relationship be with your best friend if you spoke only once a month? It is obvious that you would not last long on one meal a week, and your relationship with your friend would be almost meaningless. Jesus is both your best friend and your source of nourishment for living the Christian life. He said: " 'I am the vine; you are the branches. If a man remains in me and I in him, he will bear much fruit; apart from me you can do nothing' " (John 15:5).

Discipleship is "developing a personal, lifelong, obedient relationship with Jesus Christ."[1] You grow in your relationship with Him by spending time with Him through Bible study and prayer. As you communicate with Him and He with you, He works His will and character into you so that you grow in His likeness.

Unbelievers do not understand the purpose of Bible study and prayer, and many believers give them low priority in their lives. Here are some ways you might anticipate being questioned or challenged about the importance of Bible study and prayer.

- "Why do you Christians pray? Is it like casting a spell?"
- "The thought of people praying about other people makes me uncomfortable."

HEAR IT

Step 2 (5 mins.)

Introduce the content of this session by summarizing Defining the Question. Use the computer diskette or the overhead cel to illustrate questions and comments about Bible study and prayer.

Defining the Question

- "I read the Bible every time I get into a jam."
- "I'm already saved, and God knows it. Why do I need to study the Bible and pray?"
- "A little religion is fine, but I don't have time to get involved with a lot of Bible study and prayer."
- "People who read the Bible are religious fanatics."

Jesus knew the Scriptures thoroughly and applied them to His life. He also placed a high priority on prayer by practicing it, teaching about it, and teaching His followers to pray. Following Jesus includes emulating His commitment to Bible study and prayer. This is an important message not only for you and other believers but also for non-Christians who are willing to hear that Bible study and prayer allow you to communicate with the living God of the universe.

The Bible Speaks

The Bible itself gives us solid reasons we need regular Bible study and prayer.

Bible Study

1. The Bible teaches us about ___God___.

The Bible has been called God's love letter to human beings. The Bible is one way God chose to reveal Himself to us. Paul declared that "all Scripture is God-breathed and is useful for teaching, rebuking, correcting and training in righteousness, so that the man of God may be thoroughly equipped for every good work" (2 Tim. 3:16-17). Peter wrote, "Prophecy never had its origin in the will of man, but men spoke from God as they were carried along by the Holy Spirit" (2 Pet. 1:21). The Holy Spirit guided the process of writing the Scriptures so that their message is truly God's Word, revealing His nature and His purpose for humankind.

2. The Bible is ___living___ and ___active___.

Because the Bible is inspired by God, it is "living and active. Sharper than any double-edged sword, it penetrates even to dividing soul and spirit, joints and marrow" (Heb. 4:12). The Bible is truth, penetrating to the deep secrets of our hearts. In it we find God's answers to the questions of life. It helps us see ourselves as we really are and awakens us to what God wants us to be. It delivers what it promises, and it promises to lead us as we follow its precepts. It promises to be a lamp to our feet and a light to our path (see Ps. 119:105), to be dependable (see Ps. 19:7), to discipline us (see Prov. 6:23), and to set us free (see John 8:31-32).[2]

Step 3 (20 mins.)

Direct participants to turn to page 180 in their Journals and to fill in the blanks as you present the key points in The Bible Speaks. Use the computer diskette or overhead cels.

The Bible Speaks

3. The Bible has convicting ___power___.

Hebrews 4:12 also says that God's Word "judges the thoughts and attitudes of the heart." God's Word peers into our lives, observes, judges, and determines what is right or wrong. It is a critic of our lives, the precise standard by which we are judged.[3] God will judge us by His Word. John wrote that his Gospel was "written that you may believe that Jesus is the Christ, the Son of God, and that by believing you may have life in his name" (John 20:31). Many people have come to salvation simply by reading portions of God's Word.

4. The Bible is to be ___believed___ and ___obeyed___.

Jesus expects His disciples to believe the Word: " 'If you hold to my teaching, you are really my disciples. Then you will know the truth, and the truth will set you free' " (John 8:31-32). He also expects us to obey the Word: " 'Whoever has my commands and obeys them, he is the one who loves me. He who loves me will be loved by my Father, and I too will love him and show myself to him' " (John 14:21). A disciple knows the Word and obeys the Word. We must receive it into our lives by every possible avenue: listening, reading, studying, memorizing, meditating on, and applying it. Then we prove it in our daily lives.[4]

5. The Bible helps us ___grow___ as disciples.

Jesus wants us to grow in His likeness. A primary tool the Holy Spirit uses to produce growth is God's Word. Second Timothy 3:16-17 identifies ways the Bible is used to shape us into Christ's image.
- God uses the Word to ___teach___ us (see Ps. 119:33-34). He wants us to know the truth about Himself, His acts, His character, and the way He wants us to live.
- God uses the Word to ___rebuke___ us when we depart from His teaching (see Ps. 119:67).
- God uses the Word to ___correct___ us when we stray from His teaching (see Ps. 119:176). While a rebuke is necessary when we choose the wrong way, correction comes when we have strayed from the path.
- God uses the Word to ___instruct___ us in righteousness (see Ps. 119:35-37,105-106).[5]

Prayer

1. We pray to have ___fellowship___ with God.

Prayer is not pious, empty words but sincere, from-the-heart conversation with our Heavenly Father, the One who created us, loves us, and wants to communicate with us. Prayer is two-way communication. It is more than just talking to God; we also listen to God. Paul instructs us to "pray continually" (1 Thess. 5:17), which means constantly remaining in touch with God. He wants us to openly share our attitudes, fears, desires, and frustrations, as David did in the Psalms. Communication with God allows us to enjoy an intimate, personal relationship with Him. Jesus' regular and intense prayer life demonstrated such a close relationship with His Father (see Matt. 14:23; Mark 1:35; John 17).

2. *We pray to* **worship** *God.*

Prayer acknowledges that God is the source of all material and spiritual provision in our lives (see Jas. 1:17). We are to thank Him for His blessings (see Ps. 105:1; 107:1; Eph. 1:3-9,11; 1 Thess. 5:18), and we are to worship and praise Him for His sovereignty, power, and magnificence (see 1 Chron. 29:11-12; Ps. 86:9-10; Rev. 4:11; 5:9,12; 15:3-4).

3. *We pray to ask for God's* **provision**.

Prayer expresses our dependence on God for all our needs. Jesus taught us to ask God for what we need (see Matt. 6:9-13; 7:7-11), to believe (see Matt. 21:22), and to be persistent in our prayers (see Luke 11:5-8). We are to ask for—
- physical needs (Matt. 6:11);
- protection from evil (see Matt. 6:13; 1 Cor. 10:13);
- guidance (see Luke 6:12-13);
- wisdom (see Jas. 1:5);
- strength (see (1 Chron. 16:11; Matt. 26:40-41);
- God's help (see Phil. 4:6-7; Heb. 4:16);
- God's will to be done (see Matt. 6:10);
- healing (see Jas. 5:14-16).

4. *We pray to receive* **forgiveness** *and* **salvation**.

In prayer we confess our sin in order to be forgiven. *Confess* means *speak the same thing* or *agree with*. In prayer we agree with God about our sin and His holiness. Your FAITH gospel presentation shows that a repentant lost person can pray to receive Christ (see Rom. 10:9). When believers sin, we are to confess our sin and receive God's mercy and forgiveness (see 1 John 1:9). Then our fellowship with God is restored.

5. *We pray to join God's* **work**.

God takes the initiative in prayer by drawing us to Him. He gives us the desire to pray: "It is God who works in you to will and to act according to his good purpose" (Phil. 2:13). One reason He does this is that He wants us to join His work. God is at work throughout the world where people are praying. Jesus emphasized that we accomplish God's work by asking (see Matt. 7:7; John 14:14; 15:7; 16:24). We can cooperate with God's purposes by asking for things in prayer that will advance His kingdom. We can pray for God's work in our lives and for God's work in and through others. We can pray that spiritual strongholds will be broken down and that Jesus will be lifted up locally and around the world.[6]

6. We pray to become more like ___Christ___.

Another reason God draws us to Him through prayer is so that He can develop us into the likeness of His Son. When we identify with and respond to God in prayer, He reveals Himself and His ways to us so that we can become more like Him.

- When we confess our sin, we respond to God's holiness (see Ps. 51:1-4,10,12). He wants us to be holy like Him.
- When we praise God, we respond to God's attributes (see Ps. 145:3-7). He wants us to have the same attributes.
- When we worship God, we respond to God's glory (see Ps. 42: 1-2). He wants us to acknowledge our love, adoration, reverence, and honor for Him.
- When we give thanks to God, we respond to God's riches (Ps. 136:1,6,23-26). He wants us to be grateful at all times.

Your prayer should be directed by the Holy Spirit as He reveals the kind of person God wants you to become. Pray to grow spiritually and to become like Jesus. Pray for a life that represents the Father well. Pray for characteristics God can develop in you, like Christian virtues (see Jas. 3:17), the fruit of the Spirit (see Gal. 5:22-23), and attitudes the Lord blesses (see Matt. 5:3-11).[7]

Bible study and prayer are the believer's lifeline. Through them we place ourselves in God's presence so that we can learn more about Him and His will for our lives. As you witness and minister to others, they will be able to see evidence of a life lived in close communion with the source of all life and hope.

Entry Points in FAITH Visits

Several occasions in FAITH visits offer a person an opportunity to consider the question, Why are Bible study and prayer important?

1. As you work with Team members who are learning to lead evangelistic and ministry visits, you can model the importance of depending on the Lord for everything through a vital ___devotional___ ___life___.
2. Often, knowing that you represent the church, a person during an ___evangelistic___ or ___ministry___ ___visit___ will want to know whether Bible study or prayer makes a difference

Step 4 (5 mins.)

Direct participants to turn to page 183 in their Journals and to fill in the blanks as you summarize Entry Points in FAITH Visits. Use the computer diskette or overhead cel.

Entry Points
in FAITH
Visits

in a person's life. Many people want to know solutions to life issues they are struggling with. Many have prayed but have felt that their prayers were unheard or rejected. Others have learned concepts in Scripture but do not know how to apply them to their lives.

3. Your ____**Sunday**____ ____**School**____ ____**testimony**____ is based on the impact of Bible study and prayer in your life. Many people will think of issues in their lives that could be aided by these influences. Many other persons will ask questions about the relevance of Bible study and prayer at this point.

4. The entire FAITH ____**gospel**____ ____**presentation**____ is based on the message of the Bible. Many persons will be drawn to the Bible's message and power and will want to know more about it.

5. One of the most precious opportunities a believer has is to ____**pray**____ with another person. You may have the privilege during an evangelistic visit of leading someone to pray to receive Christ. During a follow-up or ministry visit you may pray with someone about a decision to recommit to Christ or to be assured of salvation. In ministry visits you will have many opportunities to pray about life needs or crises.

How You Can Respond

Here are possible ways you can respond to the question, Why are Bible study and prayer important? during witnessing encounters. Your response will depend on the person, the situation, and the Holy Spirit's direction in this circumstance. Always keep in mind the general principles outlined on pages 28–29 in session 1.

1. Make sure that every contact is immersed in prayer. You are learning dependency on the Lord and modeling that dependency with others.
2. Be prepared to share the impact of Bible study and prayer in your life. It will be natural to relate this during your Sunday School testimony. Also be prepared to share this as part of the *Invitation.*
3. Scripture memorization is vital for leading FAITH visits. Be able to share the outline with personal understanding and conviction. As you coach Team members, realize that memory work is difficult for many persons; however, it is important to let the words of Scripture flow as natural conversation.
4. Make sure at least one Team member silently prays (with eyes open) as another Team member talks during each visit. Also make sure prayer partners are informed of the opportunities and need for prayer before and after visits.
5. Be prepared to pray with the person being visited. Be sensitive to the

Step 5 (5 mins.)

Ask accountability partners to discuss ways they would respond to a challenge or question about the importance of Bible study or prayer, using the ideas in How You Can Respond.

If you are leading students, have accountability partners role-play a situation in which one partner asks a question about the importance of Bible study and prayer and the other partner responds.

leadership of the Holy Spirit as you look for opportunities to pray with someone.

6. Bible study and prayer are vital for believers. Look for every opportunity to enroll, engage, or reengage the person in Sunday School. Look for specific opportunities to learn and report prayer concerns of the person being visited.

7. Help your Sunday School class emphasize the need for prayer. Also accentuate the need for class leaders to model Bible study as something that transforms lives.

Visitation Time

Do It

1. Think about your personal relationship with Christ and the fellowship you have with Him through Bible study and prayer. We hope and pray that everyone will enter a relationship with God through Christ Jesus, learn from Scripture, and communicate with Him through prayer. What an awesome fact to know that we have direct access to the God of the universe and that He wants to have a relationship with us. Pray that those you visit will catch a glimpse of what that relationship can mean for them.

2. All Team members should know the FAITH presentation through the Invitation.

Celebration Time

Share It

1. Ask a Team member to take the lead in sharing reports.
2. Hear reports and testimonies.
3. Complete Evaluation Cards.
4. Complete Participation Cards.
5. Update visitation forms with the results of visits.

STUDY IT

Step 6 (5 mins.)

Overview Home Study Assignments for session 11.

Transition to assemble with FAITH Teams to prepare for home visits. (5 mins.)

DO IT (110 MINS.)

SHARE IT (30 MINS.)

Home Study Assignments

Home Study Assignments reinforce this session by helping you apply what you have learned.

Your Discipleship Journey

Journaling activities in Your Discipleship Journey are an important part of your development as a Great Commission Christian through FAITH training.

1. Review the notes you have written in your FAITH Journals. Observe ways God has answered prayers and has brought Scripture to life through your journey in FAITH. If you have not been writing prayer requests and responses, begin keeping a prayer journal.

2. Pray through some of the Psalms referenced in this session. Read the verses aloud before the Lord as praise and thanksgiving.

3. Read the Model Prayer in Matthew 6:9-13. List the elements of prayer Jesus specified.

   _____

   _____

4. Matthew 5:3-11; Galatians 5:22-23; and James 3:17 identify traits God wants you to develop as Jesus' disciple. Meditate on these verses. Then pray through the following traits and ask God to develop them in you.

Blessed Attitudes *Matthew 5:3-11*	*Fruit of the Spirit* *Galatians 5:22-23*	*Christlike Virtues* *James 3:17*
Poor in spirit— dependent on God	Love	Pure
Mourn—need the Comforter	Joy	Peace-loving
Meek—humble	Peace	Considerate
Hunger for righteousness	Patience	Submissive
Merciful— forgiving, caring	Kindness	Merciful
Pure in heart— holy, clean	Goodness	Fruitful
Peacemaker— reconciler	Faithfulness	Impartial
Persecuted because of righteousness	Gentleness	Sincere
	Self-control	

Growing as a Life Witness

Growing as a Life Witness reminds you of your responsibility to witness and minister to others during the week.

1. Talk or meet with your accountability partner and share ways you have cultivated a lost person or have witnessed or ministered on occasions other than FAITH visits.
2. Discuss ways you can apply the session 11 content in witnessing.
3. Pray for lost persons by name and for each other.

Prayer Concerns	Answers to Prayer
_____	_____
_____	_____
_____	_____
_____	_____
_____	_____
_____	_____
_____	_____
_____	_____
_____	_____
_____	_____
_____	_____
_____	_____
_____	_____
_____	_____

Your Weekly Sunday School Leadership Team Meeting

A FAITH participant is an important member of Sunday School. Encourage Team members who are elected Sunday School workers to attend this weekly meeting. Use this section to record ways your FAITH Team influences the work of your Sunday School class or department. Use the information to report during weekly Sunday School leadership team meetings. Identify actions that need to be taken through Sunday School as a result of prayer concerns, needs identified, visits made by the Team, and decisions made by the persons visited. Also identify ways you can disciple others in your Sunday School class or department and in your church.

1. Highlight FAITH visit reports and discuss ways they affect your class/department or age group. Especially highlight results of any evangelistic visits.

   _____

   _____

2. Indicate any individuals/families who might attend on Sunday as a result of FAITH ministry visits. Will a FAITH Team member meet the guest? How will other class members help newcomers feel at home? If any calls to class members or to prospects need to be made before Sunday, make assignments.

   _____

   _____

3. Participate with others on your leadership team in evaluating the previous session and in discussing ways Sunday's lesson can involve members and guests in transformational Bible study and discipleship.

   _____

   _____

4. Pray for your teacher(s), department director, and others on the leadership team. Intentionally pray for all FAITH Learners, who are at the height of their memory work and leadership in home visits.

   _____

   _____

Discipling Your Team Members

This weekly feature suggests actions the Team Leader can take to support Team members, prepare for Team Time, and improve visits. This work is part of the Team Leader's Home Study Assignments. Add any actions suggested by your church's FAITH strategy.

Support Team Members

❑ Contact Team members during the week. Remind them that you are praying for them. Discuss prayer concerns and answers to prayer.

❑ Record specific needs and concerns shared by Team members.

_____

_____

_____

_____

Prepare to Lead Team Time

❑ Overview Leading Team Time for session 12.

Prepare to Lead Visits

❑ Review the FAITH Visit Outline.

❑ Be prepared to explain the benefits of and procedures for making ministry visits.

❑ Be prepared to model a visit in which Team member(s) are asked to lead in a visit to the point of the letter _H_ (HEAVEN).

❑ Be prepared to lead your Team to participate during Celebration Time.

Link with Sunday School

❑ Participate in your weekly Sunday School leadership team meeting. Share pertinent information in this meeting, using Your Weekly Sunday School Leadership Team Meeting (p. 188) and FAITH-visit results.

❑ Most Sunday Schools have no problem majoring on Bible study. What about prayer? Encourage members to develop this discipline by providing opportunities for them to study and practice prayer in their class or department.

For Further Growth

For Further Growth may include additional reading or activities that will enhance your growth as a disciple and a discipler of others. These assignments are intended to be long-term projects and do not have to be completed during this semester of study.

1. Consider leading a Bible study targeting persons who are seeking answers but are not necessarily willing to attend traditional church events.
2. Consider leading or participating in a Bible study that targets new Christians or a Bible study that equips Christians to disciple others. One application might be to help start a new Sunday School class that focuses specifically on transforming lives.
3. Study *In God's Presence* by T. W. Hunt and Claude V. King (LifeWay, 1994).
4. Study *How to Study Your Bible* by Thomas D. Lea (Convention, 1989).
5. Read the FAITH Tip on pages 191–92.

[1]Avery W. Willis, Jr., *MasterLife 1: The Disciple's Cross* (Nashville: LifeWay, 1996), 5.
[2]Roy T. Edgemon, *The Doctrines Baptists Believe* (Nashville: LifeWay, 1988), 15–16.
[3]Ibid., 16–17.
[4]Avery T. Willis, Jr., and J. David Carter, *Day by Day in God's Kingdom: A Discipleship Journal* (Nashville: LifeWay, 1997), 22.
[5]Ibid., 93–94.
[6]T. W. Hunt and Claude V. King, *In God's Presence* (Nashville: LifeWay, 1994), 14, 52.
[7]Ibid., 14, 16–17, 68–69.

FAITH TIP

Guidelines for Prayer

Guide to Thanksgiving

Thanksgiving lays the foundation for other forms of prayer. Make thanksgiving a part of every prayer.

1. The *source* of thanksgiving is grace. Thanks is our reaction when we realize that all we have, receive, and are is a gift of God's grace. It is rejoicing at what God gave when we were undeserving (see Acts 27:35; 28:15; Rom. 6:17; 1 Cor. 1:4; Col. 1:12; Rev. 11:17).
2. The *condition* of thanksgiving is agreement. Thanksgiving means that you agree with God. Thus, the Bible encourages you to give thanks in all circumstances (see 1 Thess. 5:18) and to pray about your concerns by making petitions with thanksgiving (see Phil. 4:6).
3. The *response* of thanksgiving is worship. Thanksgiving responds to God's specific acts. Praise and thanks are thus natural partners in worship (see Ps. 100:4; Heb. 13:15). Your prayers and your actions worship your Creator. When you thank God, you enter His presence, worship Him, and present an offering to Him.
4. The *occasion* for thanksgiving is everything (see Eph. 5:20). God is active in every area of your life and can show you His direction even in the darkest hour. Thanking God frees Him to work in your life through those circumstances.
5. The *reward* of thanksgiving is the enjoyment of God's blessings: peace, joy, growth, worship, and life in Christ. If you have trouble giving thanks, ask the Spirit to fill you (see Eph. 5:18-20).[1]

Guide to Praise

Praise and thanksgiving are two ways to glorify God, but each has a different focus. Praise is adoring God for who He is—His person, character, and attributes. Thanksgiving is expressing gratitude to God for what He has done—His actions. Thanksgiving leads to praise. Thank God in everything and praise Him continually.

Why Should You Praise God?

1. God should be praised by His people (see Ps. 22:3; Rev. 19:5).
2. Praise is our gift (sacrifice) to God (see 1 Pet. 2:5; Heb. 13:15).
3. God saved us to glorify Him (see Ps. 50:23; Isa. 43:21).
4. Praise is commanded (see 1 Chron. 16:28-29; Ps. 147—150).
5. Praise prepares us for what we will do in heaven (see Rev. 5:9-14; 7:9-17).

How Should You Praise God?

1. Bless, glorify, praise, and adore God, using your own words.

2. Use scriptural prayers to glorify God.

3. Use spiritual psalms, hymns, and songs (see Eph. 5:18-19).

4. Use instruments to praise Him (1 Chron. 15:16; Ps. 150).

5. Recount God's glorious acts. This differs from thanksgiving in that it speaks of past acts as manifestations of God's glory.

What Should You Say When You Praise God?

1. Read aloud and pray the following prayers of praise and adoration.
   - Glorify God's person, character, and attributes (see Pss. 8; 19; 24; 65; 92; 104; 139).
   - Praise God's goodness (see Ps. 9; 30; 108; 138; Ex. 15:1-19; 1 Sam. 2:1-10; 1 Chron. 29:10-19; Luke 1:46-55).
   - Encourage others to honor Him (see Luke 19:37-38; Eph. 3: 20-21; 1 Tim. 1:17; Jude 25; Rev. 5:9-14; 7:9-12; 15:3-4; 19:1-7).

2. Use words of praise such as *worship*, *adore*, *bless*, *exalt*, *magnify*, *laud*, *extol*, *glorify*, and *honor*.[2]

Guide to Intercession

Intercession is the ministry of a disciple and the community of faith to bring to God the needs of the church and the world. It can result in changed lives, changed churches, and a changed world.

1. Spend much of your prayer time in intercession (see 1 Tim. 2:1).

2. Incorporate all types of prayer with your intercession, including praise, thanksgiving, and requests.

3. Intercede for all people (see 1 Tim. 2:2-4).

4. Intercede with an all-embracing purpose. Intercession is not limited to specific needs and crises. Intercession should seek salvation, peace, godliness, quietness, and holiness for all people (see 1 Tim. 2:5-7).

5. Pray in unity with other disciples (see 1 Tim. 2:8).

6. Pray on the basis of God's character.

7. Stand before God in place of the person in need, ready to sacrifice yourself to have the need met, as Moses, Paul, and Jesus did.

8. Persevere until you prevail (see Luke 11:5-13).

9. Remember that the Lord Himself is your partner in intercession (see John 17; Rom. 8:26-27).

10. Remain confident, for the promise of intercession is sure (see Matt. 7:7; Jas. 5:16).[3]

[1]Avery T. Willis, Jr., *MasterLife 3: The Disciple's Victory* (Nashville: LifeWay, 1996), 13.
[2]Ibid., 36–37.
[3]Ibid., 100.

Practicing FAITH

In this session you will—

CHECK IT by spending the entire time in extended Team Time/practice activities;

STUDY IT by overviewing Home Study Assignments;

DO IT by making visits in which a Team member may take the lead;

SHARE IT by celebrating.

In Advance

- Decide whether you wish to help Teams practice by reviewing previously viewed video segments of the FAITH Visit Outline from *A Journey in FAITH*.
- Pray for team members as they begin taking the lead in visits.

TEAM TIME

CHECK IT (60 MINS.)

CHECK IT agenda:
✔ FAITH Visit Outline

Leading Team Time

All teams remain together during this session for an extended Team Time. All Team members participate in Team Time. They are primarily responsible for reciting the assigned portion of the FAITH Visit Outline and for discussing other Home Study Assignments.

As you direct this important time of CHECK IT activities with your Team, keep in mind how Learners also look to you as a role model, motivator, mentor, and friend. Team Time activities can continue in the car as the Team travels to and from visits.

Lead CHECK IT Activities

✔ FAITH Visit Outline

Spend the entire time with your Team members, leading them to practice the entire FAITH Visit Outline. Consider rehearsing appropriate approaches to take in strengthening the skills and confidence of Learners in leading the visit. It may be helpful to suggest that the Team role-play several situations your Team or others have encountered during FAITH training.

FAITH Visit Outline

Preparation

INTRODUCTION
INTERESTS
INVOLVEMENT

Church Experience/Background

- Ask about the person's church background.
- Listen for clues about the person's spiritual involvement.

Sunday School Testimony

- Tell general benefits of Sunday School.
- Tell a current personal experience.

Evangelistic Testimony

- Tell a little of your preconversion experience.
- Say: "I had a life-changing experience."
- Tell recent benefits of your conversion.

INQUIRY

Key Question: In your personal opinion, what do you understand it takes for a person to go to heaven?

Possible Answers: Faith, works, unclear, no opinion

Transition Statement: I'd like to share with you how the Bible answers this question, if it is all right. There is a word that can be used to answer this question: FAITH (spell out on fingers).

Presentation

F IS FOR FORGIVENESS

We cannot have eternal life and heaven without God's forgiveness.

"In Him [meaning Jesus] we have redemption through His blood, the forgiveness of sins"—Ephesians 1:7a, NKJV.

A is for AVAILABLE

Forgiveness is available. It is—

AVAILABLE FOR ALL

"For God so loved the world that He gave His only begotten Son, that whoever believes in Him should not perish but have everlasting life"—John 3:16, NKJV.

BUT NOT AUTOMATIC

"Not everyone who says to Me, 'Lord, Lord,' shall enter the kingdom of heaven"—Matthew 7:21a, NKJV.

I is for IMPOSSIBLE

It is impossible for God to allow sin into heaven.

GOD IS—

- LOVE

  John 3:16, NKJV

- JUST

  "For judgment is without mercy"—James 2:13a, NKJV.

MAN IS SINFUL

"For all have sinned and fall short of the glory of God"—Romans 3:23, NKJV.

Question: But how can a sinful person enter heaven, where God allows no sin?

T is for TURN

Question: If you were driving down the road and someone asked you to turn, what would he or she be asking you to do? (change direction)

Turn means repent.

TURN from something—sin and self

"But unless you repent you will all likewise perish"—Luke 13:3b, NKJV.

TURN to Someone; trust Christ only

(The Bible tells us that) *"Christ died for our sins according to the Scriptures, and that He was buried, and that He rose again the third day according to the Scriptures"—1 Corinthians 15:3b-4, NKJV.*

"If you confess with your mouth the Lord Jesus and believe in your heart that God has raised Him from the dead, you will be saved"—Romans 10:9, NKJV.

H is for HEAVEN

Heaven is eternal life.

HERE

"I have come that they may have life, and that they may have it more abundantly"—John 10:10b, NKJV.

HEREAFTER

"And if I go and prepare a place for you, I will come again and receive you to Myself; that where I am, there you may be also"—John 14:3, NKJV.

HOW

How can a person have God's forgiveness, heaven and eternal life, and Jesus as personal Savior and Lord?

Explain based on leaflet picture, FAITH (Forsaking All, I Trust Him), Romans 10:9.

Invitation

INQUIRE

Understanding what we have shared, would you like to receive this forgiveness by trusting in Christ as your personal Savior and Lord?

INVITE

- Pray to accept Christ.
- Pray for commitment/recommitment.
- Invite to join Sunday School.

INSURE

- Use *A Step of Faith* to insure decision.
- Personal Acceptance
- Sunday School Enrollment
- Public Confession

Notes

_____

_____

_____

_____

_____

_____

_____

_____

Actions I Need to Take with Learners During the Week

_____

_____

_____

_____

_____

_____

_____

STUDY IT

Overview Home Study Assignments for session 12. (5 mins.)

Transition to prepare for home visits. (5 mins.)

DO IT (110 MINS.)

SHARE IT (30 MINS.)

Visitation Time

Do It

Throughout FAITH you have been preparing your Team members to take the lead in a visit. Make sure Team members are informed that they will take the lead in specific visits. As always, be prepared to assist, but do everything you can to encourage the person to lead the entire visit.

Celebration Time

Share It

1. Ask a Team member to take the lead in sharing reports.
2. Hear reports and testimonies.
3. Complete Evaluation Cards.
4. Complete Participation Cards.
5. Update visitation forms with the results of visits.

Home Study Assignments

Home Study Assignments reinforce this session by helping you apply what you have learned.

Your Discipleship Journey

Journaling activities in Your Discipleship Journey are an important part of your development as a Great Commission Christian through FAITH training.

1. Read the following Scripture passages. On the lines provided, list ways you can become a more effective witness and equip others to become effective witnesses even when faced with difficult questions or situations.

   Matthew 9:36-38: _____

   _____

   Matthew 28:19-20: _____

   _____

   Mark 8:1-9a: _____

   _____

   Acts 1:8: _____

   _____

   Ephesians 5:15-20: _____

   _____

   1 Peter 3:8-18: _____

   _____

2. In the following categories record some of your experiences this semester for which you can be thankful and praise God.

   Your growth as a disciple: _____

   _____

   _____

Experiences of your Team members: _____

_____

_____

_____

Persons your Team has visited: _____

_____

_____

_____

Growing as a Life Witness

Growing as a Life Witness reminds you of your responsibility to witness and minister to others during the week.

1. Talk or meet with your accountability partner and share ways you have cultivated a lost person or have witnessed or ministered on occasions other than FAITH visits.
2. Review together your responses to activity 2 in Your Discipleship Journey. Spend time thanking and praising God for results you have seen this semester in the three areas identified.
3. Pray for lost persons by name and for each other.

Prayer Concerns	Answers to Prayer
_____	_____
_____	_____
_____	_____
_____	_____
_____	_____
_____	_____
_____	_____

Your Weekly Sunday School Leadership Team Meeting

A FAITH participant is an important member of Sunday School. Encourage Team members who are elected Sunday School workers to attend this weekly meeting. Use this section to record ways your FAITH Team influences the work of your Sunday School class or department. Use the information to report during weekly Sunday School leadership team meetings. Identify actions that need to be taken through Sunday School as a result of prayer concerns, needs identified, visits made by the Team, and decisions made by the persons visited. Also identify ways you can disciple others in your Sunday School class or department and in your church.

1. As a result of FAITH visits this week, have any ministry needs surfaced? Any cultivation opportunities? Any need to share information with other departments or age groups for appropriate follow-up? Record actions that need to be taken.

   _____

   _____

   _____

2. When Christians who have previously been reluctant to share their faith become confident and intentional in doing so, 2 Timothy 2:1-2 is made personal. Celebrate as a group if any Learners took the lead in a FAITH visit and had the opportunity to share the FAITH gospel presentation. How did that Learner respond to that opportunity?

   _____

   _____

3. With others on your leadership team, evaluate last week's session. Discuss ways Sunday's lesson can involve members and guests in transformational Bible study and discipleship.

   _____

   _____

4. Evaluate the extent to which department/class leaders and members are following up on prospects being contacted through FAITH visits. What actions need to be started or strengthened to better assimilate newcomers into the Sunday School department or class?

_____

_____

_____

_____

5. Pray for your teacher(s) and department director. Also pray for any individual contacted through FAITH who is still considering a decision for Christ. Record names here.

_____

_____

Discipling Your Team Members

This weekly feature suggests actions the Team Leader can take to support Team members, prepare for Team Time, and improve visits. This work is part of the Team Leader's Home Study Assignments. Add any actions suggested by your church's FAITH strategy.

Support Team Members

❑ Pray for and personally follow up on any Learner who may need personal encouragement.

❑ Contact Team members during the week to remind them that you are praying for them and to discuss their participation in FAITH.

❑ Learners are taking the lead in making the visits from this point on. Look for opportunities to encourage each Team member about ways he or she is successfully leading in the visit. Continue to identify ways each Learner can improve.

Prepare to Lead Time Time

❑ Overview Leading Team Time for session 13.

Prepare to Participate in Visits

❑ Review the FAITH Visit Outline.

❑ Identify the Team member who will be responsible for leading specific visits.

❑ Be prepared to lead your Team to participate during Celebration Time. Look for ways to encourage Team members to take the lead in reporting during Celebration Time.

Link with Sunday School

❑ Participate in your weekly Sunday School leadership team meeting. Share pertinent information in this meeting, using Your Weekly Sunday School Leadership Team Meeting (p. 201) and FAITH-visit results.

For Further Growth

For Further Growth may include additional reading or activities that will enhance your growth as a disciple and a discipler of others. These assignments are intended to be long-term projects and do not have to be completed during this semester of study.

1. Read "Four Areas of Results (pp. 67–77) in *Evangelism Through the Sunday School* by Bobby Welch (LifeWay, 1997). As you think about these four areas of results, think about how you can handle difficult questions and help Team Learners become more confident in dealing with difficult questions.
2. Read the FAITH Tip "How Can People Be Assimilated into a Class?" (pp. 187–88) in *Building Bridges Through FAITH Journal.* Plan ways your Sunday School can intentionally assimilate new members into the class or department. Consider studying one of the resources listed at the end of the FAITH Tip.
3. Read the FAITH Tip on page 204.

FAITH TIP

The Key to Spiritual Transformation

In that stunning moment when Mary held the Baby Jesus in her arms for the first time and kissed his soft skin, did she know that she was kissing the very face of God? Did she know that, for the first time in history, a mere human was face to face, heart to heart with Almighty God?

Jesus, in whom you have placed your faith, is truly God, who became visible so that you can ultimately know Him (see John 1:14). He is Lord of all creation (see Col. 1:15-16) and the great I AM. As a follower of Jesus, you are relating one-to-one with Almighty God Himself, not a mere representative of God. Jesus is God. In John 10:30 Jesus made it dramatically clear: " 'I and the Father are one.' " In Colossians 1:17-23 Paul established that Jesus is central to all things. To know Jesus is to come face to face, heart to heart with God Himself. He is the message of hope to the lost world. And He is the key to your spiritual transformation.

Making Jesus central in your life necessitates a radical reordering of your goals, your ambitions, and your relationships. Paul summarized his own radically transformed life this way: "I have been crucified with Christ and I no longer live, but Christ lives in me. The life I live in the body, I live by faith in the Son of God, who loved me and gave himself for me" (Gal. 2:20).

Maybe you think you can never transform your life to be like Jesus. You can't, but God can. He is the key to your transformation—not you. Just as the Spirit of God used the Word of God to convict you of sin and to convince you to repent of your sin, it is God who brings spiritual transformation in your life. Paul's change from persecutor to evangelist dramatically proves what can happen when a person turns from sin and allows God to turn life around. You see, a transformed life is not simply attained by mimicking Jesus' actions. It is letting God change you from the inside out so that Christ is formed in you (see Gal. 4:19). True spiritual transformation requires a repentant heart and a faithful understanding of Jesus' statement " 'Apart from me you can do nothing' " (John 15:5).

Ask God to dispel any belief you might have that spiritual transformation is impossible. Lay your life before Him and humbly ask Him to change you from the inside out. Acknowledge that you can do nothing to make this change happen. All God requires from you is a repentant, faithful heart. He will do the rest. He did it with Paul. He will do it with you.[1]

---

[1] Roy Edgemon and Barry Sneed, "Do You Know?" *Jesus by Heart* (Nashville: LifeWay, 1999), 17–19.

What Is the Purpose of Life?

In this session you will—

CHECK IT by engaging in Team Time activities;

KNOW IT by reviewing content from session 11;

HEAR IT by affirming what the Bible says about the purpose of life;

SEE IT by viewing a video segment;

SAY IT by discussing possible applications of what you have learned in this session;

STUDY IT by overviewing Home Study Assignments;

DO IT by leading your Team in making visits;

SHARE IT by celebrating.

In Advance

- Overview content.
- Preview teaching suggestions. Prepare key points. Decide whether to use the session 13 computer slides or the overhead cels.
- Prepare the room for teaching.
- Cue the videotape to the session 13 segment, Baby Daze.
- Pray for participants and for Teams as they prepare to visit.
- As Teaching Time begins, direct participants to open their Journals to page 208.

Leading Team Time

All Team members participate in Team Time. They are primarily responsible for reciting the assigned portion of the FAITH Visit Outline and for discussing other Home Study Assignments.

As you direct this important time of CHECK IT activities with your Team, keep in mind that Learners look to you as a role model, motivator, mentor, and friend. Team Time activities can continue in the car as the Team travels to and from visits.

Lead CHECK IT Activities

✔ FAITH Visit Outline
❑ Listen while each Learner recites the FAITH Visit Outline. Because there is no new memory work, it may be best to ask Learners to recite the segment they have the most difficulty sharing during a visit.

✔ Session 11 Debriefing
❑ Because session 12 was a practice session with no new material, debrief session 11. Session 11 focused on the important time when a person is given the opportunity to personally accept God's forgiveness and salvation, so it is important that Team members be well trained. It is even more important that they grow in their sensitivity to the Holy Spirit's prompting during visitation.
❑ Discuss ways Team members are finding A *Step of Faith* helpful in prompting discussion in a visit. If time permits, allow Team members to practice the **Invitation,** using A *Step of Faith*.

✔ Help for Strengthening a Visit
❑ Discuss difficulties the Team has encountered in leading someone to hear and consider the FAITH gospel presentation. Evaluate ways the Team responded to selected experiences and identify appropriate ways to improve responses. Indicate that, while most visits go smoothly, next week's session will help all Team members better handle challenges in a visit. Difficulties are things that happen or are said that could keep you from sharing the gospel and leading someone who is ready to respond to make a commitment to Christ. Principles for dealing with difficulties relate primarily to building bridges of relationships with the person, dealing with questions and objections, and working through the obstacles and distractions that take place.
❑ As you talk with Team members during the week, share ways you are seeking to take advantage of the daily-life witnessing opportunities

you have. Also talk with them about opportunities they have to share the gospel during the week with persons they encounter.

Notes

_____

_____

_____

_____

_____

_____

_____

Actions I Need to Take with Learners During the Week

_____

_____

_____

_____

_____

_____

_____

Transition to classrooms for
instruction on the content of
the session. (5 mins.)

TEACHING TIME

KNOW IT

Step 1 (5 mins.)

Direct participants to locate A Quick Review on page 208 in their Journals and to complete the activities. Then give the answers, using the computer diskette or the overhead cel. Possible answers to question:

1. Questions during evangelistic or ministry visits
2. Sunday School testimony
3. Entire FAITH Visit Outline
4. Opportunities to pray

A Quick
Review

A Quick Review

In session 11 you learned reasons Bible study and prayer are important. Recall what you learned as you complete the following review quiz.

Bible Study

Beside each statement write *T* for *true* or *F* for *false*.

F 1. The Bible teaches us how to succeed by human initiative.

T 2. The Bible is living and active.

T 3. The Bible has convicting power.

F 4. God considers it more important for us to read the Bible than to obey it.

F 5. No matter how much you read the Bible, the primary ways to grow as a disciple are through intuition and good deeds.

Prayer

Fill in the blanks.

1. We pray to have _____**fellowship**_____ with God.
2. We pray to _____**worship**_____ God.
3. We pray to ask for God's _____**provision**_____.
4. We pray to receive _____**forgiveness**_____ and _____**salvation**_____.
5. We pray to join God's _____**work**_____.
6. We pray to become more like _____**Christ**_____.

What are two places in FAITH visits when questions about or challenges to the importance of Bible study and prayer might arise?

1. _____ 2. _____

Check appropriate ways to respond to the question, Why are Bible study and prayer important?

☐ 1. Explain that Bible study and prayer are primary ways to earn salvation.

☑ 2. Make sure every contact is immersed in prayer.

☑ 3. Share the impact of Bible study and prayer in your life.

☑ 4. Memorize the Scriptures in the FAITH Visit Outline so that they flow naturally.

☐ 5. Tell a lost person that prayer imparts magical powers to the person praying.

☐ 6. Tell a lost person that Bible study results in material wealth.

☑ 7. Make sure Team members and prayer partners pray during visits.

☑ 8. Pray with the person being visited.

☑ 9. Look for opportunities to involve persons in Sunday School.

☑ 10. Emphasize the need for prayer in Sunday School classes.

Defining the Question: What Is the Purpose of Life?

This question is one of life's most basic questions for both believers and nonbelievers. The way you answer this question determines all of your values and decisions in life:

- Your motives
- Your priorities
- The commitments you are willing to make
- The way you view yourself
- The way you relate to others
- The way you view and relate to God

Here are some ways you might anticipate being questioned or challenged about a biblical view of our purpose in life.

- "What is the meaning of life?"
- "My philosophy is eat, drink, and be merry."
- "The one who dies with the most toys wins."
- "Is there really any happiness in life?"
- "I find meaning by alleviating physical suffering."
- "Discover your inner potential in order to be all you can be."
- "There's nothing like owning your own corporation and calling all the shots."

These comments reveal a variety of life philosophies that are prevalent in our society. Many nonbelievers have discovered that these philosophies just don't satisfy. You have the opportunity to assure them that life indeed has meaning, which can be found only by fulfilling the purposes God created for them.

The Bible Speaks

The Bible shows us life philosophies that do not satisfy and teaches the profound purposes God intended us to find in a relationship with Him.

The World's Solution

Long ago King Solomon wrestled with the questions of purpose and meaning in life. He recorded his thoughts and findings in the Book of Ecclesiastes. Because of his wealth and position, Solomon was able to try a variety of pursuits in an effort to find purpose. He came to the following conclusions while searching for a sense of purpose in life.

1. __Knowledge__ *doesn't satisfy.*
Solomon was known for his knowledge and wisdom. In fact, he had

HEAR IT

Step 2 (5 mins.)

Introduce the content of this session by summarizing Defining the Question. Use the computer diskette or the overhead cel to illustrate questions and comments about the purpose of life.

Defining
the Question

Step 3 (10 mins.)

Direct participants to turn to page 209 in their Journals and to fill in the blanks as you present the key points in The Bible Speaks. Use the computer diskette or the overhead cel.

The Bible
Speaks

received a special, God-given portion of wisdom (see 1 Kings 4:29-34). However, knowledge made Solomon more aware of human pain and of the futility of human pursuits. He concluded,

> With much wisdom comes much sorrow;
> the more knowledge, the more grief (Eccl. 1:18).

In addition, both the foolish and wise die and are forgotten (see Eccl. 2:16).

2. _____Pleasure_____ *doesn't satisfy.*

Solomon pursued pleasure through laughter, wine, buildings, gardens, servants, music, and sex (see Eccl. 2:1-10). Yet the pursuit of pleasure and things results in meaninglessness. Solomon concluded,

> Yet when I surveyed all that my hands had done
> and what I had toiled to achieve,
> everything was meaningless, a chasing after the wind;
> nothing was gained under the sun (Eccl. 2:11).

Although there is some delight in the pursuit of pleasure, the feeling is short-lived and found only in the pursuit. When the pursuit ends, so does the enjoyment of it.

3. _____Work_____ *doesn't satisfy.*

We all know individuals whose careers are their lives. Solomon tried this lifestyle and came to an exciting conclusion—it isn't worth it. He stated that the results of an individual's work are not usually enjoyed by that individual but by an heir who has not earned these things and who may be a fool (see Eccl. 2:17-21). Solomon also pointed out that there is always more work to do and that the person who pursues work never finds rest (see Eccl. 2:22-23).

God's Solution

At the end of his quest for purpose Solomon concluded:

> Fear God and keep his commandments,
> for this is the whole duty of man.
> For God will bring every deed into judgment,
> including every hidden thing,
> whether it is good or evil (Eccl. 12:13-14).

Solomon admonished his readers to fear and obey God. Both ideas convey an awareness of God's judgment of our sin and an acknowledgment of God's identity as our loving Creator. Solomon recognized that God created us and that we find our purpose in relationship with Him. The Bible teaches us that we were created for three purposes.

1. We were created to have an intimate relationship with ___God___.

God created humans in His image (see Gen. 1:26). One way we are like God is that we are relational beings. God designed us to enjoy a relationship with Him, as seen in Adam and Eve's intimate fellowship with Him in the garden. Throughout history God has desired an intimate relationship of love with His children (see Deut. 6:4-5; 30:19-20). That is still His desire today, and it is possible through Jesus Christ (see John 3:16; 1 John 4:9-10,19). In Revelation 3:20 Jesus says, " 'Here I am! I stand at the door and knock. If anyone hears my voice and opens the door, I will come in and eat with him, and he with me.' "

When we have a relationship with God, we want to—
- love Him (see Mark 12:30);
- remain in His presence (see John 15:5);
- acknowledge His lordship (see Phil. 2:10-11);
- grow in knowledge of Him (see 2 Pet. 3:18);
- adopt His character (see Rom. 12:1-2; Gal. 5:22-23; Eph. 5:1-18);
- live for Him (see Phil. 1:21);
- build His kingdom (Matt. 6:33);
- thank, praise, and glorify Him (Eph. 1:12; Phil. 4:6; 1 Pet. 2:9);
- serve Him (see 1 Pet. 4:10);
- follow His commands (see John 14:21);
- show the way to Him (see Matt. 5:16);
- sacrifice for Him (see Rom. 8:17-18; 2 Tim. 2:3).

This is our purpose: to have fellowship with our Creator. Life has no meaning apart from this relationship.

2. We were created to have relationships with ___one___ ___another___.

Another purpose of life is to relate to others who are created in God's image. God created us male and female to complement and fulfill each other (see Gen. 2:20-25). Marriage is not a social arrangement but part of God's created purpose for humanity. We also enjoy relationships with parents, children, siblings, cousins, and friends.

Our relationships with others can be fully understood only in light of a relationship with God. To carry out His will for our relationships, we want to—
- love one another (see John 13:34-35);
- pray for one another (see Eph. 6:18);
- love our enemies (see Matt. 5:43-48);
- forgive one another (see Matt. 6:14);
- live at peace (see Matt. 5:21-24; 1 Thess. 5:13);

- be kind to one another (see Eph. 4:31-32);
- be patient with one another (see 1 Thess. 5:14);
- minister to others (see Matt. 19:21);
- submit to one another (Eph. 5:21);
- encourage one another (see Heb. 10:25).
- bring others to Christ (see Rom. 10:15).

Although human relationships add to our lives, they take on an eternal dimension when the individuals have personal relationships with God. As Christians, we have the same Father, the same faith, the same Holy Spirit, and the same destiny. When we are faithful to lead others to Christ, we are developing relationships that will last throughout our lives on earth and into eternity!

3. We were created to have responsibility for ___creation___ .

God ordained that human beings rule over His creation (see Gen. 1:26). Because humans are created in God's image, we are unique from the rest of creation. Humans alone have the abilities needed—intellect, emotion, spirit, and free will—to rule over God's creation.

This purpose is connected to our relationship with God. Only by relating to God can we fully understand our role and responsibility in managing His creation. To relate properly to God's creation, we want to—
- worship the Creator rather than the creation itself (see Ps. 8:3; Rom. 1:18-25);
- care for animals, plants, and natural resources (see Gen. 1:28-30);
- seek to understand science and explore how creation works (see Gen. 1:28-30);
- give proper meaning and priority to work (see Eccl. 2:24-25);
- give proper meaning and priority to material possessions (see Luke 12:16-21);
- be good stewards of time, talents, and gifts (see Rom. 12:4-8; Eph. 5:15-16);
- respect the sanctity of life (see Ps. 139:13-16; Amos 5: 7,11-12,14).

As God's creation, we find fulfillment only in a relationship with the One who created us. This relationship helps us understand who we are and why we are here. It guides our relationships with others. It establishes our responsibilities for taking care of the created order. It defines our values. It orders our priorities in life. It places all human pursuits in proper perspective. It is a relationship so valuable that God's Son gave His life to make it possible. When we share that truth, others can know the sense of purpose that a relationship with God affords.

Entry Points in FAITH Visits

Several occasions in FAITH visits offer a person an opportunity to consider the question, What is the purpose of life?

1. You can get a glimpse into the purpose of many persons' lives as you approach their house or apartment. The ____**INTERESTS**____ portion of the visit gives you an opportunity to learn a person's priorities. Occasionally, a person will be open to share values and life philosophies.

2. When conducting ____**Opinion**____ ____**Poll**____ visits, you may be asked why you are doing this. This may indicate a person's curiosity about your purpose in life.

3. As you focus on the ____**INVOLVEMENT**____ of the person in church or religious experiences, you often introduce an opportunity for a person to associate religion with a search for meaning or purpose in life.

4. ____**Sunday**____ ____**School**____ and ____**evangelistic**____ ____**testimonies**____ provide forums for you to share the basis for meaning in your life. Many persons will consider life's priorities as you or a Team member shares.

5. God uses the ____**Key**____ ____**Question**____ in many ways to help a person consider the ultimate purpose of life. As you listen to the person's response, you can identify how a person seeks meaning.

6. During ____**ministry**____ ____**visits**____ you often hear persons raise issues and questions about meaning in life. Persons experiencing crises or life transitions ordinarily reflect on the meaning of life. Many persons look for someone with whom they can share their struggles.

7. By sharing the ____**Invitation**____, you give the person an opportunity to focus on bringing purpose and meaning into life.

How You Can Respond

Here are possible ways you can respond to the question, What is the purpose of life? during witnessing encounters. Your response will depend on the person, the situation, and the Holy Spirit's direction in this circumstance. Always keep in mind the general principles outlined on pages 28–29 in session 1.

1. Listen for questions about purpose in life that may be hidden in a response to another question. Be willing to take time to depart from the FAITH Visit Outline to answer questions or to follow up on nonverbal clues indicating that a person wants to discuss this issue.

Step 4 (5 mins.)

Direct participants to turn to page 213 in their Journals and to fill in the blanks as you summarize Entry Points in FAITH Visits. Use the computer diskette or the overhead cel.

Entry Points in FAITH Visits

SEE IT

Step 5 (10 mins.)

To focus on ways witnesses can respond to questions about purpose in life, show the session 14 video segment, Baby Daze. Ask participants to make notes in the margins of their Journals. Remind members that the video vignette does not present a model that can be used in all witnessing situations. Rather, it is one example of a situation that can arise and the type of response that may be suitable in this situation.

SAY IT

Step 6 (5 mins.)

Ask accountability partners to discuss ways they would respond to a challenge or question about the purpose of life, using the ideas in the video and in How You Can Respond.

If you are leading students, have accountability partners role-play a situation in which one partner asks a question about the purpose of life and the other partner responds.

STUDY IT

Step 7 (5 mins.)

Overview Home Study Assignments for session 13.

Transition to assemble with FAITH Teams to prepare for home visits. (5 mins.)

DO IT (110 MINS.)

SHARE IT (30 MINS.)

If you are comfortable with the outline, you can deal with questions and continue with the outline as appropriate.

2. Always be prepared to share Sunday School and evangelistic testimonies. By following up these testimonies with the Key Question, you invite a person to consider ways to bring meaning to life through a relationship with God.

3. Invite persons at every opportunity to enroll in Sunday School. This provides a vehicle for a person to investigate ways to bring meaning and purpose to life by studying and applying God's Word. Encourage persons who are already Sunday School members to attend and participate in Bible study, fellowship, and ministry.

4. Share ministry opportunities available through your Sunday School class and church. Emphasize that meaning in life is discovered as they seek to apply the truth of Scripture by ministering to other believers as well as by receiving ministry.

5. Enlist supportive Sunday School members to build relationships with persons making any kind of commitment. Follow-up and discipleship will direct them to pursuits that will reinforce the decision they have made to discover meaning in life through a relationship with God.

Visitation Time

Do It

1. As you make visits with your Team, look and listen for clues about the priorities of the individuals you are visiting. Consider ways these might reveal their ideas of purpose in life.

2. Remember that a search for purpose in life without Christ is futile. You have an opportunity to point people to Christ and to help them discover purpose in life. Thank God for allowing you to have this privilege and for using you to make a difference in lives.

3. Learners should have memorized the entire FAITH outline. Provide opportunities to let them share in FAITH visits.

Celebration Time

Share It

1. Ask a Team member to take the lead in sharing reports.
2. Hear reports and testimonies.
3. Complete Evaluation Cards.
4. Complete Participation Cards.
5. Update visitation forms with the results of visits.

Home Study Assignments

Home Study Assignments reinforce this session by helping you apply what you have learned.

Your Discipleship Journey

Journaling activities in Your Discipleship Journey are an important part of your development as a Great Commission Christian through FAITH training.

1. Read Matthew 4:1-11. Record the way Jesus' knowledge of His purpose in life determined His responses to Satan in the following areas.

   Motives: _____

   Priorities: _____

   Commitments: _____

   View of self: _____

   View of God: _____

2. Read Jeremiah 29:11-13. What do these verses say about God's purpose for your life?

   What God will do: _____

   What you can do: _____

3. Consider what you have studied this week and write a purpose statement for your life.

   _____

   _____

   _____

   _____

4. Record the number of hours you spend each week on the following activities.

   Sleeping _____ Eating _____

   Working _____ Leisure _____

   Spiritual life _____ Relationships _____

How do your priorities reflect your life purpose?

_____

What adjustments do you need to make to bring your life in line with God's purpose for your life?

_____

_____

5. You can find meaning in life by growing in Christ and by helping others grow in their relationships with Him. Read 2 Timothy 2:1-2 and identify ways you can invest your life in another person's to bring encouragement, blessing, and strength.

_____

_____

Growing as a Life Witness

Growing as a Life Witness reminds you of your responsibility to witness and minister to others during the week.

1. Talk or meet with your accountability partner and share ways you have cultivated a lost person or have witnessed or ministered on occasions other than FAITH visits.
2. Discuss ways your responses to activity 5 in Your Discipleship Journey apply to your responsibilities as Team Leaders and as Sunday School members.
3. Pray for lost persons by name and for each other.

Prayer Concerns	Answers to Prayer
_____	_____
_____	_____
_____	_____
_____	_____
_____	_____

Your Weekly Sunday School Leadership Team Meeting

A FAITH participant is an important member of Sunday School. Encourage Team members who are elected Sunday School workers to attend this weekly meeting. Use this section to record ways your FAITH Team influences the work of your Sunday School class or department. Use the information to report during weekly Sunday School leadership team meetings. Identify actions that need to be taken through Sunday School as a result of prayer concerns, needs identified, visits made by the Team, and decisions made by the persons visited. Also identify ways you can disciple others in your Sunday School class or department and in your church.

1. Highlight FAITH visit results and discuss needs that affect your class/ department or age group. Are prospect-discovery activities continuing to generate good prospect information?

   _____

2. Participate with others on your leadership team in evaluating last week's session and in discussing ways Sunday's lesson can involve members and guests in transformational Bible study and discipleship.

   _____

3. How does preparation for Sunday need to consider the needs of individuals or families visited through FAITH?

   _____

4. In what ways can the truths you discovered in this session be communicated with the rest of your Sunday School leadership team? With fellow class members?

   _____

5. Discuss ways to involve members in praying for and celebrating God's leadership in raising up new persons to begin FAITH training.
6. Pray for your teacher and other leadership. Request prayer for any persons contacted through Opinion Poll visits.

Discipling Your Team Members

This weekly feature suggests actions the Team Leader can take to support Team members, prepare for Team Time, and improve visits. This work is part of the Team Leader's Home Study Assignments. Add any actions suggested by your church's FAITH strategy.

Support Team Members
❑ Contact Team members during the week. Remind them that you are praying for them. Discuss prayer concerns and answers to prayer.
❑ As you talk with Learners this week, discuss opportunities they have for witnessing during the week. Encourage them as they seek to witness to persons they encounter.
❑ Record specific needs and concerns shared by Team members.

Prepare to Lead Team Time
❑ Review Team members' Home Study Assignments.
❑ Overview Leading Team Time for session 14.

Prepare to Lead Visits
❑ Review the FAITH Visit Outline.

Link with Sunday School
❑ Participate in your weekly Sunday School leadership team meeting. Share pertinent information in this meeting, using Your Weekly Sunday School Leadership Team Meeting (p. 217) and FAITH-visit results.
❑ Ask Sunday School leaders to think about others who may become involved in FAITH training.
❑ No matter what the topic of study is in Sunday School, remember to relate lessons to God's larger purposes for members' lives. Remind members that their purposes are different from those of nonbelievers. Clearly present practical ways their priorities and values can reflect God's purposes for their lives.

For Further Growth
For Further Growth may include additional reading or activities that will enhance your growth as a disciple and a discipler of others. These assignments are intended to be long-term projects and do not have to be completed during this semester of study.
1. Participate in a group study of *Experiencing God: Knowing and Doing the Will of God* by Henry T. Blackaby and Claude V. King (LifeWay, 1990) or *Search for Significance, LIFE Support Edition* by Robert S. McGee (LifeWay, 1992).
2. As you read the Book of Ecclesiastes, list the things Solomon pursued in an attempt to find meaning. Also list reasons these things could not provide lasting meaning.
3. Read Psalm 139 and identify what the psalm teaches about our relationship with God and His purpose for us.
4. Read the FAITH Tip on pages 219–20.

FAITH TIP

Discovering God's Purpose for Your Life

Identifying God's Purpose

One blessing of being a Christian is having a purpose for living. Without Christ, life resembles a jigsaw puzzle. The pieces do not fit together when we have no vision of the finished product. A believer's completed life vision should come from God and should resemble Christ Himself. In Him we discover the meaning of our lives.

Jesus identified His purpose in John 4:34: " 'My food,' said Jesus, 'is to do the will of him who sent me and to finish his work.' " Jesus did the Father's work in complete obedience. Nothing was as important to Him as doing God's will and finishing the work He was sent to do.

A life purpose is an overarching goal for you to accomplish in your lifetime. It provides direction for everyday activities and determines your priorities. A scribe asked Jesus to summarize humanity's duty. In his reply Jesus called attention to two life purposes: " 'The most important one,' answered Jesus, 'is this: "Hear, O Israel, the Lord our God, the Lord is one. Love the Lord your God with all your heart and with all your soul and with all your mind and with all your strength." The second is this: "Love your neighbor as yourself." There is no commandment greater than these' " (Mark 12:29-31). Your life purpose should relate to these two commands regardless of your job or profession. Everything you do should glorify God (see 1 Cor. 10:31; Col. 3:17; 1 Pet. 4:11).

Other Scriptures reveal God's purpose for the world. First Timothy 2:3-4 states, "This is good, and pleases God our Savior, who wants all men to be saved and to come to a knowledge of the truth." First Thessalonians 4:3 states, "It is God's will that you should be sanctified." These verses tell us that God's will is to bring the world to Himself and to sanctify all who accept Him. This means that your life purpose should also fulfill these purposes.

God desires to reveal His purpose for you. If you remain faithful to Him, He will show you how He wants to fulfill His purpose in you. He does this through prayer and Scriptures He places on your heart.

Setting Life Goals

After you determine your life purpose, concentrate on your life goals by asking how you can best carry out God's will in specific areas of your life. While your life purpose is an overarching goal for you to accomplish in your lifetime, life goals are specific objectives for important areas of your life. They are the means by which you accomplish your life purpose. If you set life goals without first determining your life purpose, you often substitute your goals for

God's purpose. A worthy goal will bring you peace, help you look at things long-term, keep you focused, and help you measure all things in light of God's purpose. Life goals have three important characteristics:

1. Life goals are God-revealed rather than conceived by you.
2. Life goals are too big to achieve without God's power.
3. Life goals arrange your life so that you can achieve your life purpose.

Your life goals help you make decisions and order your priorities. When you make important choices in life, such as your vocation or marriage partner, ask yourself, *Will this choice help me achieve God's purpose for my life?* If so, it is worthy of your efforts to attain it.

A definite order exists for building a life under God's plan.

1. *The foundation of Christ.* Build your life on Jesus Christ (see 1 Cor. 3:11-13). Ask yourself, *Are Christ and His kingdom my first priority?*

2. *Personhood.* God is most concerned about producing in you the character of Jesus Christ (see Matt. 5:1-12; Rom. 12:1-2; 2 Cor. 5:17; Gal. 5:22-23; Eph. 5:18; Phil. 2:5; Col. 3:1-17). Ask yourself, *What kind of person am I becoming?*

3. *Life message.* Your life message is who you are as others see you. If Christ is at the center of your life, your life message reflects and honors God (see Matt. 5:16). Ask yourself: *What do others see in my life? What does my life say to others?*

4. *Ministry.* God has called you to a life of ministry (see Matt. 5:13; Acts 1:8; Rom. 12:12-13; Col. 1:28-29; Heb. 10:24-25; 1 Pet. 4:10). Concentrate on walking with Christ and becoming like Him. Learn to see people through His eyes, and He will give you a ministry. Ask yourself, *How can I share my life with others?*

5. *Home.* Your home is a natural place to demonstrate what Christ is doing in your life and can do in others' lives (see Matt. 7:24; Eph. 5:21). Ask: *How can I make my home a platform for ministry? How does God intend to use our marriage relationship in ministry together?* or *Who is the best person I can marry in order to have the most effective ministry together?* or *How can I use my singleness to minister?*

6. *Daily work.* Look at your daily work as a focal point of ministry (see Matt. 6:19-34). Work at it with all your heart, as serving the Lord. Exhibit the spirit of Christ in attitudes, relationships, work habits, and decision making. Ask yourself, *How can I allow Christ to use my career to minister?* or *What career would best enable me to have an effective ministry in the world?*[1]

---

[1]Avery T. Willis, Jr., *MasterLife 3: The Disciple's Victory* (Nashville: LifeWay, 1996), 85–103.

How Can I Find Strength for Daily Living?

In this session you will—

CHECK IT by engaging in Team Time activities;

KNOW IT by reviewing content from session 13;

HEAR IT by affirming what the Bible says about strength for daily living;

SAY IT by discussing possible applications of what you have learned in this session;

STUDY IT by overviewing Home Study Assignments;

DO IT by leading your Team in making visits;

In Advance
- Overview content.
- Preview teaching suggestions. Prepare key points. Decide whether to use the session 14 computer slides or the overhead cels.
- Prepare the room for teaching.
- Pray for participants and for Teams as they prepare to visit.
- As Teaching Time begins, direct participants to open their Journals to page 224.

TEAM TIME

CHECK IT (15 MINS.)

If the computer diskette is used, display the agenda frame for Team Time, as desired. Add other points as needed.

CHECK IT agenda:
✔ FAITH Visit Outline
✔ Session 13 Debriefing
✔ Help for Strengthening a Visit

Leading Team Time

All Team members participate in Team Time. They are primarily responsible for reciting the assigned portion of the FAITH Visit Outline and for discussing other Home Study Assignments.

As you direct this important time of CHECK IT activities with your Team, keep in mind that Learners look to you as a role model, motivator, mentor, and friend. Team Time activities can continue in the car as the Team travels to and from visits.

Lead CHECK IT Activities

✔ FAITH Visit Outline
❏ Listen while each Learner recites as much of the FAITH Visit Outline as time allows. Make sure each person has a turn. It may be best to ask Learners to recite the segment they have the most difficulty sharing during a visit.
❏ As time permits, allow for additional practice on any part of the visit presentation, sequence, and materials (*My Next Step of Faith—Baptism*, for example).

✔ Session 13 Debriefing
❏ Review: The FAITH Sunday School Evangelism Strategy is designed to help equip the Sunday School member and leader to share the gospel and minister to prospects and members. A strength of this evangelism training is that participants learn a simple yet direct approach to talking with people about the message of the gospel when visiting with a Team of three. Another wonderful benefit is that someone who learns to share the gospel becomes more aware of witnessing opportunities during encounters throughout the week. Remind Team members that, as they continue training, they will become more aware of opportunities to share both a verbal and a lifestyle witness with people whose lives they intersect.

✔ Help for Strengthening a Visit
❏ Discuss some of the difficulties Teams have encountered in leading someone to hear and consider the FAITH gospel presentation. Call attention to the fact that this session formally introduces Learners to ways to deal with difficulties and distractions. At the same time, Team Leaders and other participants will learn other ways to help their Teams respond appropriately.
❏ As time allows, consider sharing a copy of the Witness Awareness Quotient (from *Building Bridges Through FAITH*) for Team members to use at their convenience. Or discuss some things you learned as a

result. Briefly help Team members see the impact of increasing their awareness of witnessing opportunities. It is one way to focus attention on strengthening both lifestyle and verbal opportunities to witness.

Notes

_____

_____

_____

_____

_____

_____

_____

_____

_____

Actions I Need to Take with Learners During the Week

_____

_____

_____

_____

_____

_____

_____

Transition to classrooms for instruction on the content of the session. (5 mins.)

KNOW IT

Step 1 (5 mins.)

Direct participants to locate A Quick Review on page 224 in their Journals and to complete the activities. Then give the answers, using the computer diskette or the overhead cel. Possible answers to question:

1. INTERESTS
2. Opinion Poll
3. INVOLVEMENT
4. Key Question
5. Sunday School or evangelistic testimonies
6. Ministry visits
7. *Invitation*

A Quick Review

A Quick Review

Last week you examined two approaches to answering the question, What is the purpose of life?

The World's Solution

Check three pursuits that Solomon identified in the Book of Ecclesiastes as being incapable of bringing meaning to life.

❑ 1. Others' approval   ❑ 5. Writing poetry
❑ 2. Knowing God   ❑ 6. Praising God
☑ 3. Knowledge   ☑ 7. Work
☑ 4. Pleasure   ❑ 8. Having a family

God's Solution

Fill in the blanks to identify the three purposes we exist, according to the Bible.

1. We were created to have an intimate relationship with ___**God**___.
2. We were created to have relationships with ___**one**___ ___**another**___.
3. We were created to have responsibility for ___**creation**___.

What are two places in FAITH visits when questions about or challenges to a biblical view of purpose might arise?

1. _____   2. _____

Check appropriate ways to respond to the question, What is the purpose of life?

☑ 1. Be willing to depart from the FAITH Visit Outline if a person indicates that he wants to discuss the purpose of life.
☑ 2. Share a Sunday School and an evangelistic testimony, followed by the Key Question, to invite the person to consider ways to bring meaning to life through a relationship with God.
☑ 3. Enroll persons in Sunday School as a vehicle for investigating ways to bring meaning to life by studying and applying God's Word.
❑ 4. Use complex theological arguments to explain the purpose of life.
☑ 5. Share ministry opportunities available through your Sunday School as ways to discover meaning in life by helping others.
❑ 6. Criticize the person's misplaced values.
☑ 7. Enlist Sunday School members to build relationships and use follow-up and discipleship to reinforce the decision to discover meaning through a relationship with God.
❑ 8. Explain that any life purpose is permissible as long as it doesn't harm others.

Defining the Question: How Can I Find Strength for Daily Living?

Christ lives in you! What an awesome truth. He is your source of strength for daily living. Lost persons face life's challenges and problems in their own strength, without the spiritual resources a believer enjoys. As you talk with unbelievers, you can often detect their desire for spiritual strength even if they do not express it in those terms.

Here are some ways you might anticipate being questioned or challenged about sources of strength for daily living.

- "How can I keep on giving in this relationship without getting anything in return?"
- "I can't deal with any more stress. There's just so much one person can do."
- "It doesn't matter what I do. I can't please him."
- "I'm almost at the end of my rope."
- "What's the use of trying anymore?"
- "I am totally exhausted all the time."

You've probably detected or overlooked the frustration and desperation behind remarks like these. Believers aren't immune to life's frustrations, but they also know the One whose indwelling presence is their source of power for daily living. That's a message a lost person just might be willing to listen to.

The Bible Speaks

"If anyone is in Christ, he is a new creation; the old has gone, the new has come!" (2 Cor. 5:17). Your decision to accept Christ began the lifelong process of sanctification in your life. *Sanctification* means *to be set apart for God's holy purposes*. This ongoing process of growth in Christlikeness involves putting off the old, sinful self, "which is being corrupted by its deceitful desires" and putting on the new self, "created to be like God in true righteousness and holiness" (Eph. 4:22-23). As you grow in Christlikeness and allow Him to live His life through you, you gain His strength for facing your circumstances and for fulfilling God's purposes for you. Let's look at what the Bible says about ways you can grow to be more like Christ and have His strength for daily living.

1. Accept Christ as ____Savior____ and ____Lord____.
Although you have taken this step, it is the essential step lost people need to take if they hope to have a source of daily strength. There is no greater source of strength than Jesus Christ. As He demonstrated

HEAR IT

Step 2 (5 mins.)

Introduce the content of this session by summarizing Defining the Question. Use the computer diskette or the overhead cel to illustrate questions and comments about strength for daily living.

Defining the Question

If you are leading students, use these questions and challenges.
- "My parents are impossible to please."
- "What's the use of trying?"
- "I can't handle any more responsibilities."
- "My life is not fair."
- "Nobody takes me seriously or listens to my opinions because I'm just a kid."

Step 3 (20 mins.)

Direct participants to turn to page 225 in their Journals and to fill in the blanks as you present the key points in The Bible Speaks. Use the computer diskette or the overhead cels.

The Bible Speaks

through His victory over sin and death, He has the power to cancel sin.

When people accept Jesus as Savior, they also accept Him as Lord. Basically, the word *Lord* implies authority. In the Old Testament the term is one of honor, used to address God or to refer to Him. In the New Testament *Lord* implies Christ's divinity and His right to receive worship and obedience. It became the title that Christians use to describe the special place of honor and authority given to Jesus Christ. By addressing Jesus as Lord, the disciples showed that they considered Him to be God. They accepted Him as the supreme authority in life.

The early Christians' primary confession of faith was the declaration "Jesus Christ is Lord": "… that if you confess with your mouth, 'Jesus is Lord,' and believe in your heart that God raised him from the dead, you will be saved" (Rom. 10:9-10). To receive salvation, a person must recognize and accept Christ's supreme authority over every area of life. When we call Jesus Lord, then, we mean that we respect Him, that we belong to Him, and that we are committed to serving Him as our supreme Master. Even more, lordship means that we worship Him as God and give Him complete authority over our lives.

2. Learn _____**obedience**_____.

When you completely turn over your life to Jesus as Lord, you want to obey Him. Obedience to Christ's commands is the key to discipleship. When you obey these commands, you benefit because—

- you remain in His love (see John 15:10);
- the Father loves you and reveals Himself to you (see John 14:21);
- you show that you are His disciple (see John 13:34-35);
- you are blessed (see John 13:17).

Obeying Christ's commands requires two things: knowing them and doing them. Jesus said: " 'I am the vine; you are the branches. If a man remains in me and I in him, he will bear much fruit; apart from me you can do nothing' " (John 15:5). If you remain in Christ and obey Him, you will bear fruit that will lead others to a saving relationship with Him.[1]

3. Renew your _____**mind**_____.

Although you are a new creation in Jesus Christ, you still struggle with an old, sinful nature (see Rom. 7:15-20). The natural mind is the thinking process that is limited to human reason and resources (see 1 Cor. 2:14). Ephesians 4:17-18 says that people with natural minds walk in darkness and have futile thinking. Ignorance, which results because their hearts are hardened, separates them from God. They live hopeless lives of sin and self-destruction.

Paul also wrote: "Do not conform any longer to the pattern of this world, but be transformed by the renewing of your mind. Then you will be able to test and approve what God's will is—his good, pleasing and perfect will" (Rom. 12:2). The renewed mind is obedient to Christ. It enlarges your perception to include the world of the Spirit in addition to the senses. Guided by the Holy Spirit, the renewed mind thinks from Christ's viewpoint.

In 1 Corinthians 2:16 Paul claimed that believers have the mind of Christ. You can make Christ the master of your mind by filling your mind with Scripture. The more you live in the Word, the more your mind will be renewed (see Rom. 8:5-6; Col. 3:2). Think wholesome thoughts instead of evil ones (see Phil. 4:8). Replace thoughts based on your old, sinful nature with thoughts that are consistent with Scripture (see Prov. 23:7; Eph. 4:22-24).[2]

4. Master your _____ **emotions** _____ .

Natural persons want to do what their emotions tell them. Spiritual persons obey God instead of what they want to do, as a conscious act of the will. The Holy Spirit gives you direction and power to act rightly toward others even if you do not feel like doing so. Identify a biblical response to the negative or destructive emotion or a substitute for it. Try to think about ways Christ would master your emotion. He surrendered everything to God's will, even suffering and dying on the cross.

Not only do your feelings influence the way you act, but the way you act also determines how you feel. You can change your feelings by changing your actions. Jesus' solution for many emotional responses was to command an action rather than a feeling (see Matt. 5:24; 7:1-2). Acting lovingly toward someone even if you do not feel like doing so is the essence of love (see 1 Cor. 13:4-7). The Holy Spirit can help you do this. The fruit of the Spirit is more than emotions; it is stable character traits that develop in your life as you grow in Christ (see Gal. 5:22-23).[3]

5. Offer your _____ **body** _____ to God.

Paul wrote, "I urge you, brothers, in view of God's mercy, to offer your bodies as living sacrifices, holy and pleasing to God—this is your spiritual act of worship" (Rom. 12:1). You are to present each part of your body to Christ so that He can master it and use it for His glory. Your body has the capacity to do good if you allow the Spirit to control it instead of letting your sinful nature rule (see 1 Cor. 6:19; Gal. 5:19-21; Col. 3:5).

Galatians 2:20 says, "I have been crucified with Christ and I no longer live, but Christ lives in me. The life I live in the body, I live by faith in the Son of God, who loved me and gave himself for me." Because your sinful nature, with its lusts and desires, has been put to death, Christ can reign in your body. Like mastering your emotions, giving Christ control over your body is a matter of the will that is accomplished through the power of the Holy Spirit (see Rom. 6:11-14; Gal. 5:16).[4]

6. Be filled with the _____Spirit_____.

Ephesians 5:18 commands us to "be filled with the Spirit." Possessing the Spirit and being filled with the Spirit are different things. If you have received Christ, you have the Spirit living in you (see 2 Cor. 1:21-22). But the Holy Spirit wants to flow through you like a stream of living water (see John 7:38-39). You can't obey Christ's commands, witness, serve, or overcome a problem in your own strength. Christians today can be filled with the power of the Holy Spirit just as the early church was filled at Pentecost (see Acts 2:1-41).

The Holy Spirit will fill you completely only if you acknowledge Christ's lordship and submit to His authority (see 1 Thess. 5:23). Confess your sin and your need for cleansing. Present your body as a righteous instrument for God's use. Then ask God to fill, control, and empower you (see Luke 11:13). Believe that God has answered your prayer. God wants you to be filled with His Spirit so that you will be found blameless, that is, Christlike (see 1 Thess. 5:23) and will be empowered to do His work (see Acts 1:8).[5] Maybe you experienced these purposes when the Spirit has empowered you for FAITH visits.

7. Grow as a _____disciple_____.

The Greek word translated *disciple* in the New Testament means *learner* or *student*. A disciple is someone who is a committed follower of Jesus Christ. *Discipleship* is a Christian's lifelong commitment to the person, teaching, and spirit of Jesus Christ. Life under Jesus' lordship involves progressive learning, growth in Christlikeness, application of biblical truth to every area of life, responsibility for sharing the Christian faith, and responsible church membership. Growth in discipleship results in spiritual strength. Here are some ways to grow as a disciple.

- Participate in **Bible** **study** and **discipleship** **training** (see 1 Tim. 4:13; 2 Pet. 3:18). Sunday School classes and discipleship groups help transform you spiritually by providing opportunities to study the Bible in depth and to apply its teachings to your life.
- Have a daily **quiet** **time** (see Ps. 1:2; Jer. 33:3). You focused on the importance of Bible study and prayer in session 11. Fellowship with God every day is a tremendous source of spiritual strength as you talk with and listen to God.
- Memorize and meditate on **Scripture** (see Ps. 119:11). Hiding God's Word in your heart helps you handle pressure, have immediate guidance, fight sin, witness, and replace your old, sinful nature with Christlike qualities.
- Attend **congregational** **worship** (see Heb. 10:25). Corporate worship can be an uplifting and strengthening experience as the body of Christ praises God, hears His Word interpreted, and is challenged to grow.

As participants fill in the blanks on page 228 in their Journals, use the computer diskette or the overhead cel to present ways to grow as a disciple.

Growing as a Disciple

- Fellowship with other **believers** (see 1 Thess. 5:11). Members of the body of Christ need to build strong relationships with one another; share victories and struggles; and depend on, support, and encourage one another.
- Give **tithes** and **offerings** (see Mal. 3:10). A growing Christian wants to give financially to carry out God's work in the world and to express gratitude to God as the Giver of all blessings.
- Listen to spiritual **music** (see Col. 3:16). This helps you renew your mind by reinforcing scriptural teachings. It is an uplifting way to focus your attention on God's will and ways.
- **Serve** through your church (see Eph. 4:11-13). Another way to grow in Christ is to use your time, skills, and spiritual gifts to build up the body of Christ and to help other believers develop as disciples. Perhaps you began doing this by serving as a FAITH Team Leader.
- Share your **faith** (see Matt. 28:19-20). By participating in FAITH, you have probably already adopted a witnessing lifestyle. Regular witnessing is a great source of spiritual strength as you rely on the Holy Spirit more and more.

One of the most uplifting Bible passages on spiritual strength is Isaiah 40:31:

Those who hope in the Lord
will renew their strength.
They will soar on wings like eagles;
they will run and not grow weary,
they will walk and not be faint.

As a disciple of Jesus Christ, you find increasing strength for daily living as you grow in His likeness. By introducing lost persons to Christ as Savior and Lord, you give them hope that they too can live each day with a strength and faith that only He can provide.

Entry Points in FAITH Visits

Several occasions in FAITH visits offer a person an opportunity to reveal an interest in or a need for spiritual strength.
1. Many people will be curious why you and your Team have chosen to visit in homes of strangers when you could easily choose other activities. They may look for evidence of **qualities** in your life that reflect a strength worth emulating.
2. You will visit Sunday School members, many of whom know Christ but may struggle to have a life-changing relationship with the Lord. Many **ministry** **visits** will intentionally

Step 4 (5 mins.)

Direct participants to turn to page 229 in their Journals and to fill in the blanks as you summarize Entry Points in FAITH Visits. Use the computer diskette or the overhead cel.

Entry Points
in FAITH
Visits

be assigned to persons who grapple with one or more life issues for which they need God's strength. _____**Follow-up**_____ _____**visits**_____ are good opportunities to suggest ways to begin growing in Christ.

3. Many persons you visit on _____**evangelistic**_____ _____**visits**_____ will be looking for a source of strength in life.

4. As you share your _____**Sunday**_____ _____**School**_____ _____**testimony**_____, share examples of ways you have found strength for daily living through purposeful Bible study, fellowship, and the ministry of other Christians. Many persons will be influenced by the genuine impact of Christ and the church on your life.

5. Your _____**evangelistic**_____ _____**testimony**_____ pivots on the statement "I had a life-changing experience." You are seeking to whet the appetite of someone to want to know what made a practical difference in your life.

6. H is for HEAVEN; _____**HEAVEN**_____ _____**HERE**_____ piques many persons' interest in how to find strength for daily living. John 10:10 clearly states Christ's intent: " 'I have come that they may have life' " (NKJV). Many persons will become interested in how they can find strength to endure life's trials when they hear our Lord's powerful words.

7. Many persons have no idea that life can be worth living. God may be using you in a _____**divine**_____ _____**appointment**_____ to lead someone to accept the truth of the gospel. On other occasions God may have sent you to share for the first time or nurture the message that they can live with God's forgiveness, strength, and love.

How You Can Respond

Here are possible ways you can respond to a person's need for spiritual strength during witnessing encounters. Your response will depend on the person, the situation, and the Holy Spirit's direction in this circumstance. Always keep in mind the general principles outlined on pages 28–29 in session 1.

1. Be sensitive to ways persons give clues about their need for spiritual strength. Be prepared to share examples of actions you take in your journey of faith.

2. Your Sunday School testimony sets the stage for the person's further relationships with the church. Remember to keep your testimony short and concise and to focus on ways your relationship with Christ provides strength for living.

3. God will send you to many persons with whom you can relate in some way. Your previous experiences will help you understand and

SAY IT

Step 5 (5 mins.)

Ask accountability partners to discuss ways they would respond to a lost person's need for spiritual strength, using the ideas in How You Can Respond.

If you are leading students, have accountability partners role-play a situation in which one partner asks a question about spiritual strength and the other partner responds.

demonstrate Christ's compassion for persons who are looking for strength. Be sensitive to ways the Holy Spirit wants you to share examples of ways He has helped you discover strength to deal with life's difficulties.

4. During follow-up visits be prepared to share ways the person can grow in his or her commitment to follow Christ.
5. Serve as a model and encouragement for Team members as they grow in their journey of faith. Many times Team members become discouraged about the time commitment required to participate in FAITH training. Persons who are being asked to recommit to future FAITH training may need to hear that this commitment will help them grow in Christ and find greater strength for daily living. Be prepared to share personal examples of ways you are growing in your dependence on the Lord through FAITH training.

Visitation Time

Do It

1. All Team members should know the entire FAITH presentation. Are they ready to take the lead in a visit? Are they growing in their faith and in their capacity to share their faith? Are they learning to recognize when the FAITH Visit Outline needs to be adjusted in visits? Are they helping to establish bridges of relationship between the community and your Sunday School?
2. How far have Team members come since session 1? Have you taken the time to affirm them for their progress and to thank God for this mentoring experience?
3. Be sensitive to persons you visit who need spiritual strength in their lives. Be ready to hold out the hope that only Christ can supply.

Celebration Time

Share It

1. Ask a Team member to take the lead in sharing reports.
2. Hear reports and testimonies.
3. Complete Evaluation Cards.
4. Complete Participation Cards.
5. Update visitation forms with the results of visits.

STUDY IT

Step 6 (5 mins.)

Overview Home Study Assignments for session 13.

Transition to assemble with FAITH Teams to prepare for home visits. (5 mins.)

DO IT (110 MINS.)

SHARE IT (30 MINS.)

Home Study Assignments

Home Study Assignments reinforce this session by helping you apply what you have learned.

Your Discipleship Journey

Journaling activities in Your Discipleship Journey are an important part of your development as a Great Commission Christian through FAITH training.

1. Do a word study in Scripture of *strong* and *strength*. Begin with verses like Joshua 1:6-9; Psalm 28:7; Isaiah 41:10; 1 Corinthians 1:25; 2 Corinthians 12:10; Ephesians 6:10; Philippians 4:13; and 2 Timothy 2:1-7.

2. One of your greatest sources of spiritual strength is a daily quiet time. If you are not currently having a quiet time, commit now to begin one each day. Decide on the best time and place for you.

   My quiet time will be at _____ every day.

   The place of my quiet time will be _____.

3. Think about each of the following areas of your life and decide whether you have given Christ control of each area. Write problems you have in each area and spend time in prayer about them. Write what you will do to give Christ control, including Scriptures you can apply to change your thoughts or behavior.

   ### Your Mind
   The problem area: _____

   _____

   The action you will take to give Christ control: _____

   _____

   ### Your Emotions
   The problem area: _____

   _____

   The action you will take to give Christ control: _____

   _____

Your Body

The problem area: _____

The action you will take to give Christ control: _____

_____

4. Evaluate your efforts to grow as a disciple by rating yourself in each of
   the following areas. Use this rating scale: 1 = a regular practice, 2 = an
   occasional action, 3 = never or rarely do this

Participate in Bible study	1 2 3
Participate in discipleship training	1 2 3
Have a daily quiet time	1 2 3
Memorize and meditate on Scripture	1 2 3
Attend congregational worship	1 2 3
Fellowship with other believers	1 2 3
Give tithes and offerings	1 2 3
Listen to spiritual music	1 2 3
Serve through your church	1 2 3
Share your faith	1 2 3

   Place a check mark beside one action you feel the Lord would like for you
   to begin practicing immediately.

Growing as a Life Witness

Growing as a Life Witness reminds you of your responsibility to witness and
minister to others during the week.

1. Talk or meet with your accountability partner and share ways you have
   cultivated a lost person or have witnessed or ministered on occasions other
   than FAITH visits.
2. Discuss your responses to activity 4 in Your Discipleship Journey.
3. Pray for lost persons by name and for each other.

Prayer Concerns	Answers to Prayer
_____	_____
_____	_____
_____	_____
_____	_____
_____	_____
_____	_____

Your Weekly Sunday School Leadership Team Meeting

A FAITH participant is an important member of Sunday School. Encourage Team members who are elected Sunday School workers to attend this weekly meeting. Use this section to record ways your FAITH Team influences the work of your Sunday School class or department. Use the information to report during weekly Sunday School leadership team meetings. Identify actions that need to be taken through Sunday School as a result of prayer concerns, needs identified, visits made by the Team, and decisions made by the persons visited. Also identify ways you can disciple others in your Sunday School class or department and in your church.

1. Highlight FAITH visit results and implications for your class/department or age group. How can ministries of your class/department or Sunday School further extend bridges of relationship?

_____

_____

2. Pray for your teacher(s) and department director. Ask God to strengthen and encourage Team Leaders as they continue to train and equip new Learners. Record your requests.

_____

3. With others on your leadership team, evaluate last week's session and discuss ways Sunday's lesson can involve members and guests in transformational Bible study and discipleship.

_____

4. In what ways can the truths you discovered in this session be communicated with your Sunday School leadership team? How has FAITH changed your priorities? Those of your Team members? Those of new believers?

_____

_____

Discipling Your Team Members

This weekly feature suggests actions the Team Leader can take to support Team members, prepare for Team Time, and improve visits. This work is part of the Team Leader's Home Study Assignments. Add any actions suggested by your church's FAITH strategy.

Support Team Members

❑ Contact Team members during the week. Remind them that you are praying for them. Discuss prayer concerns and answers to prayer.
❑ As you talk with Learners this week, discuss opportunities they have for witnessing during the week. Encourage them as they seek to be witnesses to persons they encounter.
❑ Record specific needs and concerns shared by Team members.

_____

_____

Prepare to Lead Team Time

❑ Review Team members' Home Study Assignments.
❑ Be prepared to remind Team members to draft a "What FAITH Has Meant to Me" testimony, due in session 16.

Prepare to Lead Visits

❑ Review the FAITH Visit Outline.

Link with Sunday School

❑ Participate in your weekly Sunday School leadership team meeting. Share pertinent information in this meeting, using Your Weekly Sunday School Leadership Team Meeting (p. 234) and FAITH-visit results.
❑ Be sensitive to Sunday School members and visitors who need spiritual strength in their lives. How is your Sunday School responding to this vital need?

For Further Growth

For Further Growth may include additional reading or activities that will enhance your growth as a disciple and a discipler of others. These assignments are intended to be long-term projects and do not have to be completed during this semester of study.

1. Participate in a group study of The Mind of Christ by T. W. Hunt and Claude V. King (LifeWay, 1994) or Life in the Spirit by Robertson McQuilkin (LifeWay, 1997).
2. Study Meeting Needs, Sharing Christ by Donald A. Atkinson and Charles L. Roesel (LifeWay, 1995) to discover ways churches can provide caring ministry in Jesus' name to persons whose basic life needs are not being met.
3. Read the FAITH Tip on page 236.

1Avery T. Willis, Jr., MasterLife 1: The Disciple's Cross (LifeWay, 1996), 22.
2Avery T. Willis, Jr., MasterLife 2: The Disciple's Personality (LifeWay, 1996), 29–44.
3Ibid., 61–67.
4Ibid., 73–85.
5Ibid., 94–105.

FAITH TIP

How to Have a Quiet Time

1. Make a personal quiet time the top priority of your day. Select a time to spend with God that fits your schedule. Usually, morning is preferable, but you may want or need to choose another time.

2. Prepare the night before.
   - If your quiet time is in the morning, set your alarm. If it is difficult for you to wake up, plan to exercise, bathe, dress, and eat before your quiet time.
   - Select a place where you can be alone. Gather materials, such as your Bible, notebook, and a pen or a pencil, and put them in the place selected so that you will not waste time in the morning.

3. Develop a balanced plan of Bible reading and prayer.
   - Pray for guidance during your quiet time.
   - Follow a systematic plan to read your Bible. Use a devotional guide if desired.
   - Make notes of what God says to you through His Word.
   - Pray in response to the Scriptures you have read. As you pray, use various components of prayer. Using the acronym ACTS—adoration, confession, thanksgiving, supplication—helps you remember the components.

4. Be persistent until you are consistent.
   - Strive for consistency rather than for length of time spent. Try to have a few minutes of quiet time every day rather than long devotional periods every other day.
   - Expect interruptions. Satan tries to prevent you from spending time with God. He fears even the weakest Christians who are on their knees. Plan around interruptions rather than being frustrated by them.

5. Focus on the Person you are meeting rather than on the habit of having the quiet time. If you scheduled a meeting with the person you admire most, you would not allow anything to stand in your way. Meeting God is even more important. He created you with a capacity for fellowship with Him, and He saved you to bring about that fellowship.[1]

---

[1]Avery T. Willis, Jr., *MasterLife 1: The Disciple's Cross* (Nashville: LifeWay, 1996), 19–20.

How Can I Overcome Spiritual Obstacles?

In this session you will—

CHECK IT by engaging in Team Time activities;

KNOW IT by reviewing content from session 14;

HEAR IT by affirming what the Bible says about overcoming spiritual obstacles;

SEE IT by viewing a video segment;

SAY IT by discussing possible applications of what you have learned in this session;

STUDY IT by overviewing Home Study Assignments;

DO IT by leading your Team in making visits;

SHARE IT by celebrating.

In Advance

- Overview content.
- Preview teaching suggestions. Prepare key points. Decide whether to use the session 15 computer slides or the overhead cels.
- Be prepared to answer questions about next week's schedule.
- Prepare the room for teaching.
- Cue the videotape for the session 15 segment, Weathering Spiritual Storms.
- Pray for participants and for Teams as they prepare to visit.
- As Teaching Time begins, direct participants to open their Journals to page 240.

TEAM TIME

CHECK IT (15 MINS.)

If the computer diskette is used, display the agenda frame for Team Time, as desired. Add other points as needed.

CHECK IT agenda:
✔ FAITH Visit Outline
✔ Session 14 Debriefing
✔ Other Home Study Assignments
✔ Help for Strengthening a Visit

Leading Team Time

All Team members participate in Team Time. They are primarily responsible for reciting the assigned portion of the FAITH Visit Outline and for discussing other Home Study Assignments.

As you direct this important time of CHECK IT activities with your Team, keep in mind that Learners look to you as a role model, motivator, mentor, and friend. Team Time activities can continue in the car as the Team travels to and from visits.

Lead CHECK IT Activities

✔ FAITH Visit Outline
❏ Listen while each Learner recites as much of the FAITH Visit Outline as time allows. It may be best to ask Learners to recite the segment they seem to have the most difficulty sharing during a visit.
❏ As time permits, allow for any additional practice that is needed on the visit presentation and sequence.

✔ Session 14 Debriefing
❏ Briefly talk about distractions Team members have encountered in earlier visits.
❏ While reminding Team members that most visits go very smoothly, help them begin to recognize principles and actions for handling difficulties. As you model ways to handle difficult situations during visits, be sure to explain what you did and why. It is important to deal appropriately with difficulties that could take place at any time during the visits. Difficulties are things that happen or are said during the visit that could keep you from sharing the gospel and leading a person who is ready to respond to make a commitment to Christ. Principles for dealing with difficulties relate primarily to building bridges of relationship with the person, dealing with any questions and objections, and working through the obstacles and distractions that take place.

✔ Other Home Study Assignments
❏ Remind the group of the assignment, due next week, to write a testimony describing what FAITH has meant personally.

✔ Help for Strengthening a Visit
❏ Remind Team members to listen during each visit for ministry opportunities and for ways to follow up appropriately.
❏ If you have shared the Witness Awareness Quotient with Team members (from *Building Bridges Through FAITH*), reemphasize as follows.

- The greater the Number of Unsaved identified, the greater the potential for sharing a witness. The greater the number of Yes responses, the more someone is taking advantage of witnessing opportunities.
- If No responses are higher than Yes responses, then someone can consciously strengthen awareness of opportunities to share the gospel. If Yes responses are higher, then a witness can comfortably model for others the significance of sharing FAITH during daily-life opportunities.

Notes

_____

_____

_____

_____

_____

_____

_____

Actions I Need to Take with Learners During the Week

_____

_____

_____

_____

_____

_____

Transition to classrooms for instruction on the content of the session. (5 mins.)

TEACHING TIME

KNOW IT

Step 1 (5 mins.)

Direct participants to locate A Quick Review on page 240 in their Journals and to complete the activities. Then give the answers, using the computer diskette or the overhead cel.

Review the nine ways to grow as a disciple:

1. Participate in Bible study and discipleship training.
2. Have a daily quiet time.
3. Memorize and meditate on Scripture.
4. Attend congregational worship.
5. Fellowship with other believers.
6. Give tithes and offerings.
7. Listen to spiritual music.
8. Serve through your church.
9. Share your faith.

Challenge participants to practice these actions.

Possible answers to question:

1. Qualities you model in a visit
2. Ministry and follow-up visits
3. Evangelistic visits
4. Sunday School and evangelistic testimonies
5. HEAVEN HERE
6. Divine appointments

A Quick Review

A Quick Review

Last week you studied biblical answers to the question, How can I find strength for daily living? Check the statements that identify the way the Bible answers that question.

❑ 1. Pursue pleasure.
☑ 2. Accept Christ as Savior and Lord.
❑ 3. Practice transcendental meditation.
☑ 4. Learn obedience.
☑ 5. Renew your mind.
❑ 6. Get in touch with your inner divinity.
☑ 7. Master your emotions.
☑ 8. Offer your body to God.
❑ 9. Think about the past.
❑ 10. Take a pilgrimage to the Holy Land.
☑ 11. Be filled with the Spirit.
☑ 12. Grow as a disciple.

Name four of the nine ways you learned to grow as a disciple.

1. _____

2. _____

3. _____

4. _____

What are two places in FAITH visits when questions about or an admission of the need for spiritual strength might arise?

1. _____

2. _____

Check appropriate ways to respond to a person's need for spiritual strength.

❑ 1. Begin chanting a mantra to show that you are open to various forms of religious expression.
☑ 2. Share examples of actions you take to gain spiritual strength.
❑ 3. Suggest that the person exercise regularly.
☑ 4. Use your Sunday School testimony to focus on ways your relationship with Christ provides strength for living.
☑ 5. Be sensitive to ways the Holy Spirit wants you to share ways He has helped you discover strength to deal with life's difficulties.

☑ 6. During follow-up visits share ways the person can grow in his commitment to follow Christ.

❏ 7. If the person obviously needs spiritual strength, try not to get involved.

☑ 8. Serve as a model and encouragement for Team members as they grow in their journey of faith.

Defining the Question: How Can I Overcome Spiritual Obstacles?

This week's question is one you are most likely to hear from a believer, often a new Christian. In addition to understanding how to have spiritual strength in your life, which you learned last week, every believer needs to know how to overcome spiritual strongholds. A spiritual stronghold is "an idea, a thought process, a habit, or an addiction through which Satan has set up occupancy in your life— a place where he has the advantage."[1] Armed with the Word and prayer, you can defeat the forces of Satan and have victory in Christ.

Unbelievers also wrestle with spiritual strongholds, although they may not identify them as such. Here are some statements you might hear or signs you might detect in a witnessing visit or in daily life that signal a struggle with spiritual obstacles.

- A statement that a person wants to quit a harmful habit but lacks the strength to do so
- Strong emotions like rage, bitterness, or hatred
- An immoral lifestyle
- Unhealthy or perverted thought processes
- Abusive behavior
- Overwhelming personal problems
- Greed
- Humanistic and atheistic philosophies of life
- A love for or fascination with evil

Identifying spiritual strongholds in unbelievers' lives is important because they are instruments Satan uses to keep the lost from seeing the truth and yielding to Jesus Christ. In believers' lives, spiritual strongholds are sources of disillusionment, frustration, lack of growth, and ineffectiveness. The Bible gives guidance for overcoming spiritual strongholds that you can apply in your own Christian walk and can share with lost persons as a message of hope.

HEAR IT

Step 2 (5 mins.)

Introduce the content of this session by summarizing Defining the Question. Use the computer diskette or the overhead cel to illustrate evidence of a spiritual obstacle in someone's life.

Defining the Question

Step 3 (10 mins.)

Direct participants to turn to page 242 in their Journals and to fill in the blanks as you present the key points in The Bible Speaks. Use the computer diskette or the overhead cel.

The Bible Speaks

The Bible Speaks

Many Christians wonder why they still struggle with temptation and sin if they have a new nature in Christ. Even Paul struggled with this question (see Rom. 7:14-25). No matter how much we grow in Christ, we will always struggle with the sinful nature as long as we have an earthly existence. This means that Satan always has a foothold, an entry point into our lives. But Paul recognized that we have hope through Christ; we can be confident that "he who began a good work in you will carry it on to completion until the day of Christ Jesus" (Phil. 1:6). Let's look at the spiritual tools God provides to help us overcome sin and have victory in Him.

1. Learn to demolish spiritual _____strongholds_____.
Paul wrote in 2 Corinthians 10:3-5: "Though we live in the world, we do not wage war as the world does. The weapons we fight with are not the weapons of the world. On the contrary, they have divine power to demolish strongholds. We demolish arguments and every pretension that sets itself up against the knowledge of God, and we take captive every thought to make it obedient to Christ." All Christians engage in spiritual warfare as we confront the world, the flesh, and the devil; try to live holy lives; and fulfill God's purpose for our lives. Christ has won the victory over all evil powers, and He gives victory to Christians who totally depend on Him and use His spiritual weapons. Here is a way you can use spiritual means to demolish a stronghold in your life.

- Identify the stronghold and the reason it violates God's Word and will.
- Repent of the sin and ask for God's forgiveness.
- Declare war on the stronghold by substituting biblical truth, claiming the mind of Christ, using spiritual weapons, praying for the Holy Spirit's power and guidance, requesting others' prayers and support, boldly making God's truth clear, and claiming the victory by faith.
- Pray as you put on each piece of spiritual armor and receive God's strength to fight the obstacle.
- Win the victory in Christ by loving God, keeping His commandments, being sure that you are born of God, believing that Jesus is God's Son, and believing that God keeps you safe (see 1 John 4:4; 5:2-3,18-20).[2]

2. Put on the spiritual _____armor_____.
In Ephesians 6:10-13 Paul laid out our battle plan for spiritual warfare: "Be strong in the Lord and in his mighty power. Put on the full armor of God so that you can take your stand against the devil's schemes. For our struggle is not against flesh and blood, but against the rulers,

against the authorities, against the powers of this dark world and against the spiritual forces of evil in the heavenly realms. Therefore put on the full armor of God, so that when the day of evil comes, you may be able to stand your ground, and after you have done everything, to stand." In verses 14-17 Paul names the components of the spiritual armor we are to use.

- Put on the belt of ____**truth**____ (see v. 14). Be true to God when you fight a spiritual battle. Hold to the truth. The belt protects your inward parts, or emotions, so master your emotions and do not compromise because of your feelings. They should be guided by the truth.
- Put on the breastplate of _____**righteousness**_____ (see v. 14). The breastplate is the righteousness that you have because of Christ living in you. It protects your heart and will. Ask God to reveal any sin, confess it, and claim Christ's righteousness to cover your sin and give you right standing with Him.
- Put on the ____**gospel**____ shoes (see v. 15). The shoes, like a Roman soldier's studded sandals, represent the readiness that comes from the gospel of peace. They remind you to be prepared for battle through prayer. Also be prepared to witness. Attack the enemy through both prayer and witness.
- Take up the shield of ____**faith**____ (see v. 16). The shield protects you so that you can advance on the enemy. Claim the victory Christ has already won and advance in faith.
- Take up the helmet of _____**salvation**_____ (see v. 17). You received the helmet when you were saved. Thank God for your salvation. Praise Him for eternal life; in Him you are secure even in battle. Claim the mind of Christ, which you received when you were saved.
- Take up the sword of the ____**Spirit**____ (see v. 17). The sword is the Word of God. Grasp the Word when you wage spiritual battle. Let the Holy Spirit use His Word. Pray on the basis of the Word. Read and memorize Scriptures that apply to the situation.[3]

3. Rely on God's ____**Word**____.

Part of the process of overcoming spiritual obstacles is to replace Satan's lies with God's truth. One way God communicates His truth to you is through the Bible. Learn to listen for God's truth through His Word. You can do this by taking the following steps when you read or listen to the Word preached.

- Be alert for a Word from God (see Jas. 1:19).
- Repent of sin and pride so that the Word can be planted in your heart (see Jas. 1:21).
- Pay attention to what the Bible says about you (see Jas. 1:23-24). Take notes.

- Let the Holy Spirit lead you in truth as He illuminates or applies God's Word to your life (see John 16:13-15). Ask yourself: *What is God saying to me through this message? How does my life measure up to this Word? What actions will I take to bring my life in line with this Word? What truth do I need to study further?*
- Do the Word (see Jas. 1:25).

By receiving the Word, understanding it, bearing fruit, and seeing results in your life, you can appropriate God's truth as the solution to your spiritual obstacle.[4]

4. *Pray in* <u>faith</u>.

After outlining the spiritual weapons we can use in battle, Paul concluded: "Pray in the Spirit on all occasions with all kinds of prayers and requests. With this in mind, be alert and always keep on praying for all the saints. Pray also for me, that whenever I open my mouth, words may be given me so that I will fearlessly make known the mystery of the gospel, for which I am an ambassador in chains. Pray that I may declare it fearlessly, as I should" (Eph. 6:18-20). A spiritual warrior begins with prayer. Prayer is the way you clothe yourself with the spiritual armor and the way God strengthens you for battle. Through prayer you claim God's victory.[5]

Jesus said, " 'If you remain in me and my words remain in you, ask whatever you wish, and it will be given you' " (John 15:7). If you are living in a vital relationship with God and if He has communicated His truth to you through His Word, you are ready to pray in faith for victory over your spiritual obstacle.
- Ask according to God's will (see Matt. 7:7-8; Jas. 4:2-3). When He reveals His truth to you through His Word, you can ask on the basis of that truth.
- Accept God's will in faith (see 1 John 5:14-15). When you ask according to His will, He hears you. You can depend on God's Word in this matter by faith.
- Act on the basis of God's Word to you (see Luke 17:14; John 9:7). When you have prayed in faith, you can act even when you cannot see the answer to your request. Walking by faith means that you believe God and what He communicates through His Word, as substantiated by the Holy Spirit, even though you do not yet see physical evidence that it is true.

Praying in faith is the surest way to win spiritual victories because it aligns you with God's will and enables you to apply His truth to overcome the obstacle.[6]

5. *Resist* <u>temptation</u>.

Resisting temptation is another way to overcome spiritual obstacles. Here are some ways you can resist temptation.

- Don't feel defeated when you are tempted. Temptation is not a sin; even Jesus was tempted (see Matt. 4:1-11). If you do not give in to temptation, you do not sin.
- Don't place yourself in tempting situations. You have learned from experience the things that lure you to sin. "Resist the devil, and he will flee from you" (Jas. 4:7).
- Follow Jesus' example. Hebrews 4:15 says that He was "tempted in every way, just as we are—yet without sin." When faced with temptation, Jesus relied on the truth of God's Word, acknowledged God's authority, and rejected the devil (see Matt. 4:4,7,10).
- Depend on God's strength to resist temptation. "He will not let you be tempted beyond what you can bear. But when you are tempted, he will also provide a way out so that you can stand up under it" (1 Cor. 10:13). Hebrews 4:16 tells us to "approach the throne of grace with confidence, so that we may receive mercy and find grace to help us in our time of need."

When you fight in spiritual warfare, remember that Christ has already won the victory (see Col. 2:15). Therefore, "everyone born of God overcomes the world. This is the victory that has overcome the world, even our faith" (1 John 5:4). Jesus offers you hope for overcoming spiritual obstacles, and He offers the same victory for those who will accept His gift of salvation.

Entry Points in FAITH Visits

Several occasions in FAITH visits offer a person an opportunity to consider the question, How can I overcome spiritual obstacles?
1. During the _____**Preparation**_____ portion of the visit, you have opportunities to learn about the person's interests and involvement. Occasionally, the Holy Spirit will use your visit to open the person to share a spiritual concern or challenge.
2. As you share a _____**Sunday**_____ _____**School**_____ or _____**evangelistic**_____ _____**testimony**_____, many persons will consider spiritual challenges they face. A Christian may consider spiritual struggles as your Team shares. Many persons will begin to consider the need to start or return to involvement in Bible study, worship, and fellowship with Christians.
3. As you explain _____**God's**_____ _____**FORGIVENESS**_____, many persons will consider temptations they have experienced and sins they have committed. Many will have difficulty accepting the fact that God's forgiveness is available for them.
4. _**T**_ is for _____**TURN**_____ instructs persons that they must turn

Step 4 (5 mins.)

Direct participants to turn to page 245 in their Journals and to fill in the blanks as you summarize Entry Points in FAITH Visits. Use the computer diskette or overhead cel.

Entry Points
in FAITH
Visits

To focus on ways witnesses can respond to questions about spiritual obstacles, show the session 15 video segment, Weathering Spiritual Storms. Ask participants to make notes in the margins of their Journals.

SAY IT

Step 6 (5 mins.)

Ask accountability partners to discuss ways they would respond to a question about spiritual obstacles, using the ideas in the video and in How You Can Respond.

If you are leading students, have accountability partners role-play a situation in which one partner asks a question about spiritual obstacles and the other partner responds.

STUDY IT

Step 7 (5 mins.)

Overview Home Study Assignments for session 15.

from sin in their lives. This heightens many persons' awareness of spiritual obstacles.

5. The picture on the cover of ___**A**___ ___**Step**___ ___**of**___ ___**Faith**___ reminds many Christians of the mallets and spikes they may still carry, including sin and guilt. God can use the association with this picture to bring conviction and release for many who have already accepted God's assurance of forgiveness and eternal life.

6. When some persons hear Jesus' words in ___**John**___ ___**10:10**___, they consider obstacles to an abundant life.

7. Occasionally, God will lead you to persons who need ___**assurance**___ of ___**salvation**___, ___**reclamation**___, and ___**fellowship**___ with the church. These persons may want to discuss spiritual strongholds in connection with these needs.

How You Can Respond

Here are possible ways you can respond to the question, How can I overcome spiritual obstacles? during witnessing encounters. Your response will depend on the person, the situation, and the Holy Spirit's direction in this circumstance. Always keep in mind the general principles outlined on pages 28–29 in session 1.

1. Carefully listen for the message behind what is being shared. Often, a lost person does not know how to express a struggle with a spiritual obstacle.
2. Never come across as judgmental, but allow the Holy Spirit to speak through God's Word and the ministry of the gospel to the person's spiritual need.
3. Ask questions to encourage the person to share about spiritual obstacles.
4. Share ways you are learning to deal with spiritual obstacles in your life. Don't let it become a time to tell your entire story but to point to the solution of trusting God for forgiveness, acceptance, and peace.
5. Share Scripture verses and principles from God's Word that help a person deal with spiritual obstacles.
6. Offer to pray with the person for release from a spiritual stronghold.
7. Look for ways an individual, Team, class, or others can follow up in specific ways to minister to someone who is in bondage to a spiritual stronghold. Pray specifically for their spiritual need.
8. If the person is a believer, it is important for him or her to be surrounded by others who love the Lord and can offer encourage-

ment. Inviting the person to Sunday School is an important way to offer this support.

9. Remember that God may be using your Team to plant a seed or to reap a harvest. Always be sensitive to the leadership of the Holy Spirit in helping persons deal with spiritual obstacles.

Transition to assemble with FAITH Teams to prepare for home visits. (5 mins.)

Visitation Time

Do It

DO IT (110 MINS.)

1. Remember that this is the last week to visit before the final review. By now your learners should be accepting responsibility for the visit. You should participate as a prayer partner on the FAITH Team. Take responsibility to deal with distractions like the baby, dog, phone, and so on. Always be ready to step in if learners need assistance.

2. As you drive to assignments, talk about whom Team members have enlisted to be on their teams for the next semester of FAITH. If they have not enlisted their Team members, encourage them to do so this week.

Celebration Time

Share It

SHARE IT (30 MINS.)

1. Ask a Team member to take the lead in sharing reports.
2. Hear reports and testimonies.
3. Complete Evaluation Cards.
4. Complete Participation Cards.
5. Update visitation forms with the results of visits.

Home Study Assignments

Home Study Assignments reinforce this session by helping you apply what you have learned.

Your Discipleship Journey

Journaling activities in Your Discipleship Journey are an important part of your development as a Great Commission Christian through FAITH training.

1. When you began FAITH training, you set yourself up to go against the power of Satan. Perhaps Satan has done many things to discourage and distract you. Maybe he has brought to mind sins you have done to make you feel fearful, intimidated, and useless. Reflect on how God has used FAITH training to identify and deal with spiritual obstacles in your life.

2. Check ways your Sunday School helps equip you for spiritual warfare.
   ❏ Hearing God's Word taught
   ❏ Fellowshipping with other Christians
   ❏ Having a group hold you accountable
   ❏ Being aware that other Christians have struggled as you do
   ❏ Having a group pray with you about a task, decision, or battle
   ❏ Ministering to and serving others
   ❏ Having Christian role models to emulate
   ❏ Other: _____

3. Use the following process to overcome a spiritual stronghold in your life.

   • Identify a spiritual obstacle you would like to overcome. Explain why it violates God's Word and will.

   _____

   _____

   • Repent of the sin and ask for God's forgiveness. Claim the mind of Christ. Pray as you put on each piece of spiritual armor. Pray that the Holy Spirit will fill you and will lead you to a Word of truth that applies to your problem. When He leads you to a Scripture, write it here and state how it applies to your problem.

   _____

   _____

- Ask according to God's will, as revealed in His Word. What is your specific request?

_____

- Accept God's will in faith. What do you believe that God will do about your problem, based on the Word He has given you?

_____

- Act on the basis of God's Word to you. What actions will you take, based on the Word from God?

_____

- What actions did God take in answer to your prayer of faith?

_____

4. On a separate sheet of paper, write a "What FAITH Has Meant to Me" testimony.

Growing as a Life Witness

Growing as a Life Witness reminds you of your responsibility to witness and minister to others during the week.

1. Talk or meet with your accountability partner and share ways you have cultivated a lost person or have witnessed or ministered on occasions other than FAITH visits.
2. Discuss your responses to activity 2 in Your Discipleship Journey. Does your Sunday School help in these ways?
3. Pray for lost persons by name and for each other.

Prayer Concerns	Answers to Prayer
_____	_____
_____	_____
_____	_____
_____	_____
_____	_____

Your Weekly Sunday School Leadership Team Meeting

A FAITH participant is an important member of Sunday School. Encourage Team members who are elected Sunday School workers to attend this weekly meeting. Use this section to record ways your FAITH Team influences the work of your Sunday School class or department. Use the information to report during weekly Sunday School leadership team meetings. Identify actions that need to be taken through Sunday School as a result of prayer concerns, needs identified, visits made by the Team, and decisions made by the persons visited. Also identify ways you can disciple others in your Sunday School class or department and in your church.

1. Discuss plans for the next semester of FAITH training. Give the dates.

2. Update the group on plans to enlist a Team of new Learners from your class/department. Who are potential Learners? Invite current Team members or new Christians to share testimonies and benefits of participating as a Team Learner. Indicate other promotional efforts that are under way.

_____

_____

_____

3. With others on your leadership team, evaluate last week's session and discuss ways Sunday's lesson can involve members and guests in transformational Bible study and discipleship.

_____

_____

4. Discuss plans to keep evangelism and ministry contacts consistent and strong between semesters.

_____

_____

5. Thank the Sunday School class/department leaders for their support and encouragement throughout this semester.

6. Pray for your teacher and department director. Specifically ask God to bless and multiply your church's ministry through Sunday School.

Discipling Your Team Members

This weekly feature suggests actions the Team Leader can take to support Team members, prepare for Team Time, and improve visits. This work is part of the Team Leader's Home Study Assignments. Add any actions suggested by your church's FAITH strategy.

Support Team Members

❑ Contact Team members during the week. Remind them that you are praying for them. Discuss prayer concerns and answers to prayer.
❑ Record specific needs and concerns shared by Team members.

_____

_____

❑ Identify specific ways you can encourage Team members as they prepare for their written and verbal reviews.

Prepare for Session 16

❑ Review Team members' Home Study Assignments.
❑ Review instructions for session 16.
❑ Be prepared for your final verbal and written reviews.

Prepare to Lead Visits

❑ Review the FAITH Visit Outline.
❑ Make sure a Team member is ready to take the lead during visits.

Link with Sunday School

❑ Participate in your weekly Sunday School leadership team meeting. Share pertinent information in this meeting, using Your Weekly Sunday School Leadership Team Meeting (p. 250) and FAITH-visit results.
❑ As Sunday School members and visitors share prayer requests, you can often detect evidence of spiritual strongholds. Through caring ministry, loving relationships, and prayer, your Sunday School can begin connecting the person with God's power. Be prepared to offer spiritual counsel and to suggest helpful steps when the time is right.

For Further Growth

For Further Growth may include additional reading or activities that will enhance your growth as a disciple and a discipler of others. These assignments are intended to be long-term projects and do not have to be completed during this semester of study.

1. Consider organizing support groups to minister to persons who need to overcome problems resulting from harmful experiences or addictions.

The LIFE Support Series (LifeWay) addresses a variety of personal issues.

2. Strengthening your prayer life is a significant way to overcome spiritual strongholds. Participate in a group study of *Disciple's Prayer Life* by T. W. Hunt and Catherine Walker (LifeWay, 1997).

3. Hiding God's Word in your heart is one way to overcome spiritual strongholds. Read the FAITH Tip on pages 253–54.

[1]Avery T. Willis, Jr., *MasterLife 3: The Disciple's Victory* (Nashville: LifeWay, 1996), 9.
[2]Ibid., 23–25.
[3]Ibid., 130–31.
[4]Ibid., 33.
[5]Ibid., 129.
[6]Ibid., 76–79.

FAITH TIP

Hiding God's Word in Your Heart

Guide to Meditation

Pray
Pray for wisdom and for the Holy Spirit to make the Word come alive in your heart.

Perimeter
Read the verses before and after the verse to establish the theme and the setting, which will aid you in interpretation. Then write a summary of the passage.

Paraphrase
Write the verse in your own words. Read your paraphrase aloud.

Pulverize
1. Emphasize a different word in the verse as you read or repeat it.
2. Write at least two important words from those you have emphasized in the verse.
3. Ask these questions about the two words to relate the Scripture to your needs: What? Why? When? Where? Who? How?

Personalize
Let the Holy Spirit apply the verse to a need, a challenge, an opportunity, or a failure in your life. What will you do about this verse as it relates to your life?

Pray
Pray the verse back to God, making it personal. Vocalize or write the verse as you pray it back to God.[1]

Guide to Scripture Memorization
1. Choose a verse that speaks to your need or, if the verse is assigned, discover how it meets a particular need in your life.
2. Understand the verse. Read the verse in relation to its context. Read the verse in various Bible translations.
3. Record memory verses on a cassette tape so that you can listen to them. Leave a pause after each verse so that you can practice quoting it. Then record the verse a second time so that you can hear it again after you have quoted it.

4. Locate and underline the verse in your Bible so that you can see where it is on the page.

5. Write the verse on a card, including the Scripture reference and the topic it addresses. This allows you to relate the verse to a particular subject so that you can find it when a need arises.

6. Place the written verse in prominent places so that you can review it while you do other tasks. Put it over the kitchen sink, on the bathroom mirror, on the dashboard for review at stop lights, and on the refrigerator.

7. Commit the verse to memory. Divide it into natural, meaningful phrases and learn it word by word. If you learn it word-perfect in the beginning, it will be set in your memory, will be easier to review, will give you boldness when you are tempted, and will convince the person with whom you are sharing that he or she can trust your word.

8. Review, review, review. This is the most important secret of Scripture memorization. Review a new verse at least once a day for six weeks. Review the verse weekly for the next six weeks and then monthly for the rest of your life.

9. Use these activities to set a verse in your mind: see it in pictorial form; sing it, making up your own tune; pray it back to God; do it by making it a part of your life; and use it as often as possible.

10. Have someone check your memorization. Or write the verse from memory and then check it yourself, using your Bible.

11. Make Scripture memorization fun. Make a game of remembering verses with your family and friends. One idea is to call out a reference, and the other person must quote the verse. Take turns.

12. Set a goal for the number of verses you will memorize each week. Do not try to learn too many verses so fast that you do not have time for daily review, which is essential to memorizing Scripture.[2]

[1]Waylon B. Moore, *Living God's Word* (Nashville: LifeWay, 1997), 40–49.
[2]Avery T. Willis, Jr., *MasterLife 1: The Disciple's Cross* (Nashville: LifeWay, 1996), 112.

SESSION 16

Final Review

In this session you will—

CHECK IT by engaging in Team Time activities;

KNOW IT by taking written and verbal reviews to evaluate your learning

over the past 16 weeks;

STUDY IT by overviewing Home Study Assignments;

DO IT by leading your Team in making visits;

SHARE IT by celebrating accomplishments this semester or by announcing

plans for a FAITH Festival in which the celebration will occur.

In Advance

- Be prepared to administer the written review and to explain answers.
- Preview teaching suggestions. Prepare key points. Decide whether to use the session 16 computer slide or the overhead cel.
- Be prepared to explain the process for recognizing Learners and for certifying Team Leaders, based on information in the FAITH Administrative Guide, provided in *A Journey in FAITH Training Pack*. See your FAITH Director.
- Consult with the FAITH Director and plan to announce details for the FAITH Festival.
- Be prepared to announce dates for the next semester of training. Give Learners instructions about enlistment contacts to be made.
- Be prepared to share any special plans for Visitation Time.
- Prepare the room for teaching.
- Pray for participants and for Teams as they prepare to visit.

Leading Team Time

All Team members participate in Team Time. They are primarily responsible for reciting the assigned portion of the FAITH Visit Outline and for discussing other Home Study Assignments.

As you direct this important time of CHECK IT activities with your Team, keep in mind that Learners look to you as a role model, motivator, mentor, and friend. Team Time activities can continue in the car as the Team travels to and from visits.

Lead CHECK IT Activities

✔ *FAITH Visit Outline*

❑ Listen while each Learner recites any designated portion of the FAITH Visit Outline. It may be best to ask Learners to recite the segment they seem to have the most difficulty sharing during a visit.

❑ A brief time to practice the outline can help Team members confidently approach the verbal review.

✔ *Session 15 Debriefing*

❑ Emphasize the importance of each Team member's being available to serve as a Team Leader during future semesters. Review the potential results of choosing not to continue participating in FAITH training.

✔ *FAITH Testimonies Due*

❑ Ask participants to turn in their "What FAITH Has Meant to Me" testimonies. Present them to the FAITH director.

✔ *Help for Strengthening a Visit*

❑ Discuss some of the things that have been learned by making evangelistic, ministry, and Opinion Poll visits. Make sure Team members know who will be responsible for taking the lead in making the visits after the written and verbal reviews.

Notes

_____

_____

_____

_____

_____

_____

_____

_____

_____

Actions I Need to Take with Learners During the Week

1. Write thank-you notes to Learners. Include congratulations for
   their completion of this semester of training. Indicate your
   continued support.

_____

_____

_____

_____

_____

_____

Transition to classrooms for written
and verbal reviews. (5 mins.)

KNOW IT

Step 1 (5 mins.)

Direct participants to locate A Quick Review on page 258 in their Journals and to complete the activities. Then give the answers, using the computer diskette or the overhead cel. Possible answers to question:

1. *Preparation*
2. Sunday School or evangelistic testimony
3. *F* is for FORGIVENESS
4. *T* is for TURN
5. *A Step of Faith*
6. John 10:10
7. When you counsel persons who need assurance of salvation, reclamation, and fellowship

A Quick Review

Use the remaining ideas in A Quick Review to bring closure to this semester of training. Congratulate members for their achievement this semester. Encourage participants to continue growing by participating in future semesters of FAITH training. Announce plans for a FAITH Festival and any schedule adjustments for this session.

A Quick Review

Last week you learned ways to overcome spiritual obstacles. Test your recall by marking each statement *T* for *true* or *F* for *false*.

F 1. Always fear spiritual strongholds.
T 2. Put on the spiritual armor.
F 3. Rely on God's vengeance.
T 4. Pray in faith.
F 5. Give in to temptation as long as you can get away with it.

What are two places in FAITH visits when questions about or evidence of spiritual obstacles might arise?

1. _____

2. _____

Check appropriate ways to respond to the question, How can I overcome spiritual obstacles.

☑ 1. Listen for the message behind what the person is sharing.
☑ 2. Don't come across as judgmental, but allow the Holy Spirit to speak through God's Word and the ministry of the gospel to the person's spiritual need.
☑ 3. Ask questions to encourage the person to share about spiritual obstacles.
☑ 4. Share ways you are learning to deal with spiritual obstacles.
☑ 5. Share Scripture verses and principles that help a person deal with spiritual obstacles.
❑ 6. Ask the person to share every detail of a stronghold in his life.
☑ 7. Offer to pray with the person for release from a stronghold.
☑ 8. Look for ways others can follow up to minister to someone who is in bondage to a spiritual stronghold.
☑ 9. Invite the person to Sunday School so that he can be surrounded by others who love the Lord and can offer encouragement.
☑ 10. Be sensitive to the Holy Spirit's leadership in helping persons deal with spiritual obstacles.
❑ 11. Suggest that the person's stronghold may be too deeply entrenched for him to be released from it.

Knowing how to overcome spiritual strongholds is important for a growing disciple. The more you grow, the more Satan will attack you. But the more you rely on God for power and the more you are transformed by His truth, the more effectively you will be able to resist Satan's attacks. Then you can live a life of growth and victory that Christ made possible: "We, who with unveiled faces all reflect the Lord's glory, are being transformed into his likeness with ever-increasing glory, which comes from the Lord, who is the Spirit" (2 Cor. 3:18).

Growing in Christlikeness produces a better witness. We hope that by clarifying your beliefs and learning ways to grow as a disciple of Jesus Christ during this semester, you have become a more effective and confident witness. Congratulations for working hard and for putting forth the effort to become a stronger Great Commission Christian. We hope that you will continue your growth as a disciple and as a witness by enrolling in additional FAITH Discipleship courses.

Written Review

You will have 10 minutes to take the following written review.

Session 1: Sharing a Living Faith: An Orientation
Check the ways FAITH Discipleship will equip you as a Great Commission witness.

☑ 1. By teaching you important biblical truths you need to understand and exemplify as a growing disciple
☐ 2. By giving you an overview of the Old Testament
☐ 3. By guiding you through a process to deal with past hurts
☑ 4. By equipping you to respond to difficult questions you may encounter in witnessing
☑ 5. By helping you develop as a life witness for Christ, taking advantage of daily opportunities to share God's love
☐ 6. By helping you discover your spiritual gifts
☑ 7. By giving you opportunities to practice what you have learned in witnessing situations
☑ 8. By helping you develop as a Team Leader
☐ 9. By suggesting ways to make lost persons feel guilty
☑ 10. By suggesting ways you can help new Sunday School and church members grow as disciples

Complete the phrases to identify the three purposes of *Sharing a Living Faith*.

1. To help you develop a biblical _____**belief**_____ _____**system**_____
2. To help you become a more effective _____**witness**_____
3. To help you explore ways you can _____**disciple**_____
   _____**others**_____

Step 2 (10 mins.)

Give these instructions for the written review: Take the written review, beginning on page 259 in your Journal. You will have 10 minutes. Afterward you will grade your own work as I give the answers.

Session 2: How Do I Know the Bible Is True?

Mark each statement *T* for *true* or *F* for *false*.

__F__ 1. Jesus rejected the Old Testament as no longer relevant.

__T__ 2. Jesus considered His words to be authoritative and true.

__T__ 3. The disciples and the early believers accepted the Bible, including the letters and other writings now found in the New Testament, as from God and therefore authoritative and true.

__F__ 4. The New Testament accounts of events in the life of Jesus and the early church, though inspiring, have been proved to be unreliable secondhand reports.

__F__ 5. For the most part, historical records contradict biblical accounts of events and places.

__F__ 6. The Bible is idealistic in the way it depicts people and life.

__T__ 7. The Bible offers practical answers to real-life problems and needs.

Session 3: Does God Exist?

Check the statements that identify the ways the Bible answers the question, Does God exist?

❑ 1. We know there is a God because every person He created is basically good.

☑ 2. The universe reveals the Creator.

❑ 3. Astronauts have seen God in outer space.

☑ 4. Human beings reflect their Maker.

❑ 5. Many people who have died and been brought back to life have seen God face to face.

❑ 6. God's Word promises that people who keep His commandments will experience a divine visitation.

☑ 7. Moral values point to a just God.

☑ 8. We can experience God.

Session 4: Is Jesus Really God's Son?

Mark each statement *T* for *true* or *F* for *false*.

__F__ 1. Jesus claimed to be the promised Messiah, but we can't really be sure He was.

__F__ 2. Jesus is one of many gods.

__T__ 3. Jesus fulfilled God's purposes.

__F__ 4. Jesus lived a good life, but now He is dead.

__F__ 5. Jesus will rule His kingdom until God raises up another leader sometime in the future.

Session 5: Who Is the Holy Spirit?

Mark each of the following statements *T* for *true* or *F* for *false*.

__F__ 1. The Holy Spirit is the second Person of the Godhead.
__T__ 2. Jesus Christ sent the Counselor to us.
__T__ 3. The Holy Spirit came to be our Teacher.
__F__ 4. The Holy Spirit came to bring glory to Himself.
__T__ 5. The Holy Spirit brings conviction of sin.
__F__ 6. The Holy Spirit plays a role in salvation but not in discipleship.

Session 6: Why Does Evil Exist?

Fill in the blanks to identify reasons evil exists.

1. Evil exists because we have ____**free**____ ____**will**____.
2. Evil exists because of the intrusion of an evil ____**adversary**____.
3. The human choice to sin has affected the entire ____**created**____ ____**order**____.
4. God dealt with the problem of evil by sending His ____**Son**____ to pay the penalty for ____**sin**____.
5. God will totally and finally ____**defeat**____ evil.
6. We can ____**trust**____ ____**God**____ when we do not understand why evil things happen.

Session 7: Why Does God Permit Suffering?

Check the sources of suffering humans can control.

☑ 1. Some suffering results from evil decisions.
❏ 2. Some suffering results from the fallen state of creation.
☑ 3. Some suffering results from bad choices.
☑ 4. Some suffering results from the work of Satan.
❏ 5. Some suffering is for the sake of righteousness.
❏ 6. Some suffering is a mystery.

Fill in the blank.

No matter what the source of suffering is, God ____**cares**____ when we suffer.

Session 8: What Does It Mean to Be Lost?

Fill in the blanks to identify what it means to be lost.

1. To be trapped in ____**sin**____
2. To be spiritually ____**dead**____
3. To live under God's ____**wrath**____
4. To be separated from ____**Christ**____
5. To live without ____**God**____
6. To live without ____**hope**____
7. To be already ____**condemned**____

8. To live against _____ **Jesus** _____
9. To be _____ **dying** _____ in sin
10. To live as a child of the _____ **devil** _____
11. To live as God's _____ **enemy** _____
12. To live without _____ **peace** _____
13. To be spiritually _____ **blind** _____

Session 9: What Does It Mean to Be Saved?

Fill in the blanks to identify what it means to be saved.

1. To trust _____ **Christ** _____ as Savior
2. To be _____ **forgiven** _____
3. To be no longer _____ **condemned** _____
4. To be in a right _____ **relationship** _____ with God
5. To be _____ **born** _____ again
6. To be a new _____ **creation** _____
7. To be a _____ **child** _____ of God
8. To be _____ **free** _____ indeed
9. To be a _____ **disciple** _____ of Christ
10. To have a life of _____ **peace** _____
11. To be assured of _____ **eternal** _____ **life** _____

Session 10: Why Do I Need the Church?

Substitute the words below in the correct summary statements.

interdependent • kingdom • unity • Head • people • family
functions • body • bride • purpose

1. The church is the _____ **body** _____ of Christ.
   • Christ is the _____ **Head** _____ of the church.
   • The church is a _____ **unity** _____.
   • Each church member has a _____ **purpose** _____.
   • Church members are _____ **interdependent** _____.
2. The church is the _____ **people** _____ of God.
3. The church is a _____ **family** _____ of believers.
4. The church is the _____ **bride** _____ of Christ.
5. The church is an expression of the _____ **kingdom** _____ of God.
6. The church is responsible for fulfilling God-given
   _____ **functions** _____.

Identify five functions of the church.
1. _____ **Evangelism** _____
2. _____ **Discipleship** _____
3. _____ **Fellowship** _____
4. _____ **Ministry** _____
5. _____ **Worship** _____

Session 11: Why Are Bible Study and Prayer Important?

Beside each statement write T for *true* or F for *false*.

__F__ 1. The Bible teaches us how to succeed by human initiative.
__T__ 2. The Bible is living and active.
__T__ 3. The Bible has convicting power.
__F__ 4. God considers it more important for us to read the Bible than to obey it.
__F__ 5. No matter how much you read the Bible, the primary ways to grow as a disciple are through intuition and good deeds.

Fill in the blanks.

1. We pray to have _____**fellowship**_____ with God.
2. We pray to _____**worship**_____ God.
3. We pray to ask for God's _____**provision**_____.
4. We pray to receive _____**forgiveness**_____ and _____**salvation**_____.
5. We pray to join God's _____**work**_____.
6. We pray to become more like _____**Christ**_____.

Session 13: What Is the Purpose of Life?

Check three pursuits that Solomon identified in the Book of Ecclesiastes as being incapable of bringing meaning to life.

❏ 1. Others' approval
❏ 2. Knowing God
☑ 3. Knowledge
☑ 4. Pleasure
❏ 5. Writing poetry
❏ 6. Praising God
☑ 7. Work
❏ 8. Having a family

Fill in the blanks to identify the three purposes we exist, according to the Bible.

1. We were created to have an intimate relationship with _____**God**_____.
2. We were created to have relationships with _____**one another**_____.
3. We were created to have responsibility for _____**creation**_____.

Session 14: How Can I Find Strength for Daily Living?

Check the statements that identify the way the Bible answers the question, How can I find strength for daily living?

❑ 1. Pursue pleasure.
☑ 2. Accept Christ as Savior and Lord.
❑ 3. Practice transcendental meditation.
☑ 4. Learn obedience.
☑ 5. Renew your mind.
❑ 6. Get in touch with your inner divinity.
☑ 7. Master your emotions.
☑ 8. Offer your body to God.
❑ 9. Think about the past.
❑ 10. Take a pilgrimage to the Holy Land.
☑ 11. Be filled with the Spirit.
☑ 12. Grow as a disciple.

Name four of the nine ways you learned to grow as a disciple.

1. _____

2. _____

3. _____

4. _____

Session 15: How Can I Overcome Spiritual Obstacles?
Mark each statement T for *true* or F for *false*.

__F__ 1. Always fear spiritual strongholds.
__T__ 2. Put on the spiritual armor.
__F__ 3. Rely on God's vengeance.
__T__ 4. Pray in faith.
__F__ 5. Give in to temptation as long as you can get away with it.

Grade your written review as your Facilitator gives the answers. Each item counts one point; the highest possible score is 129. Subtract the number you missed from this total to get your score.

Highest possible score: 129

Number missed: – _____

My score: = _____

Participants could have named any four of the following ways to grow as a disciple.
1. Participate in Bible study and discipleship training.
2. Have a daily quiet time.
3. Memorize and meditate on Scripture.
4. Attend congregational worship.
5. Fellowship with other believers.
6. Give tithes and offerings.
7. Listen to spiritual music.
8. Serve through your church.
9. Share your faith.

Step 3 (5 mins.)

Give instructions for grading and scoring the written review: As I give the correct answers, place an *X* beside each incorrect response. Total the number of incorrect answers and subtract from 129 to get your overall score.

Verbal Review:
FAITH Visit Outline

❑ **Preparation**

❑ INTRODUCTION
❑ INTERESTS
❑ INVOLVEMENT
❑ **Church Experience/Background**
❑ • Ask about the person's church background.
❑ • Listen for clues about the person's spiritual involvement.
❑ **Sunday School Testimony**
❑ • Tell general benefits of Sunday School.
❑ • Tell a current personal experience.
❑ **Evangelistic Testimony**
❑ • Tell a little of your preconversion experience.
❑ • Say: "I had a life-changing experience."
❑ • Tell recent benefits of your conversion.

❑ INQUIRY
❑ **Key Question:** In your personal opinion, what do you understand it takes
   for a person to go to heaven?
❑ **Possible Answers:** Faith, works, unclear, no opinion
❑ **Transition Statement:** I'd like to share with you how the Bible answers this
   question, if it is all right. There is a word that can be used to answer this
   question: FAITH (spell out on fingers).

❑ **Presentation**

❑ F IS FOR FORGIVENESS
❑ We cannot have eternal life and heaven without God's forgiveness.
❑ *"In Him [meaning Jesus] we have redemption through His blood, the forgiveness
   of sins"—Ephesians 1:7a, NKJV.*

❑ A is for AVAILABLE
❑ Forgiveness is available. It is—

❑ AVAILABLE FOR ALL
❑ *"For God so loved the world that He gave His only begotten Son, that whoever
   believes in Him should not perish but have everlasting life"—John 3:16, NKJV.*

❑ BUT NOT AUTOMATIC
❑ *"Not everyone who says to Me, 'Lord, Lord,' shall enter the kingdom of
   heaven"—Matthew 7:21a, NKJV.*

Step 4 (15 mins.)

Explain the process for the verbal
review: Recite the FAITH Visit Outline
to your accountability partner. He or
she will listen and mark incorrect
responses in your Journal as you
present each item. Accountability
partners will have 15 minutes to recite
the outline to each other.

❏ *I* **is for IMPOSSIBLE**

❏ It is impossible for God to allow sin into heaven.

❏ **GOD IS—**
❏ •LOVE
❏ *John 3:16, NKJV*
❏ • JUST
❏ *"For judgment is without mercy"—James 2:13a, NKJV.*

❏ **MAN IS SINFUL**
❏ *"For all have sinned and fall short of the glory of God"—Romans 3:23, NKJV.*
❏ **Question:** But how can a sinful person enter heaven, where God allows no sin?

❏ *T* **is for TURN**
❏ **Question:** If you were driving down the road and someone asked you to turn, what would he or she be asking you to do? (change direction)
❏ *Turn* **means repent.**
❏ **TURN** from something—sin and self
❏ *"But unless you repent you will all likewise perish"—Luke 13:3b, NKJV.*
❏ **TURN** to Someone; trust Christ only
❏ (The Bible tells us that) *"Christ died for our sins according to the Scriptures, and that He was buried, and that He rose again the third day according to the Scriptures"—1 Corinthians 15:3b-4, NKJV.*
❏ *"If you confess with your mouth the Lord Jesus and believe in your heart that God has raised Him from the dead, you will be saved"—Romans 10:9, NKJV.*

❏ *H* **is for HEAVEN**
❏ Heaven is eternal life.
❏ **HERE**
❏ *"I have come that they may have life, and that they may have it more abundantly"—John 10:10b, NKJV.*
❏ **HEREAFTER**
❏ *"And if I go and prepare a place for you, I will come again and receive you to Myself; that where I am, there you may be also"—John 14:3, NKJV.*
❏ **HOW**
❏ How can a person have God's forgiveness, heaven and eternal life, and Jesus as personal Savior and Lord?
❏ Explain based on leaflet picture, FAITH (Forsaking All, I Trust Him), Romans 10:9.

❏ # Invitation

❏ **INQUIRE**
❏ Understanding what we have shared, would you like to receive this forgiveness by trusting in Christ as your personal Savior and Lord?

❏ INVITE

- ❏ • Pray to accept Christ.
- ❏ • Pray for commitment/recommitment.
- ❏ • Invite to join Sunday School.

❏ INSURE

- ❏ • Use *A Step of Faith* to insure decision.
- ❏ • Personal Acceptance
- ❏ • Sunday School Enrollment
- ❏ • Public Confession

Each item counts one point; the highest possible score is 67. Subtract the number you missed from this total to get your score.

Highest possible score: 67

Number missed: – _____

My score: = _____

Visitation Time

Do It

1. Your visitation schedule may be altered tonight. Allow for any schedule changes your church has agreed on.
2. Encourage Teams to return for a special Celebration Time.

Celebration Time

Share It

1. Ask a Team member to take the lead in sharing reports.
2. Hear reports and testimonies.
3. Complete Evaluation Cards.
4. Complete Participation Cards.
5. Update visitation forms with the results of visits.
6. Allow time for testimonies about what this semester of FAITH has meant to participants and to the persons they have visited.

Step 5 (5 mins.)

Give instructions for grading and scoring the verbal review: Total the number of incorrect answers your accountability partner has marked. Subtract from 67 to get your overall score.

STUDY IT

Step 6 (5 mins.)

Overview Home Study Assignments for session 16.

Close by praying for participants' further growth as disciples and as witnesses.

Transition to assemble with FAITH Teams to prepare for home visits. (5 mins.)

DO IT
(110 MINS.)

SHARE IT
(30 MINS.)

Home Study Assignments

Home Study Assignments reinforce this session by helping you apply what you have learned.

Your Discipleship Journey

Journaling activities in Your Discipleship Journey are an important part of your development as a Great Commission Christian through FAITH training.

1. Read 2 Timothy 1:7. Describe ways your confidence and love for others have increased this semester.

   _____

   _____

2. Read Paul's charge to Timothy in 2 Timothy 4:5. Write ways you can respond to each challenge as you witness.

   Keep your head in all situations: _____

   _____

   Endure hardship: _____

   _____

   Do the work of an evangelist: _____

   _____

   Discharge all the duties of your ministry: _____

   _____

3. Read 2 Timothy 2:2. We have a responsibility to teach to faithful believers what we have learned. Write the names of two persons you have enlisted or will prayerfully consider enlisting for the next semester of FAITH.

   _____

   _____

4. How have you found ways to disciple Team Learners and Sunday School members during this semester of FAITH Discipleship?

_____

_____

5. How can you encourage your current Team Learners to become Team Leaders next semester?

_____

_____

Growing as a Life Witness

Growing as a Life Witness reminds you of your responsibility to witness and minister to others during the week.

1. Talk or meet with your accountability partner and share ways you have cultivated a lost person or have witnessed or ministered on occasions other than FAITH visits.
2. Discuss your responses to activities in Your Discipleship Journey. Share your plans for future participation in FAITH training.
3. Pray for lost persons by name and for each other.

Prayer Concerns	Answers to Prayer
_____	_____
_____	_____
_____	_____
_____	_____
_____	_____
_____	_____
_____	_____
_____	_____

Your Weekly Sunday School Leadership Team Meeting

A FAITH participant is an important member of Sunday School. Encourage Team members who are elected Sunday School workers to attend this weekly meeting. Use this section to record ways your FAITH Team influences the work of your Sunday School class or department. Use the information to report during weekly Sunday School leadership team meetings. Identify actions that need to be taken through Sunday School as a result of prayer concerns, needs identified, visits made by the Team, and decisions made by the persons visited. Also identify ways you can disciple others in your Sunday School class or department and in your church.

1. Highlight needs/reports affecting your class/department or age group.

_____

_____

_____

2. List prayer requests for your teacher and department director.

_____

_____

_____

3. What are ways the department/class can celebrate the Holy Spirit's work through members who have participated in FAITH training?

_____

_____

_____

4. What actions can be taken to encourage members and leaders to prepare for the next semester of FAITH training?

_____

_____

_____

5. How does preparation for Sunday need to consider persons who might attend because they received a witness by members during the week?

_____

_____

_____

For Further Growth

For Further Growth may include additional reading or activities that will enhance your growth as a disciple and a discipler of others. These assignments are intended to be long-term projects and do not have to be completed during this semester of study.

1. Participate in a group study of *MasterLife* by Avery T. Willis, Jr. (LifeWay, 1996). This series of four six-week discipleship studies provides a comprehensive, biblical understanding of what is expected of a disciple of Jesus Christ.

2. Consider mentoring a new Christian to establish him or her in the basics of the faith. Use *Survival Kit* (LifeWay, 1996), which is designed to help new believers understand salvation and their new nature in Christ. Or use the magazine *Believe*, available by writing to Customer Service Center, MSN 113; 127 Ninth Avenue, North; Nashville, TN 37234-0113; by calling toll free (800) 458-2772; by faxing (615) 251-5933; by ordering online at *www.lifeway.com*; or by emailing *customerservice@lifeway.com*.

FAITH AT WORK

We live in a very health-conscious society today. People are careful about the types and amounts of food they take into their bodies. Nourishment is necessary for our survival, but there has to be a proper balance between taking in and giving out, or we can become physically fat and lazy. We need to discipline our bodies and exercise to remain physically fit.

Just as we need to have balance in our physical lives, I believe we need balance in our spiritual lives as well. We have a God-given need for spiritual nourishment. Our church provides many opportunities for us to be fed through the worship services, Sunday School, Bible-study times, and times of fellowship. We can feed on God's Word personally during devotional times in our own homes. If we aren't careful, though, we can become spiritually fat and lazy. I once had a pastor who said, "Sometimes we act as if we want to get all we can, can all we get, and sit on the lid." Instead, as a Christian, I believe we are called to spiritually exercise our faith. We can do that through FAITH evangelism training. FAITH is a short, clear way to present the gospel message to others. Using our hands and an acrostic is an easy way to remember the presentation and to stay on track.

Through the years I've been trained in many other witnessing programs. You would think it would be easy for me and I would jump at the chance to put some of that head knowledge to work. I wish that were so. I realize the need, and I remember that someone took the time many years ago when I was an 11-year-old girl to come to my home and share Jesus with me, but I have to discipline myself to do the same. Making a home visit is not the problem. Being bold enough to share the gospel message sometimes is. I truly have a desire for others to come to know Christ, have Him change their lives, and give them meaning and purpose as He has mine, but I have to refuse to listen to the fear that sometimes comes over me and keeps me from sharing. I must remember that He that is in me is greater than he that is in the world. When I am obedient, I receive such a blessing from God. I have been on some great visits and have had the opportunity to get to know people and answer their questions about our church and ministries here in Owasso. Some responded by coming to our Sunday School class for a visit.

Jesus said in John 20:21, " 'As the Father has sent Me, I am sending you.' " As God continues to bless our community and church with new people, it will require all of us to be obedient to go and to be found faithful in doing our Father's business.

Cheryl Butler
First Baptist Church
Owasso, Oklahoma